Arbitration in Russia

Arbitration in Russia

Andrey Kotelnikov
Sergey Kurochkin
Oleg Skvortsov

Wolters Kluwer

Published by:
Kluwer Law International B.V.
PO Box 316
2400 AH Alphen aan den Rijn
The Netherlands
E-mail: international-sales@wolterskluwer.com
Website: lrus.wolterskluwer.com

Sold and distributed in North, Central and South America by:
Wolters Kluwer Legal & Regulatory U.S.
7201 McKinney Circle
Frederick, MD 21704
United States of America
Email: customer.service@wolterskluwer.com

Sold and distributed in all other countries by:
Air Business Subscriptions
Rockwood House
Haywards Heath
West Sussex
RH16 3DH
United Kingdom
Email: international-customerservice@wolterskluwer.com

Printed on acid-free paper.

ISBN 978-94-035-0362-2

e-Book: ISBN 978-94-035-0340-0
web-PDF: ISBN 978-94-035-0351-6

Printed in the United Kingdom.

About the Authors

Andrey Kotelnikov is Lecturer in the Law School at the Robert Gordon University in Aberdeen (UK). He is a Module Leader for Dispute Resolution, Arbitration Law and Mediation in Context, and also teaches various other subjects at undergraduate and postgraduate levels, including Advanced Business Law, the Law of Obligations and Evidence, etc. Since 2014, he has been an arbitrator and a coach of RGU's mooting team in Willem C. Vis International Commercial Arbitration Moot (Vienna). He started his professional career as an in-house legal counsel for the Russian Ministry of Justice (The Ekaterinburg Legal Information Centre) then worked for the Federal Commission on the Securities Market and a large Russian telecoms company. After that, for seven years Andrey led the commercial legal team at one of the Russia's major natural monopolies in the energy sector. During the same period, he also taught Domestic and Comparative Litigation and International Commercial Arbitration in the Urals State Law Academy (Ekaterinburg, Russia). He is a graduate of Central European University (Budapest), holds an LLM in International Business Law from the University of Manchester (UK), and a PhD (candidate of Legal Studies) from the Urals State Law Academy. The title of Andrey's PhD thesis was *The Legal Nature and Effects of an Arbitration Agreement*. To date, Andrey has about twenty published research outputs in both the Russian and English languages, including journal articles, legal translations, and book chapters. Important works include the contributions to the following books: *Commentary on the Law of Russian Federation 'On International Commercial Arbitration'* (Saint Petersburg, 2007) and *Civil Procedure in Foreign Countries* (Moscow, 2013). He regularly speaks at local and international conferences and workshops on civil procedure and international arbitration. He is the Academic editor of this book and the author of Chapters 3 and 10.

Sergey Kurochkin is the Vice-Rector for International Relations of the Ural Federal University named after the first President of Russia B.N. Yeltsin (Yekaterinburg, Russia). His professional biography includes work at the University of Tyumen (Russia) as a Dean of the Institute of State and Law and at the Urals State Law University (Russia), as Associate Professor of the Civil Procedure Department, where he taught courses on Civil Procedure, Commercial Courts Procedure, Internal and International Commercial Arbitration, Alternative Dispute Resolution. In 2004, Sergey defended his PhD (candidate of Legal Studies) thesis on *The Theoretical and Legal Foundations of Arbitration in Russian Federation*. Sergey has published over one hundred monographs, textbooks, and articles on legal issues, in both Russian and English languages. The major published books include *Arbitration in Russian Federation: Theory and Practice* (Moscow, 2007), *State Courts in Arbitration Proceedings and International Commercial Arbitration* (Moscow, 2008), *Private and Public Foundations in the Civil Procedure* (Moscow-Berlin, 2012), *International Commercial Arbitration Proceedings* (Moscow, 2013), *Internal and International Commercial Arbitration* (Moscow, 2017). He regularly speaks at Russian and international conferences and workshops on civil procedure and international arbitration. He is the author of Chapters 4, 5, 7 and 9 of this book.

Oleg Skvortsov is Professor, Doctor of Law at the Saint Petersburg State University, Faculty of Law, Commercial Law Chair, as well as the Head of the Dispute Resolution practice and an advisor for the Saint Petersburg office of DLA Piper. In 2000, he defended his PhD (candidate of Legal Studies) thesis on *The Institute of Cassation in the Russian Law: Arbitral Procedure Problems of the Legal System and Legal Proceedings*. In 2006, he defended the thesis for the degree of Doctor of Law on *The Challenges of Arbitration Proceedings for Business Disputes in Russia*. He teaches the following courses: Commercial Law, International Commercial Law, Investment Law, Business Transactions with Real Estate, and the Legal Framework of Bankruptcy Proceedings. He had been a visiting Lecturer in the University of Napoli and the University of Helsinki. He has published over two-hundred monographs, textbooks, and articles on legal issues. His major works include: (1) monographs: *Action in rem in Commercial Legal Practice* (Moscow, 1998), *Protection of Rights of Entrepreneurs in Insolvency (Bankruptcy) Proceedings* (Saint Petersburg, 2003), *Arbitration Settlement of Business Disputes in Russia. Issues. Trends. Perspectives* (Moscow, 2005); (2) textbooks and teaching aids: *Privatisation Law* (1st edition, Moscow, 1999; 2nd edition, Moscow, 2000), *Business Transactions with Real Estate* (Moscow, 2006), *Arbitration Proceedings in the Russian Federation* (Moscow, 2010), *International Commercial Arbitration* (Moscow, 2012), *International Commercial Law* (Moscow, 2012); (3) comments to laws: *Comments to the Federal Law 'On Arbitration Courts in the Russian Federation'* (Moscow, 2003), *Comments to the Federal Law 'On Insolvency (Bankruptcy)'* (Moscow, 2009). Oleg has extensive experience of participation as an expert in arbitration proceedings. For example, he prepared expert opinions and gave testimony in the Arbitration Court of the Stockholm Chamber of Commerce, London Court of International Arbitration, and Zurich Arbitration Court under the Zurich Court of Commerce on numerous occasions. In 2016, he became a member of the Council for the Development of Arbitration of Russian Federation under the decree of the Ministry of Justice. He is the Chairman of the Russian Centre for the Assistance to Arbitration. He is the author of the Preface, Chapters 1, 2, 6, 8, 11, and 12 of this book.

Table of Contents

Preface

The regulation of arbitration in the Russian Federation has a difficult history. Over the past quarter of a century, two diametrically opposite models of arbitration have been tested in Russia – the liberal and the conservative. The liberal model of arbitration dominated from the 1990s until about 2015. This has led to widespread abuse and has largely discredited arbitration. The need for a change in legal regulation was evident.

Russia's entry into the era of 'conservative arbitration' was the consequence of the reform that took place in 2015-2017. The reform led to the extensive control of the state over the activities of both domestic and international commercial arbitration, the awards of which are enforced in the territory of the Russian Federation. The notification system for creating arbitral institutions has been replaced by licensing. As a result, arbitral institutions are under the state supervision at all stages of their existence: during creation, operation, as well as at the stage of recognition and enforcement of awards. This control is vested in both competent state courts and the executive authorities, particularly the Ministry of Justice.

In the course of the reform, several thousand arbitration centres ceased to exist. Only a handful of permanent arbitral institutions in the country obtained permission to operate. As for the foreign and international commercial arbitral institutions, they can carry out their activities in Russia but only with the permission of the executive branch. Only those arbitral centres with a widely recognised international reputation can obtain such permission.

At the same time, the national arbitration law continues to follow to a significant extent the international legal standards, including the New York Convention 1958, the European Convention 1961, and the recommendations of the UNCITRAL Model Law. The legislative provisions concerning judicial control of arbitration, grounds for setting aside of arbitral awards and their enforcement also remained largely intact in the course of the reform.

Thus, the Russian Federation has created a model of arbitral regulation where the state adopts a paternalistic approach.

In preparing this publication, the authors used both the national legislation that governs arbitration and the international legal instruments in this area. One of the principles on which the presentation of materials relies is combining an academic approach with a practical orientation of the book. For these purposes, the text takes account of both the most significant Russian works on the theory of arbitration law and the relevant judicial and arbitration practice.

The authors considered it necessary to highlight the history of arbitration's development in Russia, in order to provide the reader with a more comprehensive understanding of this institution of the jurisdictional sphere.

The different parts of the book cover all the major areas of the Russian arbitration law: regulatory sources, arbitrability of disputes, arbitration agreement, interim measures, procedure, arbitral acts, challenging of arbitral awards and their enforcement.

List of Abbreviations

Arbitration Act 2002	Federal Law 'On Arbitration in the Russian Federation' of 24 July 2002 No. 102-FZ
Arbitration Act 2015	Federal Law 'On Arbitration (Arbitral Proceedings) in the Russian Federation' of 29 December 2015 No. 382-FZ, Collection of Legislative Acts of the Russian Federation, 4 January 2016, No. 1 (Part I), Article 2.
CC	Commercial Court of a republic, autonomous republic, territory, region, cities of Moscow and Saint Petersburg, autonomous region (Commercial Court of a First Instance)
CC RF	Constitutional Court of the Russian Federation
CCA	Commercial Court of Appeal
CIS	Commonwealth of Independent States
Civil Code	Civil Code of the Russian Federation: Part One of 30 November 1994, Part Two of 26 January 1996, Part Three of 26 November 2001, Part Four of 18 December 2006
Code of Civil Procedure	Code of Civil Procedure of the Russian Federation of 14 November 2002, Collection of Legislative Acts of the Russian Federation 2002, No. 46, Article 4532
Code of Inland Water Transport	Code of Inland Water Transport of the Russian Federation of 7 March 2001, Collection of Legislative Acts of the Russian Federation 2001, No. 11, Article 1001
Commercial Procedure Code	Commercial Procedure Code of the Russian Federation of 24 July 2002, Collection of Legislative Acts of the Russian Federation, 2002, No. 30, Article 3012
ECHR	The Convention for the Protection of Human Rights and Fundamental Freedoms (the European Convention on Human Rights) (Rome, 4 November 1950)

ECtHR	European Court of Human Rights
EDI	Electronic Data Interchange
Enforcement Proceedings Act	Federal Law 'On Enforcement Proceedings' of 2 October 2007 No. 229-FZ
European Convention 1961	European Convention on International Commercial Arbitration (Geneva, 21 April 1961; ratified by the Decree of the Presidium of the Supreme Soviet of the USSR of 14 May 1962 No. 67-VI)
FCC	Federal Commercial Court of a Circuit (Commercial Court of Cassation)
FTAC	Foreign Trade Arbitration Commission
HKIAC	Hong Kong International Arbitration Centre
IBA	International Bar Association
IBA Guidelines on Conflicts of Interest	International Bar Association Guidelines on Conflicts of Interest in International Arbitration 2014
IBA Rules of Evidence	International Bar Association Rules on the Taking of Evidence in International Arbitration 2010
ICA Act 1993	Law of the Russian Federation 'On International Commercial Arbitration' of 7 June 1993 No. 5338-1, Bulletin of the RF Congress of People's Deputies and the Supreme Council of the RF, 1993, No. 32, Article 1240.
ICAC, ICAC at the RF CCI	International Commercial Arbitration Court at the Chamber of Commerce and Industry of the Russian Federation
ICC	International Chamber of Commerce
IMA	Institute of Modern Arbitration
LCIA	London Court of International Arbitration
MAC, MAC at the RF CCI	Maritime Arbitration Commission at the Chamber of Commerce and Industry of the Russian Federation
Merchant Shipping Code	Merchant Shipping Code of the Russian Federation of 30 April 1999 No 81-FZ, Collection of Legislative Acts of the Russian Federation 1999, No. 18, Article 2207
Moscow Convention	Convention on Resolution by Arbitration of Civil Law Disputes Arising from Economic and Scientific Cooperation (Moscow, 26 May 1972)
New York Convention 1958	Convention on the Recognition and Enforcement of Foreign Arbitral Awards (New York, 1958; ratified by the Decree of the Presidium of the Supreme Soviet of the USSR of 10 August 1960)
NGO	Non-governmental Organisation
RAO UES	RAO Unified Energy Systems of Russia

RF	Russian Federation
RF CCI	Chamber of Commerce and Industry of the Russian Federation
RF CCI Rules on Impartiality	Rules on Impartiality and Independence of Arbitrators (approved by the President of RF CCI on 27 August 2010)
SC RF	Supreme Court of the Russian Federation
SCC	Arbitration Institute of the Stockholm Chamber of Commerce
SCC RF	Supreme Commercial Court of the Russian Federation
SIAC	Singapore International Arbitration Centre
UNCITRAL	United Nations Commission on International Trade Law
UNCITRAL Model Law	UNCITRAL Model Law on International Commercial Arbitration 1985 (with amendments as adopted in 2006)
UNCITRAL Rules	UNCITRAL Arbitration Rules (15 December 1976, as revised in 2010, with new Article 1, paragraph 4, as adopted in 2013)
USSR	Union of Soviet Socialist Republics

CHAPTER 1

Arbitration Reform in Russia

§1.01 THE HISTORY OF ARBITRATION IN RUSSIA

Legal scholars widely agree that, historically, private justice predates judicial process of a state.[1] Arbitration was widespread in the era of customary law. In the past, arbitration as a method of conflict resolution held prominent positions in many countries, including ancient Russia. The willingness to submit individual disagreements to arbitrators had its roots in the popular belief that such an approach agreed particularly well with the notions of justice.

One of the first monuments and sources of the Old Russian law, 'Russkaya Pravda' of the eleventh century, introduced a court of twelve representatives, which was also 'the oldest way of dealing with disputed cases among the Anglo-Saxons, Danes, Swedes and Norwegians. Such a court was in existence among these peoples, first by custom, then according to the law, and consisted of each the plaintiff and the defendant appointing six judges to decide in the dispute'.[2] The charters and treaties of the Russian princes testify that the custom of appointing a third person was one of the first civilised ways, and subsequently the most common method, of resolving disputes among the Slavs.[3] Historical sources indicate that the personality of arbitrators and

1. *See*, e.g., Roberts S., Palmer R., *Dispute Processes: ADR and the Primary Forms of Decision-Making*, 11-13 (2nd ed., Cambridge University Press 2005).
2. Mikhailov M.M., *The History of the Formation and Development of the System of Russian Civil Proceedings up to the Code of 1649*, 40, in Mikhaylov M.M., *Selected Works* (Moscow, 2014) [Mikhailov M.M. Istoriya obrazovaniya i razvitiya sistyemy russkogo grajdanskogo sudoproizvodstva do Ulojyeniya 1649 goda. // Mikhailov M.M. Izbrannyye proizvyedyeniya. - M., 2014. S. 40].
3. Mirkhuseeva S.D., *Formation of an Arbitral Tribunal: A Historical Comparative Study*, 1 (97) Treteysky Sud, 21 (2015) [Mirkhuseeva S.D. Formirovaniye tryetyeiskogo suda: istoriko-komparativistskoye isslyedovaniye. // Treteysky Sud. 2015. No. 1 (97). S. 21].

their good reputation were of utmost importance in the constitution of an arbitral tribunal.[4]

During the Middle Ages, the Moscow state was striving to establish a uniform manner of government and administration. For this reason, the state authorities refused to support alternative methods of resolving legal disputes. Moreover, during some historical periods, the central authorities directly opposed arbitration. As a result, arbitration – grounded in the principles of private initiative – was unpopular at the times of the Moscow state.

Another reason for arbitration not being as widespread in Russia as it was in Western Europe was the weakness of the Russian merchant class that until mid-nineteenth century remained in serfdom of the landowner nobility.

At the same time, it is impossible to deny that private 'courts' continued to exist throughout the entire Russian history. Thus, in the times of Ivan the Terrible, from 1552 onwards, the so-called favourite judges acting as peasants' judges started to appear in the communities. There remains plenty of preserved information about the selection of those judges and their work.[5]

The Council Code 1649 (*Sobornoe Ulozhenie 1649*) laid down the rules permitting disputants to resort to arbitration in its Article 5 'On the Arbitration Court'. With the adoption of the Council Code, arbitration began to acquire its 'classical' features: arbitral awards were recognised as final and immediately enforceable, and it was prohibited to review them on appeal. The Council Code also introduced some novel solutions: arbitral awards were deemed equal to the decisions of state courts, sanctions were introduced for their non-performance and so on.[6]

During the reign of Peter the Great, the Regulations of the Chief Magistrate were drafted, the main purpose of which was to strengthen the merchant class. Among the measures introduced to this end, it was ordained that merchants should establish the merchants' court,[7] which by its constitution and decision-making mechanisms was similar to an arbitration tribunal. In 1727, the Customs Charter provided for the possibility of creating 'legalised' arbitration courts.

From the eighteenth century, it became possible to certify an arbitration clause by registering it in special books maintained by provincial chancelleries. One could also certify an arbitration clause with a notary. This was the position until the middle of the nineteenth century when the magistrate courts took over the certification of agreements that purported to submit a dispute to arbitration.

4. *Collection of the Most Important Monuments on the History of Ancient Russian Law* 18 (St Petersburg, 1859) [Sobraniye vajnyeishih pamyatnikov po istorii Dryevnyego russkogo prava. – SPb., 1859. S.18], cited in: Mirkhuseeva S.D., *Formation of an Arbitral Tribunal: A Historical Comparative Study*, 1 (97) Arbitration Journal 20-31 (2015) [Mirkhuseeva S.D., Formirovaniye tryetyeiskogo suda: istoriko-komparativistskoye issledovaniye. // Tryetyeiskii sud. 2015. No. 1 (97). S. 20-31].
5. Drozhzhin V., *Court of the Tsar Ivan the Terrible*, 6 Russian Justice, 59-62 (1996) [Drozhzhin V., Sud carya Ivana Groznogo // Rossiiskaya yusticiya. 1996. N 6. S. 59-62].
6. Mankov A.G., *Commentary to the Council Code 1649*, 73 (Leningrad, 1987) [Sobornoye ulojyeniye 1649 goda. – L., 1987. S.73 (avtor kommyentariya – A.G. Mankov)].
7. Udintsev V.A., *Selected Works on Trade and Civil Law*, 49 (Moscow, 2003) [Udintsev V.A. Izbrannyye trudy po torgovomu i grajdanskomu pravu. M., 2003. S. 49].

A peculiar variety of arbitral dispute resolution of that period was the so-called courts of conscience. These were established in 1775 in the course of the Catherine II's judicial reform. It is known that the Russian Empress was influenced by works of both French (Voltaire, Diderot, D'Alembert, Rousseau) and Russian (S.E. Desnitsky) intellectuals of the enlightenment, whose ideas laid the foundation for these courts. However, the courts of conscience remained unpopular, as they faced resistance and incompetence in the provinces and lower levels of government.

In 1801 (according to other sources, in 1803),[8] the famous Russian poet and Minister of Justice G.R. Derzhavin, on the request of Emperor Alexander I, compiled and submitted to the Emperor the Statute of the Arbitration Court of Conscience.[9] It is possible that the idea of establishing the legislative framework for arbitration in Russia was a consequence of another report of the Senate to the Emperor concerning the arbitration proceedings between the foreign Asians in Astrakhan. Language difficulties prompted the Astrakhan city magistrate to petition the supreme authorities to permit the resolution of disputes between these persons by arbitration. The Emperor approved the Senate's report. This became the arrangement in Astrakhan, and it was later extended to Asians living in Moscow and St. Petersburg.

Derzhavin's draft never made it to the statute books, but one could feel its influence on the Russian legal agenda throughout the next century.

Between 1817 and 1826, the well-known Russian historian and statesman N.M. Karamzin drafted a rescript for the Minister of Justice Lobanov-Rostovsky. The basis of this project was a sociological study of sorts conducted by Prince Repnin, the governor of Little Russian territories. The essence of Prince Repnin's experiment was that arbitrators – the so-called marshals of the nobility – resolved legal disputes between residents of two small provinces in Little Russia. Within a short time, 574 disputes reached a successful resolution. The results of the experiment were highly acclaimed, and as a result, Repnin received the imperial 'excellent favour', and his experience was brought to the attention of all provinces.

One of the main directions of development of arbitration in the Russian Empire was via a grant of entitlements to arbitrate disputes within certain social classes, as well as at some areas on the outskirts of the state. For example, the Regulations on the Administration of the Don Cossack Host Lands 1804 granted the disputants in these lands the right to arbitrate their disagreements.

In 1831, the Russian Imperial government carried out an arbitration reform. The Regulation on Arbitration Courts 1831 became the cornerstone for the development of arbitration in Russia. This Regulation was based on the article of the Council Code 1649 dealing with arbitration (which became the legal basis for voluntary arbitration) and the Emperor Peter II's Customs Regulations. Thus, there remained a continuity in the regulation of arbitration.

8. Dzhanshiev G.A., *Basic Principles of Judicial Reform*, 218 (Moscow, 2004) [Dzhanshiev G.A. Osnovy sudyebnoi ryeformy. M., 2004. S. 218].
9. Derzhavin G.R., *Statute of the Arbitration Court of Conscience, drawn up in 1801* [Derzhavin G.R. Ustav tryetyeiskogo sovyestnogo suda, sostavlyennyi v 1801 g.] (Unpublished manuscript; a copy is available in the library of the Law Faculty of St Petersburg State University).

The adoption of the Regulation on Arbitration Courts 1831 marked the beginning of the period of prevalence for the arbitral 'tribunals of conscience'. These courts resolved disputes on the basis of equitable considerations rather than the law.[10]

In turn, it was ordered that the 'legalised' arbitration courts should resolve disputes according to trade customs.

The idea of 'legalised' arbitration courts was soon discredited. The parties were reluctant to refer disputes to them. Moreover, the procedure of the 'legalised' arbitration court became burdensome not only for disputants but also for arbitrators. It became difficult to find arbitrators willing to take up a case, which resulted in frequent appointments of government officials. In turn, officials were reluctant to perform their arbitral duties. In the end, according to contemporaries, arbitration degenerated into an instrument of heavy and endless delay.[11]

Following the decline of 'legalised' arbitration courts, they were abolished during the judicial reform of 1864. The new Charter of Civil Procedure laid down the rules for arbitration. In the Explanatory Notes to the Charter, its drafters noted that 'the form of arbitration should be as light and easy as possible'.[12] During the debates on the draft Charter, an entire volume of materials on the transformation of the judiciary was devoted to conciliatory proceedings. These documents were also accompanied by letters and opinions from the public concerning the regulation and activities of arbitration courts. For instance, the materials explaining the legislative motives for judicial reform contain a note of the 'Committee of Shareholders of the Board of the Fire Insurance Society' about the structure and procedures of an arbitration court.[13]

The reform was not easy to design and implement. There were different, often contradictory views on arbitration. Some respondents expressed very radical opinions advocating for the total abolition of this institution. Thus, during the consultation preceding the legislative reform, chairpersons of courts had to answer the question about the merits and demerits of arbitration. All the interviewed chairmen of commercial courts expressed the unanimous opinion that 'the rules of legalised arbitration not only fail to facilitate conciliation, but they merely provide an avenue for evading the court and delaying the resolution of cases; in practice, they are hardly ever used ... In short, with the current regulation, arbitration in general, and legalised arbitration in particular, does not achieve its objectives'.[14]

---

10. Annenkov K., *The Experience of Commenting on the Charter of Civil Procedure*, Vol. 6, 276 (St Petersburg, 1887) [Annenkov K. Opyt kommyentariya k Ustavu grajdanskogo sudoproizvodstva. T. 6. SPb., 1887. S. 276].
11. Potekhin P.A., *Excerpts from the Memoirs of a Lawyer*, 47 The Law Journal (1900) [Potekhin P.A. Otryvki iz vospominanii advokata // Pravo. 1900. N 47].
12. *The Judicial Charters of November 20, 1864, Outlining the Reasoning on Which They Are Based, Published by the State Chancellery*, Part 1, 653 (St Petersburg, 1867) [Sudyebnyye ustavy 20 noyabrya 1864 g. s izlojyeniyem rassujdyenii, na kotoryh oni osnovany, izdannyye gosudarstvyennoi kancyelyariyei. CH. 1. SPb., 1867. S. 653].
13. G. Dzhanshiev, *Foundations of the Judicial Reform* (Moscow, 1891) [Djanshiyev G. Osnovy sudyebnoi ryeformy. M., 1891].
14. Opinion of the Chairman of One of the Commercial Courts on Our Arbitration Courts, 13 Journal of the Ministry of Justice, Vol. 13, Part 2, 187 (1862) [Mnyeniye pryedsyedatyelya odnogo iz kommyerchyeskih sudov o nashih tryetyeiskih sudah // Jurnal Ministyerstva yusticii. 1862. T. 13. CH. 2. S. 187].

Abuses in the field of arbitration proceedings were of diverse nature, but they were most significant in disputes over immovable property. Often, interested parties would initiate fictitious, staged arbitration, attempting thereby to establish a title to some real property. In other cases, through arbitral proceedings, unscrupulous parties tried to avoid payment of the duties for the transfer of ownership in real estate.

The development of commercial arbitration dealing with disputes between merchants was dynamic. Exchange arbitration became especially widespread in the late nineteenth century. Dealings at the exchanges were very complex and required qualified lawyers who could resolve disputes arising from such transactions.[15] Naturally, this type of proceedings was very attractive for traders who were interested in the speedy resolution of conflicts. The high level of exchange arbitration was evidenced by the fact that merchants from all over Europe, including Berlin, Hamburg, Liverpool, London, requested the assistance of the Arbitration Commission at the Kalashnikov Grain Exchange in St. Petersburg in settlement of their disputes.

From the second half of the nineteenth century, arbitration became a subject of serious academic research. A.I. Vitsyn's book *On Arbitration in Russian Law* became a distinctive landmark in the literature devoted to arbitration.[16]

However, optimistic views of arbitration coexisted with opinions that were more critical of it. Prominent pre-revolutionary Russian lawyers also reported negative, anti-arbitration attitudes. For example, Professor I.E. Engelman pointed out that arbitration, due to the strict formalities of legislation and excessively suspicious attitudes of the judiciary, has, in fact, become removed from the resolution of civil disputes.[17]

Nevertheless, despite the diverging positions, arbitration continued to exist as an institution of non-governmental dispute resolution, to some extent independent of public authorities, especially in the commercial sphere.

In the Soviet period, the legal system rejected many 'bourgeois' legal institutions. As far as arbitration is concerned, throughout the entire history of Soviet law, the legislator never refused to regulate the activities of arbitral tribunals. However, arbitration did not become widespread.

According to the Decree on the Court (No. 1) of 24 November 1917, interested persons were entitled to refer disputes to arbitration in all civil cases and in private criminal cases (a category of criminal cases where a private party and not a designated public authority had to maintain prosecution). The Decree of the All-Russian Central Executive Committee on Arbitral Tribunals of 16 February 1918 became one of the first actions of the Soviet authorities in the area of justice. This decree was in force until 16 October 1924 when the newly adopted Regulation on Arbitration Tribunals replaced it. The Regulation, in turn, considerably limited the possibilities for the use of arbitration.

---

15. Volkov A.F., *Exchange Law: Exchange Court and the Rules of Exchange Trade in Grain Products*, Vol. 1, 1-16 (St Petersburg, 1905) [Volkov A.F. Birjyevoye pravo. Birjyevoi sud i pravila birjyevoi torgovli hlyebnymi tovarami. T. 1. SPb., 1905. S. 1-16].
16. Vitsyn A.I., *On Arbitration in Russian Law* (Moscow, 1856) [Vitsyn A.I. O tryetyeiskih sudah po russkomu pravu. M., 1856].
17. Engelman I.E., *Textbook on Russian Civil Procedure*, 400 (Yuriev, 1904) [Engelman I.E. Uchyebnik russkogo grajdanskogo sudoproizvodstva. - Yuryev, 1904. S. 400].

First, it became possible to arbitrate only the civil disputes 'between private individuals, including collectives' – thereby the criminal cases of private prosecution were withdrawn from arbitral jurisdiction. Second, the parties now could only refer the existing disputes to arbitration but not those that might arise in the future. Third, the law only stipulated for the existence of arbitration tribunals for the resolution of a single dispute (ad hoc) but not institutional arbitration centres.

With the strengthening of a socialist economy in the Soviet Union, arbitration virtually disappeared from the domestic legal agenda and remained in existence, essentially, only insofar as international commercial contracts of socialist enterprises were concerned. Some Soviet lawyers opined that arbitration had outlived itself.[18]

Meanwhile, the Soviet government was developing international commerce and cooperation, and thus could not ignore the established institutions, not least of which was international commercial arbitration. In 1932, the Foreign Trade Arbitration Commission (FTAC) was established. Its current successor is the International Commercial Arbitration Court at the Chamber of Commerce and Industry of the Russian Federation (ICAC at the RF CCI). The Maritime Arbitration Commission (MAC) established in 1930 at the All-Union Chamber of Commerce became another longstanding and authoritative arbitral institution.

The 1950s and 1960s saw the revival of economic activity in the USSR. The ideas about community control and management grew in popularity. These factors drew the attention of the legislator to arbitral forms of dispute resolution in economic life. The need to involve members of the public in the exercise of public functions traditionally performed by government authorities led to the increase of the role arbitration played in the life of the society.[19] Arbitration was considered one of the steps on the path of the development of socialist statehood into public self-government.[20]

On 23 July 1959, the Council of Ministers of the USSR adopted a Resolution 'On Improving the Work of State Arbitration' permitting arbitration between companies and other legal entities. The idea behind this step was to increase the involvement of the public in the resolution of commercial disputes, in certain large and complex cases between socialist enterprises.

Implementing this Resolution, on 31 August 1960 the State Arbitration at the Council of Ministers of the USSR approved the Provisional Rules for the Resolution of Economic Disputes by an Arbitration Tribunal,[21] which regulated the main issues relevant for the arbitration of disputes between socialist enterprises.

18. Avdeenko N.I., *On the Jurisdiction of Comradeships Courts in Property Disputes*, 1(5) Bulletin of Leningrad State University, 124 (1961) [Avdeenko N.I. O podvyedomstvyennosti imushyestvyennyh sporov tovarishyeskim sudam // Vyestnik Lyeningradskogo gosudarstvyennogo univyersityeta. 1961. Vyp. 1. N 5. S. 124].
19. Volin A.A., *Resolution of Economic Disputes in Arbitration*, 9 (Moscow, 1962) [Volin A.A. Razryeshyeniye hozyaistvyennyh sporov tryetyeiskimi sudami. M., 1962. S. 9].
20. Lieberman F.H., *The New Issues in the Arbitration Process*, 8 Soviet State and Law, 128 (1962) [Lieberman F.H. Novoye v arbitrajnom procyessye // Sovyetskoye gosudarstvo i pravo. 1962. N 8. S. 128].
21. 15 *Collection of Instructions of the State Arbitration at the Council of Ministers of the USSR*, 72-74 (Moscow, 1961) [Sbornik instruktivnyh ukazanii Gosudarstvyennogo arbitraja pri Sovyetye Ministrov SSSR. Vyp. 15. M., 1961. S. 72-74].

According to the traditions of the time, it was a widespread practice to hold a public hearing of disputes in arbitration (the so-called offsite meetings). For instance, in one reported case arbitration proceedings between the Kuibyshev Office of Energy Sales and a metallurgical plant took place in a conference hall, in the presence of the representatives of thirty city enterprises specially invited to the session of the arbitration tribunal. Such events were considered from the positions of their educational influence on the public and as a form of public participation in self-government.

In 1975, the State Arbitration of the USSR approved the Statute of the Arbitral Tribunal for resolving economic disputes between associations, enterprises, organisations and institutions.

Nevertheless, with the prevalence of administrative methods of managing the economy, arbitration could not become widespread. In 1969, arbitration tribunals in Russia resolved 183 disputes between economic entities and in 1970, this number fell to 94.[22] The relative unpopularity of arbitration allowed legal researchers to question whether there was any need to preserve arbitration as an institution.[23]

From this brief overview, one can see that the development of arbitration in Russia had been uneven and varied from one historical period to another.

§1.02 ARBITRATION REFORM IN RUSSIA AND ITS PREREQUISITES

From the beginning of the 1990s, a liberal model of arbitration dominated in Russia. This led to serious abuses. One negative phenomenon that entrepreneurs and lawyers had to face was the proliferation of so-called pocket arbitration centres. A commercial organisation would typically create such a centre, and unscrupulous businesses utilised them to resolve their problems in illegal ways. As a result, the Ministry of Justice of the Russian Federation implemented a reform of arbitration based on conservative principles and assuming a thorough governmental oversight over the creation and operation of arbitral institutions.

Initially, the idea of an arbitral reform originated with the expert community in 2011. The '*Arbitration*' (*Treteysky Sud*) journal that for many years had been a uniting force for the specialists in this field surveyed public opinion on ways to improve the law on arbitration. The survey revealed that 82% of the respondents were in favour of radical changes in legal regulation. In 2012, the first working groups began to draft a bill for the new federal law 'On Arbitration'. The influential Russian Union of Industrialists and Entrepreneurs joined the drafting process. In the second half of 2012, on the initiative of the editorial board of the '*Arbitration*' journal, the Expert Council of Arbitration Community was created that comprised of the prominent academics and

22. Kallistratova R.F., *State Arbitration*, 25 (Moscow, 1973) [Kallistratova R.F. Gosudarstvyennyi arbitraj. M., 1973. S. 25].
23. Pobirchenko I.G., *Economic Jurisdiction: General Teaching*, 197 (Kyiv, 1973) [Pobirchenko I.G. Hozyaistvyennaya yurisdikciya: Obshyeye uchyeniye. Kiyev, 1973. S. 197]; Khutiz M.H. *Historism in the Study of Problems of Civil Procedural Law*, 1 Jurisprudence, 95 (1984) [Khutiz M.H. Istorizm v isslyedovanii problyem grajdanskogo procyessualnogo prava // Pravovyedyeniye. 1984. N 1. S. 95].

practitioners of arbitration. One of the main tasks within the remit of the Expert Council was to prepare the proposals for the arbitral reform.

In 2012, a board meeting took place at the Russian Union of Industrialists and Entrepreneurs, in which Dmitry Medvedev, the Chairman of the Government of the Russian Federation, took part.

After that, the Government of Russia instructed the Ministry of Economic Development and the Ministry of Justice to form a working group consisting of representatives of interested executive agencies and the judiciary, to foster the development of the institution of arbitration in Russia, as well as to formulate appropriate proposals to that effect. A little later, President of Russia Vladimir Putin instructed the Government to develop, in consultation with business associations, a set of measures to improve the functioning of arbitration in the Russian Federation. These events marked the beginning of the arbitration reform.

In April 2012, the Ministry of Economic Development published a document entitled 'The Concept of the Development of Arbitration'. However, experts in the arbitration community, as well as the Ministry of Justice officials, heavily criticised this document. As a result, an interdepartmental commission was set up, headed by Deputy Minister of Justice of Russia Elena Borisenko.

The next stage of the reform was marked by the release of the document 'Complex of Measures for the Development of Arbitration in the Russian Federation'. It was radically conservative. Despite criticism from the expert community, the Government of Russia adopted this document as the basis for the reform.

By 2014, the first package of draft legislation was ready, consisting of four bills. Arbitration experts met those bills with a barrage of heavy criticism. However, the Ministry of Justice rejected the overwhelming majority of critical remarks.

In the course of the discussion with the official authorities, the public created a permanent conference of the Russian arbitration community, uniting the leading arbitral institutions of the country. The conference set itself a goal to monitor the progress of the draft legislation and to prepare expert opinions on the aspects of the reform. The conference included the Russian Centre for the Assistance to Arbitration, the Russian Union of Industrialists and Entrepreneurs, the Interregional Arbitration Centre and others. Eventually, the conference published an unfavourable conclusion on the Ministry of Justice's package of bills.

In May 2014, the Council on Codification and Improvement of Civil Legislation under the President of the Russian Federation also prepared its opinion on the bill. Although the Council supported the draft law as a whole, it made many significant critical remarks; such criticism originated with the Council itself and with other bodies.[24] In particular, the Administration of the President of the Russian Federation wrote a negative opinion. As a consequence, the bills were re-drafted, and in 2015 the new versions of the bills entered in the State Duma for consideration.

After the adoption by the State Duma on 29 December 2015, the President of the Russian Federation signed the Arbitration Act 2015 into force.

---

24. All comments on the draft laws were summarised and published in a special issue of the 'Arbitration' journal – *see* 2/3 Treteysky Sud (2014) [Treteysky Sud. 2014. No. 2/3].

§1.03 THE CURRENT STATE OF ARBITRATION IN RUSSIA

The transitional period following the enactment of the Arbitration Act 2015 took almost two years. When the arbitration reform began, there were, according to various estimates, between 2,000 and 3,000 permanent arbitration centres in Russia. By the time the reform was over – and 1 November 2017 can be regarded as its completion date – there were four arbitral institutions left in the entire country.

As a result of the reform, an extremely conservative arbitration model was created in Russia implying rigorous government oversight over the creation of arbitral institutions and the operation of arbitration in general. The Ministry of Justice of the Russian Federation is responsible for exercising this control.

In contrast to the pre-existing notification procedure for the setting up of arbitral institutions, a new system has now been introduced requiring a permission to create one. There are three stages in the process of obtaining a permit: (1) verification of formalities in the application and supporting documents by the responsible department within the Ministry of Justice; (2) receiving a recommendation from the Council for the Development of Arbitration at the Ministry of Justice; (3) getting a permit to operate as a permanent arbitral institution from the Government of the Russian Federation.

In the two years since the enactment of the Arbitration Act 2015, only two permanent arbitral institutions – the Institute of Modern Arbitration (IMA) and the Arbitration Centre at the Russian Union of Industrialists and Entrepreneurs – have obtained such a license. Two arbitral institutions (International Commercial Arbitration Court at the Chamber of Commerce and Industry of the Russian Federation (ICAC at the RF CCI) and the Maritime Arbitration Commission at the Chamber of Commerce and Industry of the Russian Federation (MAC at the RF CCI)) were the creatures of statute and did not need to apply for a permit from the Government to exercise the functions of a permanent arbitral institution.

As of 21 December 2017 (i.e., within two years of the adoption of the new law), the Ministry of Justice of Russia received applications for the permit to exercise the functions of a permanent arbitral institution from about fifty non-profit organisations located on the territory of the Russian Federation. In total, there were eighty-eight applications because some non-profit organisations applied several times. In most cases, applications and supporting documents were returned to applicants due to the discovery of inaccurate information in them.

The goals declared from the early days of the reform – promoting the image of arbitration that would be on par with the world's leading arbitration institutions and free from the use of fraudulent schemes – determined the choice of the conservative model of arbitration in Russia.

Among the directions of further development of arbitration, the Ministry of Justice intends to create the incentives for the existing arbitration institutions to develop their regional networks. Arbitration institutions that have the right to administer arbitration have already set up some new regional centres. International Commercial Arbitration Court (ICAC) opened its branches in Rostov-on-Don, Irkutsk, Ufa and Kazan on the basis of pre-existing permanent arbitral institutions at regional Chambers of commerce and industry. The IMA launched its Far Eastern branch with offices in Vladivostok and Petropavlovsk-Kamchatsky and the Department for Dispute Resolution in the Nuclear Energy of the IMA's Arbitration Centre. According to the ICAC information, the Chamber of Commerce and Industry of the Russian Federation plans to expand the geography of the ICAC further and open new branches. Such branches will most likely be interregional, each serving the needs of more than one territory within the Russian Federation.

At the end of 2018, a statutory amendment to Article 44 of the Arbitration Act 2015 simplified the procedure of obtaining a permit to exercise the functions of a permanent arbitral institution. From the day that the amendment entered into force (29 March 2019), the third stage of the licensing procedure involving the Government of the Russian Federation had been abolished, making an order of the Ministry of Justice the final stage of the process. At the same time, the requirements relating to foreign arbitral institutions with a widely recognised international reputation were also somewhat relaxed. Shortly after those amendments entered into force, on the basis of the Council for the Development of Arbitration recommendation dated 4 April 2019 and the Ministry of Justice's order dated 25 April 2019, the Hong Kong International Arbitration Centre (HKIAC) became the first international arbitral institution to obtain official permission to operate in Russia. Together with the new Russian arbitration centre, the Sports Arbitration Chamber – the creation of which was prescribed by the Federal Law 'On Physical Culture and Sport in the Russian Federation' and which obtained the Council's recommendation on the same day – the HKIAC's application brought the overall number of permanent arbitral institutions with a permission to operate in Russia to six. Although it is too early to judge the effects of these developments, after the 'lull' of the first years following the reform, this was a step forward welcomed by the Russian arbitration experts.

§1.04 PLACE OF ARBITRATION WITHIN THE SYSTEM OF CIVIL JURISDICTION

As a legal institution, arbitration finds itself at the juncture, on the one hand, of public and private law, and on the other – of substantive and procedural law, and comprises both international law and national legislation as its sources. Local rulemaking by arbitral institutions (regulations, charters, rules, etc.), as well as the agreements of private parties, is also of great significance for this institution.

The institution of arbitration is an exception to the state monopoly to the administration of justice. This monopoly has its roots in the understanding of power, including judicial power, as a prerogative of public authorities. By authorising arbitration, the state agrees that private parties in civil legal relations are entitled to establish such rules for resolving disputes between them as they deem appropriate.

The points above essentially determine the understanding of legal relations in this sphere. Procedural rules, usually very detailed and mandatory (such as the court rules), acquire in this case a contractual character because it is the agreement of private parties that lays the foundation for the entire procedure of arbitration. Hence, in arbitration law the *lex voluntaris* principle – the autonomy of the parties – becomes paramount. Autonomy of the parties is essential not only for the substantive but also for the procedural legal relations between the parties because it shapes the arbitral procedure without regard to any regulation by a public authority.

At the same time, one should not forget that the state does not entirely forfeit its control over arbitration. The legislation lays down the specific parameters within which actors in arbitration can exercise their procedural rule-making powers. But just like, for example, in the civil-law regulation of contractual rulemaking, these legislative parameters only outline those boundaries that the parties cannot trespass. This reasoning led to the emergence of a doctrine of public policy, which serves as a limit for the realisation of the interests of private parties. The unauthorised intrusion of private actors into the public sphere is suppressed in the manner prescribed by law. Control over the activities of private actors in arbitration is, to some extent, entrusted to state courts. Thus, when a party challenges an arbitral award, the competent state court can verify the validity of an arbitration agreement, i.e., the compliance of a contract whereby private actors refer the dispute to arbitration, to the legislative framework requirements for arbitration agreements. For example, where the parties did not comply with the statutory requirements prescribing the written form for the arbitration agreement, this will be a ground for challenging the award or refusing to enforce it because of the violation of a mandatory legal rule.

The need for an adequate description of arbitration's legal nature is important not just for the sake of its study as a social and legal phenomenon. This description is also essential for the legislative process, the primary purpose of which is to place legal institutions correctly within the regulatory system, to optimise the forms of their normative expression, to determine the relationships between adjacent legal institutions. One of the crucial dimensions of legislative work is the optimal structuring of normative material via statutory acts. Such optimisation is based, as a rule, on the analysis of patterns in legal evolution and on the drafting of regulations that reflect such patterns and drive the development of the society in the desired direction.

The intertwining of the public and private elements in arbitration is evident from the fact that private actors, at their discretion, change publicly significant relations – the jurisdiction in civil cases. The mechanism of jurisdiction helps the government to perform one of its traditional functions, the administration of justice and protection of individual rights. This situation, almost impossible in public legal proceedings, proves to be admissible in the sphere of private dispute settlement. Moreover, the possibility of altering the jurisdiction to hear a dispute is a fundamental principle of arbitration, without which it would be hard to imagine its existence. By its resolution, a private person is changing the seemingly unshakable foundation of public authority – the exclusive right of a state to resolve conflicts. The arbitration agreement, i.e., the act of two private parties that changes the procedure for the resolution of disputes between them, is one of the critical elements of the institution of arbitration. However, the discretion of individuals who are altering the public organisation of the dispute settlement system is only valid up to a certain limit. It remains possible only while attempts to resolve a private-law conflict proceed with the recognition of the rights of the opposing party, including the voluntary compliance with an award of the arbitral tribunal. As soon as one side of the conflict demonstrates a disregard for the rights of its counterparty by failing to comply with an arbitral award, this 'period of unfettered discretion' ends. The state intervenes by providing the person concerned with the means to enforce the decision of the arbitral tribunal. The parties' agreement can no longer govern the enforcement procedure; it has to rely on the mandatory requirements of the law. Such a division of spheres is entirely understandable. The confusion between the regimes of free and regulated activity, the extension of the rules designed for the first type of activity ('everything is allowed that does not contradict certain public interests') to the second ('only that is allowed which is prescribed by law') and vice versa is unacceptable. It leads either to the arbitrariness, government dictatorship and the violation of the rights and freedoms of individuals (civil society) or to the anarchy for all private actors and the violation of the interests of the public and the state.[25] For arbitration, this means that the state is a 'sleeping guardian' for private actors who are entitled to 'invent' arbitral process at their discretion, provided that it does not infringe public policy, the rights of the counterparty or the rights of any third parties. If such infringement occurs, the state (i.e., the judiciary on its behalf) 'awakens' and interferes in private relations, trying to make them stable again.

In the Russian legal scholarship, the study of the problems concerning arbitral process traditionally belongs within the framework of civil procedure, because arbitration is seen as a procedural activity aimed at the resolution of civil disputes. This approach leads some experts to the conclusion that the institution of arbitration is an integral part of the civil procedural law,[26] which in turn serves as the basis for the so-called 'procedural theory' of the legal nature of arbitration. The latter concept is based on the prevalence of procedural legal rules in arbitration. In the general legal theory, the classification of mixed legal institutions as belonging to one branch of law or another is often said to depend on the origins (from a particular branch of law) of the predominant part of legal rules comprising this legal institution.[27] However, the very idea of putting the question this way has already been criticised in the Russian legal literature as confusing the system of law with its internal classification.[28]

For our current subject, this means that from the quantitative dominance of procedural norms it does not follow that there is any need for a categorical qualification of the institution of arbitration as an element of the procedural law. The combination of rules with different origins in a single legal phenomenon militates against its treatment as having a monistic legal nature and testifies to its complex nature.

25. Popondopulo V.F., *The System of Public Relations and Their Legal Forms (To the Question of the System of Law)*, 4 Jurisprudence, 83 (2002) [Popondopulo V.F. Sistyema obshyestvyennyh otnoshyenii i ih pravovyye formy (k voprosu o sistyemye prava) // Pravovyedyeniye. 2002. No. 4. S. 83].
26. *See*, e.g., Kurochkin S.A., *The Theoretical and Legal Foundations of Arbitration in Russian Federation: An Abstract of a Doctor of Law Dissertation*, 6 (Ekaterinburg, 2004) [*Kurochkin S.A. Tyeoryetiko-pravovyye osnovy tryetyeiskogo razbiratyelstva v Rossiiskoi Fyedyeracii: Avtoryef.diss...k.yu.n.* – Ekaterinburg, 2004. S. 6].
27. Alekseev S.S., *On the Theoretical Basis for the Classification of Branches of Soviet Law*, 7 Soviet State and Law, 104 (1957) [*Alekseev S.S. O tyeoryetichyeskih osnovah klassifikacii otraslyei sovyetskogo prava. // Sovyetskoye gosudarstvo i pravo.* 1957. No. 7. S. 104].
28. Tolstoy Yu.K., *On the Theoretical Foundations of the Codification of Civil Legislation*, Jurisprudence, 47 (1957) [Tolstoy Yu.K. O tyeoryetichyeskih osnovah kodifikacii grajdanskogo zakonodatyelstva. // Pravovyedyeniye. 1957. S. 47].

Meanwhile, the procedural theory of the legal nature of arbitration becomes the theoretical basis for modelling such a legislative civil procedure system that treats arbitration as an element of civil procedure. Accordingly, arbitration is seen through the prism of the civil procedural law. Such views are quite numerous.

The outlined approach to arbitration and its correlation with the civil procedural law is questionable. Yes, there is every reason to say that there is a connection between arbitration and civil procedure. The aim of both civil procedure and arbitration is the resolution of disputes; such disputes are resolved in a specific procedural format. The enforcement of an arbitral award is only possible with the sanction of a competent state court that acts according to the norms established by civil procedural law; likewise, parties are entitled to challenge arbitral awards before the state courts. This list can continue. As a matter of form, the relationship between arbitration and civil process manifests itself in the fact that the both Code of Civil Procedure and the Commercial Procedure Code of Russian Federation contain chapters dealing with the enforcement of arbitral awards, the procedure for their challenge and certain other arbitration-related matters.

At the same time, the qualification of arbitration as a constituent element of civil procedure does not reflect the reality of social relations in this area. Several considerations evidence this fact.

First, the two legal phenomena – civil procedure and arbitration – are based on different principles. If civil procedure and arbitration share some principles between them, these are the principles that have general legal significance (legality, adversarial character, freedom of choice, equality of parties). They are not specific only to these legal phenomena but also apply to other areas of law.

At the same time, the specific internal principles of civil justice and arbitration are different. For example, publicity of proceeding is a principle of civil procedure. Confidentiality in the civil judicial process is an exception to the general principle of its publicity and is permissible only where the law thus provides, e.g., to safeguard the interests of minors, to prevent the disclosure of intimate details of personal life, to protect state and commercial secrets. In arbitration procedure, on the contrary, confidentiality is a governing principle, and the openness of hearings is treated as *jus singulare* (the rule for special cases) since it is permissible only where the participants in the process so agree.

Besides, there are other principles of arbitration, even if the statute does not name them as such – for example, the competence-competence principle and the principle of autonomy of the arbitration agreement. Researchers note that these two principles are special[29] since they are not expressly named as the principles of arbitration but have normative significance as the central categories of the arbitration procedure.

29. *Commentary to the Federal Law 'On Arbitration Courts in the Russian Federation'* (Makovsky A.L., Sukhanov E.A., eds) 77-78 (Moscow, 2003) (author of the commentary – E.A. Vinogradova) [Kommyentarii k Fyedyeralnomu zakonu 'O tryetyeiskih sudah v Rossiiskoi Fyedyeracii'. / Otv. ryed. A.L. Makovsky, E.A. Sukhanov. - M., 2003. S. 77-78 (avtor komm. - E.A. Vinogradova)].

Additionally, the content and the meaning of principles with the same name in civil procedure and arbitration differ. For example, freedom of choice in arbitration provides the parties with much broader powers than those of the litigants in civil process. The discretionary powers of the arbitral tribunal – a consequence of this freedom – acquire a different character than the corresponding powers of a state court.

The same goes for the adversarial character of the procedure.

Second, the heterogeneous groups of social relations that are the object of legal regulation also testify to the different nature of the two legal phenomena (i.e., civil/commercial civil justice and arbitration). The civil procedural law is a set of rules governing the social relations concerning the administration of justice,[30] while arbitration law is a set of rules governing the resolution of disputes in arbitration, which is not justice but instead an alternative method of resolution of legal disputes.

The essential components of arbitration include elements of both substantive (e.g., contractual) and procedural legal nature. This circumstance makes it impossible to consider arbitration solely from the positions of procedural law and, consequently, does not allow one to treat arbitration law as an integral part of the procedural law, where the latter is understood as a systemic commonality of rules with a single (procedural) orientation. The genetic dominance of substantive legal elements in arbitration makes it impossible to consider this institution as belonging unequivocally in the bosom of the procedural system.

Third, there is a difference in the legal regimes of regulation, i.e., the set of methods for regulating the relevant social relations. The civil procedural law adopts a relatively homogeneous mandatory method of regulation, whereas the approach of arbitration law is not uniform at all. It combines various methods of regulation, both imperative and permissive, using mandatory as well as default rules. Furthermore, the subjects of regulation (the parties) in arbitration establish the rules themselves, so that subsequently the third party (the arbitral tribunal) could apply such self-imposed rules to them.

Thus, attempts to describe the regulatory method of arbitration law from the standpoint of trying to identify its 'classical', non-mixed method are doomed to failure. At the same time, it is practically impossible to draw a line between imperative and permissive methods of regulation in arbitration law.

One must also note that arbitral tribunal can have certain delegated public law functions. For example, it has the authority to order interim measures, including the imposition of a security arrest on vessels (Article 388 of the Merchant Shipping Code of the Russian Federation 1999). In this case, arbitral tribunal – a creature of private law – wields public authority.

Thus, *arbitration can be described as a complex legal institution, the sources of which are the rules of both substantive and procedural law, public and private law, as well as the rules formulated by arbitral institutions and the parties themselves.* The qualitative distinctiveness of this institution stems from the inseparable connection

30. *Civil Procedure* (Musin V.A., Chechin N.A., Chechot D.M., eds) 128 (Moscow, 1996) (author of the chapter – D.M. Chechot) [Grajdanskii procyess. / Pod ryed. V.A. Musina, N.A. Chechinoi, D.M. Chechota. – M., 1996. C. 128 (avtor glavy – D.M. Chechot)].

and interaction of its elements. The place of arbitration in the system of Russian law is determined by its independence from the civil procedural law, with which, however, there is a close relationship.

Genetically, arbitration is conceived in the system of private and substantive law on the basis of a contract (arbitration agreement) and later transforms into a system of procedural rules governing the relations of the disputing parties. In its final stages, the arbitration process acquires the features of exclusive public legal nature, since the implementation of an arbitral award requires the involvement of state courts.

At the same time, since the jurisdiction of an arbitral tribunal and the arbitration procedure itself are determined by the parties and derive from the will of the parties, no relations of power and subordination arise here in such a form as they exist in the civil procedure.[31]

§1.05 LEGAL REGULATION OF ARBITRATION IN RUSSIA

In the modern history of Russia, one can identify three stages in the development of arbitral legislation: Stage 1 (1992-2002) – the operation of Provisional Regulations on the Court of Arbitration for the Resolution of Economic Disputes;[32] Stage 2 (2002-2016) – the legal regulation under the Arbitration Act 2002; Stage 3 (from 2016 onwards) – since the coming into force of the Arbitration Act 2015.

The modern Russian legislation on arbitration includes the Arbitration Act 2015 as its central element, with the procedural codes (the Code of Civil Procedure and the Commercial Procedure Code) regulating the process of challenging and enforcing arbitral awards and various other arbitration-related matters. At the same time, since 1993 to this day the Law on International Commercial Arbitration (the ICA Act 1993) has been in force, as amended over the past two and a half decades, in parallel with the legislation on domestic arbitration. Thus, the regulation of arbitration in Russia is dualistic, which entails separate legal regimes for domestic and international arbitration.

There is a strong link between the Arbitration Act and the procedural codes since the implementation of the provisions of the Act is often impossible without further detailed regulation of the procedures for the civil and commercial courts to follow. This consideration is especially important in the context of challenging and enforcing arbitral awards.

Besides the main statute in this area, other federal laws may also contain rules on arbitration. Examples include the Federal Law 'On Chambers of Commerce and Industry in the Russian Federation', the Federal Law 'On State Registration of Immovable Property Rights and Transactions ', the Federal Law 'On Mortgage (Pledge of

31. Morozov M.E., *Arbitration among the Branches of Law,* 1 The Law, 45 (2008) [*Morozov M.E. Otraslyevaya priroda tryetyeiskogo suda. // Zakon. 2008.* No. 1. S. 45].
32. Decree of the Supreme Council of the Russian Federation of 24 June 1992 No. 3115-1 'On the approval of the Provisional Regulations on the Court of Arbitration for the Resolution of Economic Disputes.'

Immovable Property)', the Federal Law 'On Self-Regulating Organisations', the Federal Law 'On Organised Trade (Exchanges)' and some others.

The system for legal regulation of arbitration in Russia also includes by-laws and statutory instruments enacted on the basis of the Arbitration Act. Many such instruments were adopted by the Ministry of Justice of the Russian Federation.

CHAPTER 2
Theoretical Foundations of Arbitration in Russia

§2.01 TERMINOLOGY

There are several peculiarities in the terminology of Russian law. In particular, it operates with two terms: '*arbitrazh*' (a calque of the French '*l'arbitrage*') and '*treteysky sud*' (literally, 'a court of the third'), which both mean 'arbitration'. The word 'court' can sometimes legitimately refer to an arbitral tribunal.

Within arbitration law proper, the term '*arbitrazh*' has four meanings. First, it is one of the ways to protect an individual civil right, an alternative to state judicial remedies. Second, it denotes the body that organises the resolution of disputes (an arbitral institution). Third, '*arbitrazh*' means one or more arbitrators considering a specific dispute (an arbitral tribunal). Finally, '*arbitrazh*' can refer to the arbitral proceedings in general.

Also, the term '*arbitrazh*' recently acquired another meaning, which to some extent has overshadowed the original one. Due to historical reasons, regular state courts dealing with economic disputes between entrepreneurs received an official designation of '*arbitrazh* courts'. At the same time, the previous meaning of this term – an out of court mechanism where private parties agree to resolve a civil dispute through a final and binding award – remains in use as well.

Thus, the term '*arbitrazh*' may sound ambiguous, especially to those who obtained their legal training outside Russia. In order to avoid misleading the reader, this book will refer to the state '*arbitrazh* courts' as 'commercial courts'. Following the conventional English usage, a 'court' will mean a state judicial authority, and a 'tribunal' will refer to an arbitral tribunal – unless otherwise specified. The terms 'arbitration, 'arbitral institution', 'arbitral tribunal' and 'arbitral proceedings' shall also be used in their respective conventional meanings.

§2.02 THE ESSENCE OF ARBITRATION

Arbitration finds itself at the junction of several legal domains. On the one hand, it intertwines public and private law, and on the other, substantive and procedural law. The law of arbitration encompasses both the international rules and the national legislation. Also, the rules of arbitral institutions, as well as the norms generated by private parties' agreements, are essential for arbitration.

This institution is an exception to the state monopoly to the administration of justice, which presumes that any power, including judicial power, has to be a prerogative of public authorities. Through this exception, the state grants commercial parties, in their private relations, the right to lay down their own rules for the resolution of disputes. The state treats the procedural relations in this private sphere as contractual, because it is the agreement of disputing parties that lies at the heart of these procedural relations. Arbitration law holds in high regard the principle of *lex voluntaris*, i.e., the idea of the autonomy of the parties. The autonomy of the parties is essential not only in substantive contract law but also in the procedural relationships of the parties, since the parties determine the latter independently, or almost independently, from the will of public authorities. Here lies the similarity between civil law and arbitration. Parties in civil contracts acquire and exercise their rights by their will and in their interest, and the parties of disputed legal relations also enter into arbitration agreements by their will and in their interest.

However, the state does not leave arbitration entirely outside its control. The legislation defines framework parameters wherein private procedural rule-making is allowed. This approach stems from the doctrine of public policy, the boundaries of which delineate what individual parties can do. Invasion of private parties into the public sphere will be suppressed in ways prescribed by the law. In Russia, supervision of the private parties' activities in arbitration rests with state courts and the Ministry of Justice. For example, hearing an application to set aside an arbitral award, the competent court can check the validity of the arbitration agreement, i.e., the compliance of the private parties' contract with the current legislation on arbitration and the civil procedural law. Non-compliance, e.g. failure to put the agreement in writing, will lead to setting aside an award or refusal to enforce it because of the violation of mandatory legal rules. As for the Ministry of Justice, it conducts an audit during the establishment of an arbitral institution. It also has the right to oversee the activities of arbitral institutions and to demand that they remedy any non-compliance with the law the Ministry might discover.

Private and public principles intertwine in arbitration. Private parties, by their agreement, alter the publicly important rules on jurisdiction in civil cases, which the state establishes in the exercise of one of its functions – the administration of justice. The will of a private party thus modifies the seemingly unshakable foundation of public authority, the exclusive right of a state to resolve disputes. The arbitration agreement, i.e., the act of two private law subjects changing the method of resolving disputes between them, is the arbitration's vital element. However, the influence of individual discretion on the public dispute settlement system is only possible up to a limit – only while attempts to resolve a private-law conflict are based on mutual recognition of the opponent's rights, including the voluntary compliance with the arbitral award. As soon as one of the parties demonstrates a disregard for the rights of their counterparty, fails to recognise an arbitral award, the 'period of individual discretion' ends. The public authority intervenes by providing the person concerned with the means to enforce the award. This procedure cannot be subordinated to the agreement of the parties; it has to rely on mandatory rules of civil procedural law. In the case of arbitration, this means that the state acts as a 'dormant guard' for the private parties who can 'create' arbitral process at their discretion, so long as it does not violate public policy, the rights of their counterparty and the third parties. As soon as such a violation occurs, the state (in this case, the judiciary) 'wakes up' and interferes in private relations, taking them back to stability.

The unique position of arbitration law in the legal system stems from the fact that its normative basis includes fewer national legislative provisions than other areas of law, and comparatively more contractual rules, customs and rules of international law. Moreover, the importance of contractual rules in arbitration is higher than that of the legislative prescriptions. In this respect, it is unsurprising that the so-called autonomous theory of arbitration, which considers its legal nature to reflect the practical needs of trade, and thus allows the business community to experiment with it regardless of any direct government regulation, gained some prominence.[1] At the same time, the pragmatism of this approach aligns surprisingly well with the deep humanitarian principle underlying the alternative methods of dispute resolution. As Norbert Rouland correctly noted, 'the category of the contract is preferable to the category of coercion: in this way, it is possible to resolve a significant number of conflicts with greater efficiency and at a smaller cost'.[2] The plurality of arbitration's sources is one of the most convincing arguments showing that it does not fit into the framework of the strictly procedural law. Among the sources of law, there are sources involving no rule-making power of the state, being exclusively a product of the private actors' will. The normative activity of private individuals, based solely on the coordination of their wills, gives arbitration its private legal character, takes it out of the sphere of total public control.

The quantitative dominance of procedural norms in arbitration law does not mean that one has to classify this institution as part of the procedural law. The combination of norms from different legal areas in a single phenomenon militates against treating it as monistic and testifies to its complex legal nature. The essential components of arbitration include elements of both substantive and procedural nature. This circumstance makes it impossible to assess arbitration solely from the standpoint of procedural law and, therefore, to consider it as an integral part of procedural law understood as a systemic commonality of norms with a single (procedural) orientation.

1. Minakov A.I., *Arbitration Agreement and the Practice of International Trade Dispute Settlement*, 84-85 (Moscow, 1985) [*Minakov A.I. Arbitrajnoye soglashyeniye i praktika rassmotryeniya vnyeshnyeekonomichyeskih sporov*. - M., 1985. S. 84-85].
2. Rouland N., *Legal Anthropology*, 180 (Moscow, 1999) [*Rulan N. Yuridichyeskaya antropologiya*. - M., 1999. S. 180].

The genetic dominance of substantive legal elements in arbitration precludes the qualification of this institution in the bosom of the procedural system.

Note that arbitration can perform certain delegated public-law functions. For example, the arbitral tribunal has the authority to order interim measures, including the imposition of a security arrest on vessels (Article 388 of the Merchant Shipping Code of the Russian Federation, 1999). In this case, the arbitral tribunal, a creature of private law, wields public authority. This makes it possible to endow the acts of an arbitral tribunal with a coercive power. At the same time, the competent state court retains control over the implementation of public functions by the arbitral tribunal. Interim security measures are to some extent in conflict with the principles of arbitration, which rely on voluntary submission of the parties to the jurisdiction of the tribunal. However, the legislator in the case had to make an exception. This is because 'measures to secure a claim are, as a rule, carried out against the will of one of the parties, and therefore their implementation requires coercive power'.[3] No litigant is thrilled by the prospect of some measures restraining his ability to use property or dispose of money, which is why parties will always resist the application of interim security measures. Overcoming these obstacles requires an enforcement mechanism.

Thus, *arbitration is a complex legal institution, the sources of which are the norms of both substantive and procedural law, public and private law, as well as the rules of arbitration institutions and the rules formulated by the parties.* The inseparable connection and interaction between its elements determine the qualitative specificity of this institution. The place of arbitration in the system of Russian law is determined by its independence from the civil procedural law, with which, however, there is a close relationship. The mechanical transfer of the categorical and conceptual apparatus of the public civil process to arbitration is a pervasive mistake, which results in a distorted view of arbitration.[4]

Genetically, arbitration originates in the system of private and substantive law on the basis of a contract (arbitration agreement) and transforms into a system of procedural rules governing the parties' relations in the resolution of the dispute. In its final stage, the arbitration process becomes a matter of public law, since the enforcement of an award that was not complied with voluntarily requires the intervention of public authorities – the competent state courts.

One should also note that since the jurisdiction of the arbitral tribunal and the arbitration procedure itself are determined by the parties and derive from the will of the parties, this does not lead to the emergence of power-subordination relations in the form in which they exist in the civil procedure.[5]

3. Musin V.A., *Security Measures for Arbitral Claims*, 48 (Arbitration Court at the Saint Petersburg Chamber of Commerce and Industry, 2001) [*Musin V.A. Myery po obyespyechyeniyu iska, pryedyavlyayemogo v tryetyeiskom sudye. // Tryetyeiskii sud pri Sankt-Pyetyerburgskoi torgovo-promyshlyennoi palatye.* SPb., 2001. S. 48].
4. Valeev D.H., *Commentary to the Federal Law of 24 July 2002 No 102-F 'On Arbitration in the Russian Federation'* 33 (Moscow, 2015) [Kommyentarii k Fyedyeralnomu zakonu ot 24 iyulya 2002 goda No. 102-FZ «O tryetyeiskih sudah v Rossiiskoi Fyedyeracii» - M., 2015. S. 33 (avtor kommyentariya D.H. Valeev)].
5. Morozov M.E., *The Legal Classification of the Nature of Arbitration*, 1 Zakon, 45 (2008) [*Morozov M.E. Otraslyevaya priroda tryetyeiskogo suda. // Zakon*. 2008. No. 1. S. 45].

§2.03 THE LEGAL NATURE OF ARBITRATION

Discussions about the legal nature of arbitration have been going on for more than a century. These discussions took place in Russia as well.

Doctrines on the legal nature of arbitration date back to the ancient Rome. The Roman law distinguished a public judge (judex) and a private arbitrator (arbiter) appointed by the parties and approved by the praetor. The legal basis of arbitration consisted of two contracts: (1) an agreement whereby the parties accepted an obligation to submit to the arbitrator's decision and (2) a parties' contract with the arbitrator, according to which the arbitrator assumed the responsibility to resolve the dispute. The law classified both of these contracts as private legal agreements.[6]

Holistic theories of the legal nature of arbitration were formulated in the nineteenth-century Germany. Russian jurisprudence saw the arrival of these doctrines in the middle of the nineteenth century, brought in by the young lawyers the Emperor sent to study in Germany. The most significant work in this field was the book by A.I. Vitsyn *On Arbitration in Russian Law: Historical and Dogmatic Discussion.*[7] In this work, he laid out for the first time in the Russian legal literature the principal doctrines of the legal nature of arbitration. Following him, A.F. Volkov studied the legal nature of arbitration in great depth in the early twentieth century.[8] His research and the questions he raised remain relevant until this day.

Over the century and a half since the release of A.I. Vitsyn's book, the debate lost none of its relevance and urgency. The discussions about the legal nature of an arbitration agreement and arbitration itself continued throughout the twentieth century, in many countries of the world[9] including Russia.[10]

The lack of undisputed, generally accepted approaches to the legal nature of arbitration is not merely a theoretical problem. Failure to resolve it leads to severe difficulties in the application of the law. One of the central practical problems resulting from the understanding of the legal nature of arbitration is the need to determine which areas of law should apply to the arbitration agreement and the arbitral proceedings. The selection of an appropriate group of rules to govern the relationship between the parties must be based on the genetic nature of arbitration.

6. Volkov A.F., *Trade Arbitration*, 1-27 (St Petersburg, 1913) [Volkov A.F. Torgovyye tryetyeiskiye sudy. - SPb., 1913. S. 1-27].
7. Vitsyn A.I., *On Arbitration in Russian Law: Historical and Dogmatic Discussion* (Moscow, 1856). Reprinted in Treteysky Sud journal, issues 2-3, 4-6 (1999), issues 1, 3, 6 (2000). [Vitsyn A.I. Tryetyeiskii sud po russkomu pravu. Istoriko-dogmatichyeskoye rassujdyeniye. - M., 1856. Pyeryeizdaniye v jurnalye «Treteysky sud». 1999. Nos 2-3, 4-6; 2000. Nos 1, 3, 6.]
8. Volkov A.F., *Trade Arbitration. Historical and Dogmatic Study* (St Petersburg, 1913). Reprinted in Treteysky Sud journal, issues 2-3, 4-6 (1999), issues 1, 2, 4 (2000), issues 1, 2, 3-4, 5-6 (2001) [Volkov A.F. Torgovyye tryetyeiskiye sudy. Istoriko-dogmatichyeskoye isslyedovaniye - SPb., 1913 (pyeryeizdaniye v jurnalye «Tryetyeiskii sud». 1999. Nos 2-3; 4-6; 2000. Nos 1, 2, 4; 2001. Nos 1, 2, 3-4, 5-6)].
9. *See*, e.g., the literature review in: Lew J., Mistelis L., Kroll S., *Comparative International Commercial Arbitration*, 71-81 (The Hague, 2003).
10. Anurov V.N., *Arbitration Agreement* (Moscow, 2009) [Anurov V.N. Tryetyeiskoye soglashyeniye. M., 2009].

A study of the legal nature of arbitration in Russia was traditionally carried out by experts in international law. This inevitably left an imprint on the debate, because the problem of understanding this legal phenomenon had to be complicated by the need to evaluate the relations between international private law and national law. This situation is fraught with the danger that the desire to achieve the uniformity of regulation on the international level may lead to the isolation of arbitration from the traditional principles of the country's national legal system.[11]

In addition, the competition between the theories is brought about by the objective fact that arbitration is at an intersection of the substantive and procedural law and has both public and private legal aspects.[12]

To date, the approaches to the explanation of the nature of arbitration do not have a common denominator, and no tendency is currently detectable that one might emerge. It has a visible adverse effect on the courts and legal practice. Perhaps this may be why some Russian experts expressed their doubts as to the practical value of theories explaining the legal nature of arbitration?[13]

We cannot agree with these doubts. From our point of view, the pragmatic consequences of the lack of unity in theoretical ideas about the nature of the arbitration agreement and the arbitration proceedings are: (1) significant uncertainties in the legal regulation of arbitration;[14] (2) tangible contradictions in arbitral and judicial practice concerning the challenge and enforcement of arbitral awards, because the courts do not have sufficient guidelines. In turn, this dictates the urgent need to understand arbitration in the framework of the existing ideas about the law and the place of arbitration in the legal system.

One of the most influential theories in the Russian jurisprudence is the contractual, or consensual, theory of arbitration. This doctrine emphasises the fact that the arbitration agreement is a civil contract that entails civic obligations and liabilities for its parties, including the obligation to abide by the award.

---

11. *See* Anurov V.N., *The Legal Nature of International Commercial Arbitration. Theory and Practice*, 7 (Moscow, 2000) [Anurov V.N. Yuridichyeskaya priroda myejdunarodnogo kommyerchyeskogo arbitraja. Voprosy tyeorii i praktiki. – M., 2000. S. 7].
12. An American lawyer Lawrence M. Fridman noted once that arbitration is comparable to 'a cocktail consisting of a mixture of public and private law'. *See* Friedman L., *Introduction to American Law*, 25 (Moscow, 1993) [Friedman L. Vvyedyeniye v amyerikanskoye pravo. – M., 1993. S 25].
13. Karabelnikov B.R., *Recognition and Enforcement of Foreign Arbitral Awards: Academic and Practical Commentary to the New York Convention 1958*, 62 (Moscow, 2001); Petrov M.V., *Interaction Between the State Court and the International Commercial Arbitration: Abstract of a Ph.D. Dissertation*, 6 (St Petersburg, 2003) [Karabelnikov B.R. Priznaniye i privyedyeniye v ispolnyeniye inostrannyh arbitrajnyh ryeshyenii: Nauchno-praktichyeskii kommyentarii k Nyu-Iorkskoi konvyencii 1958 goda. – M., 2001. S. 62; Petrov M.V. Vzaimodyeistviye gosudarstvyennogo suda i myejdunarodnogo kommyerchyeskogo arbitraja: Avtoryef. diss. ... k.yu.n. – SPb., 2003. S. 6].
14. For example, the French authors point out the difficulty of regulating arbitration arising from the necessity to position the relevant rules, on the one hand, in the Civil Code, and, on the other hand, in the Code of Civil Procedure. *See* Delvolve J.-L., Pointon G.H., Rouche J., *French Arbitration Law and Practice. Dynamic Civil Law Approach to International Arbitration*, 16 (Wolters Kluwer, 2009).

In its structure, an arbitral contract is a complex phenomenon. It includes as its essential elements the arbitration agreement and the arbitral award. By entering into an arbitration agreement, the parties undertake to submit in the future award of an arbitral tribunal. Thus, in the context of this theory, the relationship between the parties acquires the character of a civil contract. All stages of arbitration, from the conclusion of an arbitration agreement to the rendering of an award, are the stages in a single process.[15]

This civilian interpretation of the legal nature of arbitration finds its radical expression in the doctrine that explains the relationship between the arbitrator and the parties in terms of an agency agreement, or a contract for the provision of services between them.[16] This theory proceeds from the premise that the participants in arbitration conclude two kinds of agreements: the parties' agreement to submit a dispute to arbitration (*compromissum*) and the agreement between the parties and the arbitrators (*receptum*).[17] In turn, the arbitral agreement with the arbitrators is interpreted as a mandate, which certifies the right of the arbitration tribunal to resolve the dispute. Fulfilling this assignment, the arbitrators act as agents of the parties. It has been pointed out in the literature that such identification of an arbitration agreement with one of the types of civil contracts is a radical notion.[18] For this reason, an arbitrator is sometimes referred to as a 'hired judge'.[19]

Critics of the 'hired judge' theory highlight the fact that the powers of an arbitrator, determined by his discretion, conflict with the duty of an agent to follow the principal's instructions. An agent completes his task with a report laid out before the principal, which would be incompatible with the functions of an arbitrator who is independent of the parties.[20]

15. Luntz L.A., Marysheva N.I., *The Course of Private International Law. Volume 3. The International Civil Process*, 217 (Moscow, 1976) [Luntz L.A., Marysheva N.I. Kurs myejdunarodnogo chastnogo prava. V 3-h tomah. Tom 3. Myejdunarodnyi grajdanskii procyess. - M., 1976. S. 217].
16. *See* Valeev D.H., *Commentary to the Federal Law of 24 July 2002 No 102-F 'On Arbitration in the Russian Federation'*, 26-27 (Moscow, 2015). One of the consistent supporters of the view of arbitration as a service A.I. Muranov wrote ironically on the subject: 'We cannot fail to note that in Russia, many notaries, lawyers, arbitral institutions and arbitrators are bashful about accepting that their role in dispute resolution is a provision of services, "proudly" attempting to present it instead as an publically significant activity. Surely this activity is publically significant, but by no means that precludes it from being a provision of services.' *See* Muranov A.I., *In Support of the Ministry of Justice's Arbitration Bills*, 2/3 Treteysky Sud. Number, 281 (2014) [Muranov A.I. V poddyerjku tryetyeiskih proyektov Minyusta Rossii. // Treteysky Sud. 2014. No. 2/3. S. 281].
17. Keilin A.D., *Judiciary and Civil Process of the Capitalist States. Part 3: Arbitration*, 44 (Moscow, 1961) [Keilin A.D. Sudoustroistvo i grajdanskii procyess kapitalistichyeskih gosudarstv. Chast 3: Arbitraj. - M., 1961. S. 44].
18. Anurov V.N., *Arbitration Agreement: A Monograph*, 22 (Moscow, 2009) [Anurov V.N. Tryetyeiskoye soglashyeniye: monografiya. - M., 2009. S. 22].
19. Friedman L., *Introduction to American Law*, 26 (Moscow, 1993).
20. Keilin A.D., *Judiciary and Civil Process of the Capitalist States. Part 3: Arbitration*, 45 (Moscow, 1961) [Keilin A.D. Sudoustroistvo i grajdanskii procyess kapitalistichyeskih gosudarstv. Chast 3: Arbitraj. - M., 1961. S. 45].

Another approach to the interpretation of an arbitration agreement as a type of civil transaction treats the arbitrators as representatives of the parties in the proceedings. If the two 'arbitrator representatives' do not come to a consensus, they choose the third arbitrator (super-arbitrator), whose opinion is decisive.

An important practical consequence of the contractual theory is the application of civil-law rules to the validity and invalidity of an arbitration agreement. Thus, where one needs to determine whether the arbitration agreement was concluded between the parties, this inquiry should proceed by examining the subject matter and the necessary terms of the arbitration agreement. When considering an amendment, cancellation, or termination of an arbitration agreement, one should apply the rules of the Civil Code governing amendment, cancellation, and termination of civil contracts. Should the question of possible invalidity of the arbitration agreement arise, the appropriate evaluation should proceed according to the rules on the invalidity of civil contracts as expressed in the civil legislation in force.

From the point of view of the private international law, the contractual theory provides the basis for using a connecting factor in relation to the arbitration procedure, i.e., the possibility of applying foreign law to procedural matters.

However, the proponents of this theory fail to give due consideration to the fact that, strictly speaking, the arbitration agreement itself does not produce any civil-law effects.[21] The legal effect of an arbitration agreement lies in the realm of procedural law, leading to the ousting of the competent state court's jurisdiction to resolve the dispute.

The justification of the civilian nature of an arbitration agreement sometimes boils down to a statement that it provides both parties with the means to protect their rights and interests, and it influences the creation, modification and termination of legal relations indirectly.[22]

However, one must keep in mind that arbitration agreement is an act of private law. In other words, an arbitration agreement is a private-law contract, which, however, is not the same as a civil-law contract. The concept of private-law contract is broader than the concept of a civil contract; the civil contract is a species of private-law contract. One must agree with the proponents of the contractual theory that arbitration agreement is a means of ensuring the efficiency and effectiveness of civil contracts, but this does not affect its legal nature.

Critics of the contractual theory also say that the parties' common will does not find its expression in arbitration – either in the procedure or in the award. Thus, the

21. One can find court decisions expressly stating that the arbitration agreement does not aim to establish, modify or terminate civil rights and obligations. *See* the Decree of the Federal Commercial Court for the Central Circuit of 5 March 2009 No. A35-6404/08-C4. According to another judge, 'an agreement to refer the dispute to an arbitral tribunal is a results of the parties disposing of their procedural rights and obligations'. *See* the Decree of the Federal Commercial Court for the North-Western Circuit of 16 June 2005 No. A56-21019/2004. In yet another decision, the court said that the arbitration agreement is not an agreement that governs the parties' mutual civil rights and obligations. *See* the Ruling of the RF Supreme Court of 2 November 2016 No. 306-ES16-4741.
22. Rozhkova M.A., *Settlement Agreement: The Use in Commerce*, 36-37 (Moscow, 2005) [Rozhkova M.A. Mirovaya sdyelka: ispolzovaniye v kommyerchyeskom oborotye. – M., 2005. S. 36-37].

lack of the parties' common will militates against the contractual nature of arbitration.[23] There were objections to the practical implementation of the contractual theory, especially with regard to treating arbitration as 'conventional' services as the civil law defines this notion, during the latest arbitration reform in Russia. That would be inconsistent with 'the approach of the European Court of Human Rights and the position of the Russian Federation Constitutional Court, regardless of the fact that in many Western pro-arbitration jurisdictions arbitration is equivalent to a service in terms of its taxation and is recognised as such in various economic classifiers (including that of WTO)'.[24]

Russian court practice is inconsistent in its application of the contractual theory. On the one hand, there are numerous instances where the civil-law rules had been applied in cases concerning the invalidity of arbitration agreements.

On the other hand, the state court will revoke a penalty imposed by the tribunal on a party in the arbitration, even if the Rules of arbitration and the parties' agreement expressly provide for such a penalty.[25]

At the heart of the argument behind the jurisdictional (procedural) theory is the thesis that the conclusion of an arbitration agreement only produces one effect, which is procedural. From this, it follows that arbitration agreement is a procedural contract. The purpose of this agreement is to eliminate the possibility of the dispute ending up in a state court, i.e., the modification of the default jurisdictional rules. Also, the activity of an arbitrator is similar in its form to the procedural form in which the state judges act.

Thus, arbitration is a set of procedures carried out in a specific procedural format. Unlike the adepts of the contractual theory, supporters of the jurisdictional theory claim that the arbitration agreement does not produce any substantive effects.

Although arbitration procedure is substantially different from the procedure in state courts, it does not cease to be a procedure, i.e., a normatively organised activity aimed at settlement of a dispute in arbitration.

One of the significant differences between the jurisdictional theory and the contractual theory is that the latter treats the arbitration agreement and arbitral award as the two inextricably linked stages in a single process. In contrast, the procedural doctrine assumes that although arbitration agreement does indeed express the will of the parties, the arbitral award is the product of the arbitrators' will, which is independent of the discretion of the parties. Unlike an arbitration agreement, 'award

23. Luntz L.A., Marysheva N.I., *The Course of Private International Law. Volume 3. The International Civil Process*, 218 (Moscow, 1976) [Luntz L.A., Marysheva N.I. Kurs myejdunarodnogo chastnogo prava. V 3-h tomah. Tom 3. Myejdunarodnyi grajdanskii procyess. – M., 1976. S. 218].
24. Savranskiy M.Y., *Do We Need a Revolution in Russian Arbitration*, 2/3 (92-93) Treteysky Sud, 16 (2014) [Savranskiy M.Y. Nujna li ryevolyuciya v rossiiskom tryetyeiskom razbiratyelstvye? // Treteysky Sud. 2014. No. 2/3 (92-93). S. 16].
25. The Ruling of the Supreme Court of 14 June 2016 No. 305-ES16-5449, case No. A40-131620/2015; the Ruling of the Supreme Court of 9 August 2016 No. 305-ES16-8895, case No. A40-173700/2015; the Ruling of the Supreme Court of 15 August 2016 No. 305-ES16-9450, case No. A40-79284/2015.

may be reviewed or amended by an appeal court which, according to supporters of this theory, strongly confirms that it is a court decision, not a contract'.[26]

Opponents of the jurisdictional theory argue that the arbitration agreement does not as such entail any procedural consequences. The chain of causation that starts with the action of the parties must also include the actions of the state court.[27]

In addition, opponents of the procedural theory say that this doctrine gives the arbitration agreement uncharacteristically public procedural content.

Meanwhile, the *compromis* (the arbitration agreement) is neither a public contract in general nor a procedural agreement in particular, because it cannot produce public relations and does not aim to create procedural consequences (to alter the procedural position of the parties and initiate arbitration).[28]

A practical consequence of the jurisdictional theory is the position that the rules governing substantive aspects of the contract between the parties are not applicable to the arbitration clause. Proponents of this approach, for instance, point to the fact that the arbitration clause cannot be a foreign economic transaction, since it does not regulate civil-law relations between the parties but only deals with procedural relations.[29] The regulations governing the form of foreign trade transaction (in particular, the previously existing rule that required two signatures from each party, by a director and a chief accountant, on a foreign economic contract) cannot apply to the arbitration clause. Those arguments formed the basis of the widely known arbitral award of the Foreign Trade Arbitration Commission in *Soyuznefteexport v JOC Oil Limited (a Bermuda company)*.

In Russian judicial practice, one can also find arguments based on the procedural theory. In one case, the competent national court pointed out that the parties' agreement to submit the dispute to arbitration cannot be treated as a transaction in the sense of Article 153 of the Civil Code. The court explained this conclusion by pointing out that the *arbitration agreement is procedural in nature and does not constitute a transaction as a matter of substantive civil law*, because it does not aim to achieve any legal consequences in this area. The arbitration agreement has legal consequences only in the field of procedural law; therefore, civil-law rules cannot be used as grounds for its annulment. An arbitration agreement is an agreement of the parties to refer the dispute to arbitration, i.e., an agreement that determines the jurisdiction to hear a

26. Kurochkin S.A., *International Commercial and Domestic Arbitration*, 11 (Moscow, 2013) [Kurochkin S.A. Myejdunarodnyi kommyerchyeskii arbitraj i tryetyeiskoye razbiratyelstvo. – M., 2013. S. 11].
27. Rozhkova M.A., *Settlement Agreement: The Use in Commerce*, 143 (Moscow, 2005) [Rojkova M.A. Mirovaya sdyelka: ispolzovaniye v kommyerchyeskom oborotye. – M., 2005. S. 143].
28. Novikov E.Y., *Arbitration of Disputes Within the Jurisdiction of the General Courts of General Jurisdiction: Regulatory Issues*, 195, in: *Contemporary Problems of Civil Procedure* (Musin V.A., ed., St Petersburg, 2002) [Novikov E.Y. Tryetyeiskoye razbiratyelstvo sporov, podvyedomstvyennyh sudam obshyei yurisdikcii: Problyemy normativnogo ryegulirovaniya. // Aktualnyye problyemy grajdanskogo procyessa. / Pod ryed. V.A. Musina. – SPb., 2002. S. 195].
29. Vaneev A.S., Dyakin D.B., *Validity of the Arbitration Clause in the Russian and Foreign Practice*, 1 Bulletin of International Commercial Arbitration, 39 (2010) [Vaneev A.S., Dyakin D.B. Dyeistvityelnost arbitrajnoi ogovorki v rossiiskoi i zarubyejnoi praktikye. // Vyestnik myejdunarodnogo kommyerchyeskogo arbitraja. 2010. No. 1. S. 39].

dispute. This agreement only indicates that the parties disposed of their *procedural* rights and obligations.[30]

The mixed theory of arbitration doctrine combines the postulates of the contractual (consensual) doctrine and the jurisdictional (procedural) theory.

This theory arose as a kind of conciliatory attempt to resolve the seemingly insoluble contradictions between the supporters on the contractual and the jurisdictional theories.

It is conventional to trace the origins of the sui generis theory (from the Latin expression meaning 'one of its kind') to the report by the Swiss professor J. Sauser-Hall presented at the 44th session of the Institute of International Law held in April 1952, which summarised his views on the legal nature of arbitration.[31]

The main content of this theory lies in the fact that some of the elements of arbitration are governed by substantive law and some by procedural law. Thus, the validity of the arbitration agreement and legal capacity of its participants are in the field of contract law, and therefore may be resolved with the recourse to civil law. The matters that concern arbitral proceedings are in the realm of procedural law.[32] At the same time, there is an inextricable link between substantive and procedural aspects of arbitration, because the relevant parts complement each other, and their autonomous existence within the framework of this institution would be meaningless. Proponents of this theory point out that the coexistence of the two elements is marked by their mutual influence and dependence determined by the nature of this institution. One can recognise certain priorities within this system: first come the civil, i.e., substantive (contractual) elements, then, at the subsequent stages, the procedural legal elements.[33]

These features of arbitration, which manifest themselves as the interconnection and interaction between its substantive and procedural elements, allow one to speak of this theory as the sui generis doctrine.

At the same time, the criticism of the mixed theory proceeds from the assertion that it does not offer any criteria to determine the limits of substantive and procedural legal regulation of arbitration.[34] An attempt to declare a legal phenomenon sui generis is an attempt to avoid analysing the complex legal phenomenon, which is essentially an

---

30. The Decree of the Federal Commercial Court for the Volgo-Vyatsky Circuit of 10 May 2011, case No. A11-6675/2010.
31. Lebedev S.N., *The Selected Papers on International Commercial Arbitration, International Trade Law, Private International Law, Private Law of the Sea*, 65 (Compiled by Muranov A.I., Moscow, 2009) [Lebedev S.N. Izbrannyye trudy po myejdunarodnomu kommyerchyeskomu arbitraju, pravu myejdunarodnoi torgovli, myejdunarodnomu chastnomu pravu, chastnomu morskomu pravu. / Sost. A.I. Muranov. – M., 2009. S. 65].
32. *Clause-by-Clause Academic and Practical Commentary to the Federal Law 'On Arbitration in the Russian Federation*, 2 Treteysky Sud, 6 (2003) (author of the comment - Yarkov V.V.) [Postatyeinyi nauchno-praktichyeskii kommyentarii k Fyedyeralnomu zakonu «O tryetyeiskih sudah v Rossiiskoi Fyedyeracii». // Treteysky sud. 2003. No. 2. S. 6 (avtor kommyentariya V.V. Yarkov)].
33. Anufrieva L.P., *Private International Law. Volume 3: Cross-Border Bankruptcy. International Commercial Arbitration. International Civil Procedure*, 146 (Moscow, 2001) [Anufrieva L.P. Myejdunarodnoye chastnoye pravo. Tom 3: Transgranichnyye bankrotstva. Myejdunarodnyi kommyerchyeskii arbitraj. Myejdunarodnyi grajdanskii procyess. - M., 2001. S. 146].
34. Popov M.A., *Theoretical and Practical Problems of the Russian Model of Regulating the Arbitration: An Abstract of the Doctor of Law Dissertation*, 11 (St Petersburg, 2002) [Popov M.A.

interdisciplinary institution that at the same time cannot be reduced to the simple sum of elements.[35]

The autonomous theory of commercial arbitration (the *sui juris* doctrine) arose as a denial of contractual, jurisdictional, and mixed theories. It became a consequence of the refusal to continue the unsuccessful attempts to find a single principle uniting all the above theories.

The idea behind this theory is that arbitration is an independent phenomenon, which does not fit into the Procrustean bed of traditional legal concepts. The legal nature of arbitration must be explained from the vantage point of the convenience of commercial dispute resolution. Most of all, this is in the interests of the entrepreneurs and business people, especially those who are involved in international economic relations. Arbitration procedures are defined by the needs of commerce, which act as the source of this institution's development.

The dynamics of commercial turnover require specific forms of dispute resolution that cannot be explained not only from the standpoint of the substantive or procedural theories but even in the context of the mixed theory of arbitration because arbitration itself continually evolves under the influence of pragmatic considerations. This means that the rules formulated by the parties and arbitrators play the leading role in arbitration, and the role of national legislation is diminished. Thus, the autonomy of the parties becomes dominant in commercial arbitration, independent of the public authorities in all its aspects.

At the same time the autonomous theory, based on the bitter criticism of the competing doctrines, itself does not answer the question about the place of arbitration in the legal reality. This theory refuses to explain the nature of arbitration. This, in our view, makes autonomous theory purely speculative, divorced from the realities of the understanding of social life.

One must note that the autonomous theory developed in relation to international commercial arbitration and deals primarily with its international legal aspects, without explaining those of its features that are peculiar to domestic arbitration.

In the Russian legal scholarship, the representatives of the Yekaterinburg School have considered the problems of the concession theory of arbitration.[36]

The original idea from which the concession theory grew is the justification of the immunity of arbitrators. Hence, its other name is the theory of immunity.

Tyeoryetichyeskiye i praktichyeskiye problyemy rossiiskoi modyeli ryegulirovaniya dyeyatyelnosti tryetyeiskih sudov: Avtoryef. dis. ... kand.yurid.nauk. – SPb., 2002. S. 11].

35. *See* Anufrieva L.P., *Private International Law. Volume 3: Cross-Border Bankruptcy. International Commercial Arbitration. International Civil Procedure*, 145-146 (Moscow, 2001) [Anufrieva L.P. Myejdunarodnoye chastnoye pravo. Tom 3: Transgranichnyye bankrotstva. Myejdunarodnyi kommyerchyeskii arbitraj. Myejdunarodnyi grajdanskii procyess. - M., 2001. S. 145-146]; Anurov V.N., *Arbitration Agreement: A Monograph*, 46-47 (Moscow, 2009) [Anurov V.N. Tryetyeiskoye soglashyeniye: monografiya. – M., 2009. S. 46-47].

36. Kotelnikov A.G., *The Legal Nature and Effects of an Arbitration Agreement: The Doctor of Law Dissertation*, 80 (Ekaterinburg, 2008) [Kotelnikov A.G. Pravovaya priroda arbitrajnogo soglashyeniya i poslyedstviya yego zaklyuchyeniya: Diss. ... k.yu.n. – Ekaterinburg, 2008.]; Chupahin I.M., *Arbitral Award: Theoretical and Applied Problems*, 34 (Moscow, 2015) [Chupahin I.M. Ryeshyeniye tryetyeiskogo suda: tyeoryetichyeskiye i prikladnyye problyemy. – M., 2015. S. 34].

The concession theory relies on the fact that state authorises arbitration ('grants it a concession') to carry out a function of a judicial nature.

The concession theory argues that the arbitral award and its effects are 'the result of a concession from the state. These effects exist within the well-defined limits set by the legislator where the latter considers it expedient to admit individuals to the sphere of law enforcement at a certain stage of development of the economy, while the judicial acts are a direct manifestation of state power'.[37]

This doctrine, if consistently developed and embodied in legislation, may have significant implications for the public authorities. In particular, if the regulator were to admit that the state delegated to a certain extent the implementation of public functions to arbitration, then would become liable (including the financial liability) for the improper performance of their duties by arbitral tribunals. In turn, this becomes the basis to justify the state's careful supervision of arbitration, perhaps going so far as an invasion to the application of law by arbitral tribunals. This ideology is unlikely to be attractive for the state that would assume additional responsibilities, as well as for arbitration that largely loses its independence, being drawn into the official jurisdictional system. This approach is unattractive for parties in arbitration as well, since the substantial control of the state significantly narrows the party autonomy in the formation of the tribunal and determining the rules of arbitration.

One must admit that the concession theory has not been widely recognised in Russian jurisprudence and does not represent a convincing opposition to the other doctrines of the legal nature of arbitration.

The theory of private procedural law has been put forward in the context of the discussion between Russian arbitration experts about its legal nature.[38]

The ideas about procedural relations of contractual character were the forerunner of this theory.[39]

According to supporters of this theory, private self-regulation in general and self-regulation of arbitration in particular has a number of features, including: (1) the

37. Chupahin I.M., *Arbitral Award: Theoretical and Applied Problems*, 40 (Moscow, 2015) [Chupahin I.M. Ryeshyeniye tryetyeiskogo suda: tyeoryetichyeskiye i prikladnyye problyemy. – M., 2015. S. 40].
38. Kurochkin S.A., *On the Question of Private Procedural Law*, 3 Treteysky Syd (2010) [Kurochkin S.A. K voprosu o chastnom procyessualnom pravye. // Tryetyeiskii sud. 2010. No. 3]; Morozov M.E., *Private Procedural Law: A Dead-End Branch of Law or a New Vector in Its Development?*, 6 Treteysky Sud (2010) [Morozov M.E. Chastnoye procyessualnoye pravo: tupikovaya vyetv prava ili novyi vyektor yego razvitiya? // Treteysky Sud. 2010. No. 6]; M.K. Suleimenov, *Private Procedural Law as an Independent Branch of Law*, 3 Treteysky Sud (2011) [Suleimenov M.K. Chastnoye procyessualnoye pravo kak samostoyatyelnaya otrasl prava. // Treteysky Sud. 2011. No. 3]; Sevastyanov G.V., *The Legal Nature of Arbitration as an Institution of Alternative Dispute Resolution (Private Procedural Law)* (St Petersburg, 2015) [Sevastyanov G.V. Pravovaya priroda tryetyeiskogo razbiratyelstva kak instituta altyernativnogo razryeshyeniya sporov (chastnogo procyessualnogo prava). – SPb., 2015]; Sevastyanov G.V., *The Legal Nature of Arbitration and the Competence of the Arbitral Tribunal in the Field of Real Estate: Abstract of a Doctor of Law Dissertation* (Moscow, 2013) [Sevastyanov G.V. Pravovaya priroda tryetyeiskogo razbiratyelstva i kompyetyenciya tryetyeiskogo suda v sfyerye nyedvijimosti: Avtoryef. diss. ... kand. yurid. nauk. – M., 2013].
39. Tarasov V.N., *Arbitration Procedure*, 15 (St Petersburg, 2002) [Tarasov V.N. Tryetyeiskii procyess. – SPb., 2002. S. 15].

private legal regime; (2) the procedural orientation. These features determine the appropriate specificity of the relevant group of norms that constitute private procedural law.[40]

Proponents of the theory of private procedural law proceed from the assumption that the arbitral procedure is generated solely by the will of participants in arbitration. From our point of view, this is not the case. The legislation contains mandatory provisions that determine the duties of the participants in arbitration (e.g., the rule requiring an odd number of arbitrators). These mandatory rules cannot be changed by the parties' discretion.

Also, the doctrine of private procedural law, as we see it, ignores the question about the nature of those relationships that arise in a competent state court hearing an application to set aside or enforce an arbitral award.

The diversity of doctrines that explain the legal nature of arbitration creates difficulties both for the consistent legal regulation and for legal practice. Nevertheless, currently there does not seem to be a prospect in sight that the experts debating the nature of arbitration proceedings, their principles, and the place of arbitration in the legal system might be united within a single theory.

§2.04 TYPES OF ARBITRATION

[A] International Commercial Arbitration and Domestic Arbitration

International commercial arbitration and domestic arbitration are the species of the same legal phenomenon. However, one should bear in mind that while any international commercial arbitration is essentially an arbitral mechanism, not every kind of arbitration meets the definition of international commercial arbitration.

Additionally, there is a strong tendency for unification on a global level in international commercial arbitration, whereas domestic arbitration largely reflects the characteristics of the national legal order.

Russia, unlike some other jurisdictions, adopted a dualistic approach to the regulation of international commercial and domestic arbitration. In practical terms, this means the adoption of two statutes – the ICA Act 1993 and the Arbitration Act 2015.

The main difference between international commercial and domestic arbitration is that disputes involving parties from different states (or with their places of business in different states) are considered in the former, while domestic arbitration deals with disputes involving parties of the same nationality. However, this definition is too broad. There may be multiple grounds for determining the domestic or international

40. Sevastyanov G.V., *The Legal Nature of Arbitration as an Institution of Alternative Dispute Resolution (Private Procedural Law)*, 45 (St Petersburg, 2015) [Sevastyanov G.V. *Pravovaya priroda tryetyeiskogo razbiratyelstva kak instituta altyernativnogo razryeshyeniya sporov (chastnogo procyessualnogo prava)*. – SPb., 2015. S. 45]; Sevastyanov G.V., *The Legal Nature of Arbitration and the Competence of the Arbitral Tribunal in the Field of Real Estate: Abstract of a Doctor of Law Dissertation*, 14 (Moscow, 2013) [Sevastyanov G.V. *Pravovaya priroda tryetyeiskogo razbiratyelstva i kompyetyenciya tryetyeiskogo suda v sfyerye nyedvijimosti: Avtoryef.diss. …kand.yurid.nauk*. – M., 2013. S. 14].

nature of a dispute, depending on the specific regulation in the national law of any given country.[41] National statutes governing international commercial arbitration formulate the provisions that specify which entities are eligible to make use of it within this jurisdiction, and thereby distinguish between international and domestic arbitration.

Thus, according to Article 1(3) of the Russian ICA Act 1993, the parties by their agreement may refer to international commercial arbitration the disputes resulting from contractual and other civil-law relationships arising in the course of foreign trade and other forms of international economic relations, provided that:

- the place of business of at least one of the parties is situated abroad; or
- if any place where a substantial part of the obligations out of the relationship of the parties is to be performed is situated abroad; or
- the place with which the subject matter of the dispute is most closely connected is situated abroad;
- as well as disputes arising in connection with the foreign investments in the territory of the Russian Federation or Russian investments abroad.

International commercial arbitration is regulated by international law and the national laws that work in tandem with it (usually the statutes on international commercial arbitration), whereas the central source of regulation for domestic arbitration, as a rule, is the national arbitral legislation.

The Russian statutory law on domestic arbitration uses two terms to refer to 'non-Russian' arbitral institutions – a 'foreign arbitral institution' and 'international commercial arbitration'.

A foreign arbitration institution is an organisation established outwith the Russian Federation and administering arbitration on a permanent basis, regardless of whether or not it has an independent legal personality. Thus, it is possible that a foreign arbitral institution within the meaning of the Arbitration Act 2015 may not be an international commercial arbitration, being instead a domestic arbitral institution resolving disputes within its particular national legal order. The need to enforce the award of such a domestic arbitration from another jurisdiction may arise if there is the property of a respective party in arbitration on the territory of Russia.

[B] Permanent Arbitral Institutions and Ad Hoc Arbitration

In the course of the historical development of arbitration, its two main forms crystallised – *a permanent arbitral institution (institutional arbitration) and the arbitration created to settle a particular dispute (arbitration ad hoc).*

The Arbitration Act 2015 provides the following definition of a *permanent arbitral institution* – it is a subdivision of a non-profit organisation that performs the functions of the administration of arbitration on a permanent basis. The permanent

41. Belohlavek A.I., *Arbitration, Ordre Public and Criminal Law: Volume 1*, 422 (Kiev, 2009) [Belohlavek A.I. Arbitraj, ordre public i ugolovnoye pravo. Tom 1. – Kiyev, 2009. S. 422].

arbitral institution is also called institutional arbitration. Institutional arbitration uses the infrastructure provided by its founding organisation. The institutional arbitration performs its functions on a regular basis. The disputes are resolved by the arbitrators on the institution's list (if the list is exclusive, arbitrators from the list resolve all the disputes), as well as by the arbitrators not included in the list but chosen by the parties (where the list of arbitrators is not exclusive).

Ad hoc arbitration is an arbitral tribunal constituted by the parties to settle a particular dispute, or, in other words, an arbitral tribunal that acts without any administration by a permanent arbitral institution (except where the parties' agreement provides that a permanent arbitral institution will perform certain individual functions to assist the ad hoc arbitration). After the arbitration proceedings are complete and the tribunal rendered an award, an ad hoc arbitration ceases to function.

Ad hoc arbitrations are established to handle a single dispute, and upon its resolution, they cease to exist. It means that specific rules are necessary in order to ensure that the procedure in such a tribunal is effective. Since the initiative to set up an ad hoc arbitration rests solely with the parties, they also bear the burden of determining the rules for its functioning. As one researcher put it, 'the advantage of ad hoc arbitration is that the procedural rules can be tailored individually to suit each specific case. At the same time, an arbitral tribunal established to resolve a single dispute has certain disadvantages in comparison with a permanent institution. The source of these disadvantages lies in the fact that if the parties are reluctant to cooperate, the effectiveness ad hoc arbitration is greatly reduced. In addition, if in the course of proceedings before the ad hoc tribunal some problems arise (such as the need to appoint an arbitrator), their resolution will, as a rule, fall within the competence of the state courts, which often have little experience of dealing with arbitration cases'.[42]

The Arbitration Act 2015 established different legal regimes for institutional and ad hoc arbitration activity. The differences include the following:

(1) corporate disputes cannot be resolved in ad hoc arbitration;
(2) ad hoc arbitration tribunals are not entitled to apply to the competent state court for assistance in obtaining evidence;
(3) the parties cannot agree that an ad hoc arbitration award shall be final, which means that the grounds for setting aside an ad hoc award are broader than for an institutional arbitration award.

Thus, the current Russian regulation provides institutional arbitration with a much wider range of possibilities than ad hoc arbitration.

An ad hoc arbitral tribunal, being created to resolve a single dispute, does not have a specific permanent location. Its location, as well as the seat of arbitration, is

42. Liebscher K., *Memorandum: How to Agree on Dispute Resolution in International Commercial Arbitration*, 3/3 Treteysky Sud, 201 (2002) [Liebscher *K. Myemorandum: kak pravilno dogovarivatsya o rassmotryenii spora v myejdunarodnom kommyerchyeskom arbitrajye. // Tryetyeiskii sud. 2002. No. 3/3. S.201*]. *See also* Bruntseva E.V., *International Commercial Arbitration*, 105-106 (St Petersburg, 2001) [Bruntseva *E.V. Myejdunarodnyi kommyerchyeskii arbitraj. – SPb.*, 2001. S. 105-106].

determined by agreement of the parties or the arbitral tribunal, taking into account the convenience of the parties and other circumstances relevant for the fast, efficient, and cost-effective resolution of a dispute.

It has been pointed out that the international trend of convergence between institutional arbitration and ad hoc arbitration is noticeable in Russia as well.[43] This trend seems to be, to some extent, objectively predetermined – although, in the end, it does not erase the demarcation line that separates the two forms of arbitration. This is due to the different opportunities that the two forms of dispute resolution can offer to the parties.

The practice of international ad hoc tribunals could be useful for their Russian counterparts. In particular, there is a rich body of experience generated by the international ad hoc tribunals acting in accordance with the United Nations Commission on International Trade Law (UNCITRAL) Arbitration Rules, adopted by the United Nations Commission on International Trade Law in 1976 (revised in 2010).[44] These Rules contribute to a quicker resolution of disputes and provide a way out of the impasse for the event that the respondent fails to appoint its arbitrator or where the two arbitrators cannot reach an agreement on the presiding arbitrator.[45] As B.R. Karabelnikov notes, these Rules 'provide the combination of predictability in the resolution of procedural issues that are characteristic to institutional arbitration, with the organisational autonomy and flexibility of ad hoc arbitration'.[46]

[C] Arbitration *Ex Aequo Et Bono* (Tribunals of Conscience)

The modern Russian legislation abandoned the idea of an arbitration tribunal of conscience (in Western countries it is customary to talk about arbitration *ex aequo et bono*). Meanwhile, arbitration tribunals of conscience (*ex aequo et bono*) have a long tradition in the Russian history of justice, and are widespread in other jurisdictions. Prominent Russian legal scholars pointed out that the right of an arbitrator to be guided in resolution of disputes by his own sense of justice, but not to follow the law to the

43. Boguslavsky M.M., *Contemporary Trend of Broadening the Applications of Institutional Arbitration*, in: *Topical Questions in International Commercial Arbitration*, 50 (Komarov A.S., ed., Moscow, 2002) [Boguslavsky M.M. *Sovryemyennyye tyendyencii rasshiryeniya sfyery dyeistviya institucionnyh arbitrajnyh sudov. // Aktualnyye voprosy myejdunarodnogo kommyerchyeskogo arbitraja. / Otv. ryed.* A.S. Komarov - M., 2002. S.50].

44. For the drafting history of the UNCITRAL Arbitration Rules and the commentary thereto, *see* Nikiforov I.V., *UNCITRAL Arbitration Rules 2010 (With New Article, Paragraph 4, as Adopted in 2013: A Workbook* (Moscow, 2015) [*Nikiforov I.V. Arbitrajnyi ryeglamyent UNSITRAL 2010 goda (s novym punktom 4 stati 1, prinyatym v 2013 godu. Rabochaya tyetrad. – M., 2015*].

45. Shmittgoff K.M., *Ad Hoc Arbitration and Institutional Arbitration*, in: *Export Law and Practice of International Trade*, 345 (Komarov A.S., ed., Moscow, 1993) [Shmittgoff K.M. *Arbitraj ad hoc i institucionnyi arbitraj. // Eksport: pravo i praktika myejdunarodnoi torgovli. / Otv. ryed.* A.S. Komarov. - M., 1993. S.345].

46. Karabelnikov B.R., *Recognition and Enforcement of Foreign Arbitral Awards: Academic and Practical Commentary to the New York Convention 1958*, 22 (Moscow, 2001) [Karabelnikov *B.R. Priznaniye i privyedyeniye v ispolnyeniye inostrannyh arbitrajnyh ryeshyenii: Nauchno-praktichyeskii kommyentarii k Nyu-Iorkskoi konvyencii 1958 goda. - M.: ZAO Yuridichyeskii dom Yusticinform, 2001. S.22*].

letter is one of the main advantages of arbitration.[47] In modern literature, one can encounter some proposals to revive the arbitration tribunals of conscience,[48] but there is some scepticism as well.[49]

The tribunals of conscience, or *bonae fidei iudicia*, are known since Roman times. Their development had a very interesting explanation. They were regarded as a natural phenomenon resulting from the development of the commercial turnover. The sustainability of the turnover requires, on the one hand, the integrity of its participants, and on the other – some mechanisms for resolving conflicts based on the principles of justice. Thus, S.A. Muromtsev wrote that 'as the 'conscience' of the civil turnover, i.e., the custom of the law-abiding, honest people, was developing and becoming more sophisticated, more and more circumstances became subject to legal regulations in this tribunal, which increased the scope and complexity of the parties' mutual obligations. Widening thereby its jurisdiction, the 'conscience judge' merely responded to the demand of the commerce itself, sometimes bringing into the tribunal the things that life already developed in other realms, and sometimes leading the aspirations that life was only beginning to envisage.[50]

During the Russian court reforms in 1864, the drafters of the Charter of Civil Procedure indicated in their Explanatory Notes to the Charter that arbitrators in the resolution of a dispute could well base their decisions on a 'natural sense of justice'.[51]

The possibility of arbitration *ex aequo et bono* is enshrined in Article 28 of the UNCITRAL Model Law. However, Russian law did not implement this provision, although in other respects the ICA Act 1993 is an almost complete replica of the UNCITRAL Model Law. Meanwhile, other countries designed arbitral legislation based on their own historical traditions, and the principle of *bonae fidei iudicia* has been implemented in their statutory texts.

47. Volkov A.F., *Trade Arbitration and Its Importance in Commerce*, XII, in: *North-Western Arbitration Commission: A Report on the Activities of the North-Western Regional Chamber of Commerce and the Leningrad Mercantile Exchange for the Year 1922-1925* (Leningrad, 1925) [*Volkov A.F. Torgovyye tryetyeiskiye sudy i ih znachyeniye v torgovom oborotye. // Syevyero-Zapadnaya arbitrajnaya komissiya: Otchyet o dyeyatyelnosti Syevyero-Zapadnoi oblastnoi torgovoi palaty i Lyeningradskoi tovarnoi birji za 1922-1925 goda.* – L., 1925. S. XII].

48. Tarasov V.N., Baronov O.V., *The Arbitration of Conscience*, 1 Treteysky Sud 28-33 (2000) [*Tarasov V.N., Baronov O.V. Tryetyeiskii sud po sovyesti.* // Treteysky Sud. 2000. No. 1. S. 28-33]; *Alternative Dispute Resolution: Compendium*, 146-147 (Zaitsev A.I., ed., Moscow, Exam, 2007) [Altyernativnoye razryeshyeniye sporov: uchyebno-myetodichyeskii komplyeks / Pod ryed. A.I. Zaitseva. – M. «Ekzamyen», 2007. S. 146-147]; Balashov A.N., Zaitsev A.I., Zaitseva Yu.A., *Arbitration in the Russian Federation: Textbook* (Moscow, 2008) [Balashov A.N., Zaitsev A.I., Zaitseva Yu.A., *Tryetyeiskoye sudoproizvodstvo v Rossiiskoi Fyedyeracii: Uchyebnoye posobiye. – M., 2008*]; Chupahin I.M., *Arbitral Award: Theoretical and Applied Problems*, 12-13 (Moscow, 2015) [Chupahin I.M. Ryeshyeniye tryetyeiskogo suda: tyeoryetichyeskiye i prikladnyye problyemy. – M., 2015. S. 12-13].

49. Kurochkin S.A., *Arbitration of Civil Cases in the Russian Federation: Theory and Practice*, 230 (Moscow, 2007) [Kurochkin S.A. *Tryetyeiskoye razbiratyelstvo grajdanskih dyel v Rossiiskoi Fyedyeracii: tyeoriya i praktika.* - M., 2007. S. 230].

50. Muromtsev S.A., *Civil Law of the Ancient Rome*, 478 (Moscow, 2003) [Muromtsev S.A. *Grajdanskoye pravo Dryevnyego Rima.* – M., 2003. S. 478].

51. Lawsuits Statutes 20 November 1864 setting out the arguments on which they are based, issued by the State Chancellery. 2 nd ed., Ext. Part 1. - SPb., 1867. S. 652.

The essence of arbitration tribunals of conscience is evident from their name. If the dispute resolution in arbitration has its basis in moral principles that lack any formal legislative expression, such arbitration is a tribunal of conscience. Thus, the demarcation line between the two kinds of arbitration lies at the dominant idea guiding the tribunal – either morality (justice) as a basis for decision-making or the positive law (legislation).[52] This premise is fundamental for both the arbitration tribunal of conscience and the arbitral tribunal that relies on the law. The nature of an arbitral tribunal will dictate different requirements to the circumstances the parties need to prove, to the evidence, reasoning and motives for the award, etc. A.I. Vitsyn noticed this when he wrote: 'Here is one of the essential differences between the tribunal of conscience and the tribunal of law: the very verdict of an arbitration tribunal, when it relies on conscience, is not arbitrary, but there are reasons that lead the arbitrators to that or another opinion. Those reasons are evidence. But what constitutes evidence? In the court of conscience, this is left for the arbitrators to decide, and it may be that they will not require any further proof, relying on the person's statement alone. In the tribunal of law, on the contrary, the belief of the arbitrators in the truthfulness of a statement means nothing. They must consider the statement as proved when the evidence is sufficient under the legal requirements.'[53]

Currently, the tribunals in Russia have no legal basis for the adoption of arbitral awards on an equitable basis or, in the words of Professor A.A. Kostin,[54] unmotivated from the vantage point of legal requirements to arbitral awards. This practice is impossible even in the framework of international commercial arbitration seated in Russia since their awards are also subject to the requirement of legality. Failure to comply with these rules will result in unenforceability of an award. At the same time, it has been pointed out that in the West, the influence of the popular doctrine *Lex mercatoria* is growing. The provisions of arbitration Rules that allow the parties to withdraw their disputes from the strictly legal sphere and have them considered on the basis of 'law and justice' (*ex aequo et bono*) are becoming more popular.[55] As a general rule, the need to resolve the dispute on the basis of 'equity and good conscience' arises

52. It would be unproductive to treat morality and law as completely opposite notions. The law, in our view, usually reflects the basic moral ideas. However, a conflict between those two regulatory institutions is also not unthinkable. With regard to our current topic, we must emphasise that the arbitration tribunals of conscience do not represent an opposite of 'legalised' arbitration, but reflect a forward-looking philosophical and legal concept of what is fair and ought to exist, as opposed to what presently exists and may be unfair.
53. Vitsyn A.I., *On Arbitration in Russian Law: Historical and Dogmatic Discussion*, 40 (Moscow, 1856) [*Vitsyn A.I. Tryetyeiskii sud po russkomu pravu. Istoriko-dogmatichyeskoye rassujdyeniye.* – M., 1856. S. 40].
54. Kostin A.A., *Correlation of the Laws 'On International Commercial Arbitration' and 'On Arbitration in the Russian Federation'*, 4(28) Treteysky Sud, 32 (2003) [Kostin A.A. *Sootnoshyeniye Zakonov «O myejdunarodnom kommyerchyeskom arbitrajye» i «O tryetyeiskih sudah v Rossiiskoi Fyedyeracii». //* Treteysky Sud. 2003. No. 4 (28). S. 32].
55. Kanashevsky V.A., *International Rules and the Civil Law of Russia*, 128 (Moscow, 2004) [Kanashevsky V.A. *Myejdunarodnyye normy i grajdanskoye zakonodatyelstvo Rossii.* – M., 2004. S. 128].

when, due to the change of circumstances, the performance of the contract on the same terms becomes impossible or would be unfair for a party, and the resolution of a dispute on the basis of a strict application of the law is also unfair.[56]

56. Bruntseva E.V., *International Commercial Arbitration*, 130 (St Petersburg, 2001) [Bruntseva E.V. *Myejdunarodnyi kommyerchyeskii arbitraj.* – SPb., 2001. S. 130].

CHAPTER 3
The Arbitration Agreement*

§3.01 NATURE AND SIGNIFICANCE OF THE ARBITRATION AGREEMENT

It is a well-established rule that commercial arbitration stems from an agreement to arbitrate, which is a prerequisite and a basis for the arbitral procedure. The entire process, from its inception to the award, originates in the agreement of the parties. A valid agreement determines whether the courts can assist arbitration, e.g., in adopting interim measures, obtaining evidence, and enforcing arbitral awards.[1]

[A] Voluntary and Compulsory Arbitration

Arbitration is compulsory when the law requires certain disputes to be resolved by an arbitral tribunal, whether or not the parties consent to forego the usual legal remedies. This sometimes takes place on a statutory basis, and in some jurisdictions, such as England and Scotland,[2] statutory arbitration remains prominent. In Russia, it is virtually unknown. The highest courts of Russia – the Supreme Commercial Court,[3] the

---

* The author is grateful to Dr Gloria Alvarez and David Christie for their helpful comments on the earlier draft of this chapter.

1. *Commentary to the Federal Law 'On Arbitration (Arbitral Proceedings) in the Russian Federation' (Clause-by-Clause, Academic and Practical Commentary)*, Commentary to Article 7, §4 (O.Yu Skvortsov, M.Yu. Savransky, eds) (Moscow, 2016) [Kommyentarii k Fyedyeralnomu zakonu 'Ob arbitrajye (tryetyeiskom razbiratyelstvye) v Rossiiskoi Fyedyeracii' (postatyeinyi, nauchno-praktichyeskii) / pod ryed. O.Yu. Skvortsova, M.Yu. Savranskogo. M.:, 2016. Kommyentarii k statye 7, §4].
2. *See*, e.g., Harris B., Planterose R., Tecks J., *The Arbitration Act 1996: A Commentary*, 406-409 (5th ed., Wiley Blackwell, 2014).
3. Decree of the Presidium of the RF Supreme Commercial Court of 13 December 2011 No. 9807/11; *The Review of the Legal Positions of the Presidium of the RF Higher Commercial Court on Private Law Matters (February 2012)*, 4 The Herald of the Supreme Commercial Court (2012) [*Obzor*

Supreme Court,[4] and the Constitutional Court[5] – often emphasised that parties must refer their disputes to arbitration voluntarily.

There are two possible exceptions in Russia to the general rule against compulsory arbitration. The first one is a legacy of the Soviet times – the Moscow Convention 1972 'On the Resolution by Arbitration of Civil Law Disputes Resulting from Relations of Economic, Scientific and Technical Cooperation'. Concluded between governments of socialist countries under the auspices of the Council for Mutual Economic Assistance, this Convention required the disputes arising between organisations from the contracting states in the course of economic and scientific-technical cooperation to be resolved in the Court of Arbitration at the Respondent's national Chamber of Commerce. The jurisdiction of state courts in such cases would be ousted regardless of whether or not the parties ever agreed to arbitrate; in other words, arbitration was compulsory.

Most of the signatory countries have repealed the Convention during the 1990s, after the fall of the Soviet Union and the dismantling of the Council for Mutual Economic Assistance. As a formal matter, Bulgaria, Mongolia, Cuba, Slovakia, and Russia remain bound by the Convention, although in a very long time there had been no opportunities for Russian courts to apply it. Many Russian[6] and foreign[7] commentators argued convincingly that the Convention, at least de facto, was no longer in force. Some reports suggest, however, that the ICAC at the RF CCI continues, from time to time, to establish its jurisdictions under this Convention.[8] Many of the ICAC awards published within the last twenty years (in a redacted form) did consider the Convention, but there was invariably also a written arbitration agreement between the parties,

pravovyh pozicii Pryezidiuma VAS RF po voprosam chastnogo prava. Fyevral 2012 g. Vyestnik Vysshyego Arbitrajnogo Suda RF, 2012, N 4].

4. Ruling of the RF Supreme Court of 24 April 2017 No. 305-KG17-323, case No. A40-179125/2016; Ruling of the RF Supreme Court of 16 August 2016 No. 304-ES16-9029, case No. A03-20164/2015.
5. Decree of the RF Constitutional Court of 18 November 2014 No. 30-P 'On Verification of the Constitutionality of the Provisions of Article 18 of the Federal Law 'On Arbitration in the Russian Federation', Clause 1 of Section 3 of Article 239 of the Commercial Procedure Code of the Russian Federation and Section 3 of Article 10 of the Federal Law 'On Non-Commercial Organisations' in Connection with a Complaint by the Open Joint Stock Company 'Sberbank of Russia'.
6. *See*, e.g., Belov A.P., *International Commercial Law*, 240-241 (Moscow, 2001) [Belov A.P., Myejdunarodnoye pryedprinimatyelskoye pravo. - M., 2001. S. 240-241]; Khvalei V., *History, Fate and Role of the Moscow Convention*, Arbitraz I Mediacja. Ksiega Jubileuszowa, 7 (Warsaw, 2012) [Vladimir Khvalei, Istoriya, sudba i znachyeniye Moskovskoi Konvyencii. Arbitraz I Mediacja. Ksiega Jubileuszowa (Warsaw, 2012)] http://www.arbitrations.ru/userfiles/file/Publications/Publications/MoscowConventionArticle.pdf (accessed 13 June 2018).
7. *See*, e.g., *Fouchard, Gaillard and Goldman on International Commercial Arbitration*, 145 (Gaillard E., Savage J., eds), (The Hague, 1999) and the sources cited therein.
8. Petrosyan R.A., *Procedural and Connected Matters in the Work of the International Commercial Arbitration Court at the RF Chamber of Commerce and Industry*, in: *International Commercial Arbitration: Contemporary Problems and Solutions. A Compilation of Articles Dedicated to the 80th Anniversary of the International Commercial Arbitration Court at the RF Chamber of Commerce and Industry*, 302-304 (Kostin A.A., ed., Moscow, 2012) [Petrosyan R.A., Procyessualnyye i svyazannyye s nimi voprosy v dyeyatyelnosti MKAS pri TPP RF / Myejdunarodnyi kommyerchyeskii arbitraj: sovryemyennyye problyemy i ryeshyeniya: Sbornik statyei k 80-lyetiyu Myejdunarodnogo kommyerchyeskogo arbitrajnogo suda pri Torgovo-promyshlyennoi palatye Rossiiskoi Fyedyeracii / pod ryed. A.A. Kostina. M., 2012. S. 302-304].

which spared the arbitrators a necessity to reach any conclusion as to whether the Convention could still be a sole basis for the tribunal's jurisdiction.[9]

Thus, there remains some room for debate about the legal force and importance of the Moscow Convention 1972, although it becomes harder and harder to come across a published example of its application.

The second possible exception to the rule against compulsory arbitration concerns investor-state dispute resolution. This kind of arbitration, where the relevant international treaty requires a host state to arbitrate if a private investor brings an arbitral claim, remains a special case. Jan Paulsson famously termed it 'arbitration without privity',[10] and some Russian commentators consider it compulsory.[11] However, in investment arbitration, the host state does consent to the possibility of future arbitral claims by investors, albeit not in a contract with every particular investor but a treaty with a fellow state. The considerations determining whether it would be appropriate to classify investor-state arbitration as compulsory are the same for Russia as in their wider international context.

[B] Regulation of the Arbitration Agreement

The amount of statutory material devoted to arbitration agreements increased significantly in the Arbitration Act 2015 compared to its predecessor – the Arbitration Act 2002, as well as compared to the UNCITRAL Model Law on International Commercial Arbitration.[12] Article 7 of the 2002 Act (Form and Substance of an Arbitration Agreement) included only four sections, whereas the equivalent Article 7 of the current Act (Definition, Form and Interpretation of an Arbitration Agreement) now contains no less than twelve.

This increase in the volume of regulation was partly a consequence of adopting the 2006 amendments to the Model Law. The Russian legislature implemented some of the Model Law Article 7 (option I) provisions in the Arbitration Act 2015 Article 7(1) to 7(5), albeit doing so in a somewhat conservative manner.[13] Another reason for the increased length of Article 7 was the inclusion of the novel rules on interpretation of arbitration agreements.[14]

9. *See*, e.g., ICAC award of 26 June 2007, case No. 98/2006; ICAC award of 2 June 2005, case No. 131/2004.
10. Paulsson J., *Arbitration Without Privity*, 10 ICSID Rev.-Foreign Investment L.J. 232 (1995).
11. Zvereva N.S., *The Interplay Between Alternative Methods of Dispute Settlement and Civil Procedure in Russian and French Law*, §74(6) (V.V. Yarkov, ed., Moscow, 2017) [Zvereva N.S. Vzaimodyeistviye altyernativnyh myetodov uryegulirovaniya sporov i grajdanskogo sudoproizvodstva v prave Rossii i Francii / pod ryed. V.V. Yarkova. M., 2017].
12. Text of the Model Law is available at http://www.uncitral.org/uncitral/en/uncitral_texts/arbitration/1985Model_arbitration.html (accessed 13 June 2018).
13. *See* below, §3.03.
14. *See* below, §3.05.

[C] Arbitration Agreement in the Domestic and International Context

The legislation on domestic and international arbitration in Russia remains, at least in some aspects, dualistic. Two different statutes regulate arbitration: the Arbitration Act 2015 and the Law of the Russian Federation 'On International Commercial Arbitration' of 7 June 1993 (the ICA Act 1993). One might call this a dualism of international and domestic arbitration regimes, although the relationship between the two statutes is more complicated than that.

First, the ICA Act 1993 applies to international commercial arbitration, while the Arbitration Act 2015 governs all its other types, i.e., any arbitration that does not satisfy the statutory definition of 'international commercial arbitration' – for example, the non-commercial international arbitration. Thus, the 2015 Act governs arbitration in the 'residual' category of cases.

Second, the 2015 Act applies to international commercial arbitration in enumerated matters, for which the ICA Act 1993 contains no specific rules, i.e., those arising in connection with:

- the establishment and operation of permanent arbitral institutions in the territory of the Russian Federation;
- the custody of materials concerning the past cases;
- the making of entries in official registers in the Russian Federation where it is necessary for the enforcement of arbitration awards;
- the relationship between mediation and arbitration;
- the requirements to arbitrators;
- the liability of arbitrators and permanent arbitral institutions.

The concluding provisions in Chapter 12 of the Arbitration Act 2015 dealing with matters such as its application to pre-existing arbitration agreements and arbitration proceedings ongoing at the date of its entry into force also apply to both kinds of arbitration.

Before 2015, the dualism was very significant. It resulted, among other things, in the different definitions and legal regimes of an arbitration agreement in the context of international commercial arbitration, and arbitration agreement in the 'residual' category of cases. The legal term in Russian for an arbitration agreement in international commercial arbitration was '*arbitrazhnoe soglasheniye*', which was a calque (a literal word-for-word translation) of the term 'arbitration agreement'. The legal term in Russian for an arbitration agreement in the 'residual' category of cases was '*treteyskoye soglashenie*' representing another, more 'complete' way of translating the term 'arbitration agreement' into Russian – equally acceptable linguistically, but slightly different in form. The text of the relevant articles in the two statutes diverged, so the difference went beyond the mere linguistics, sometimes resulting in a de facto differential treatment of very similar legal phenomena. The Russian procedural codes – the Code of Civil Procedure and the Commercial Procedure Code – used the term '*treteyskoye soglashenie'* to refer to both kinds of agreement, which further complicated the matters and led to more confusion in the court practice.[15]

With the enactment of the Arbitration Act 2015, the legislator attempted to simplify this conundrum. First, the terminology in both statutes was streamlined, so currently both Acts use the same term '*arbitrazhnoe soglasheniye*'. Second, the 2015 amendments to Article 7 of the ICA Act 1993 made it resemble very closely Article 7 of the 2015 Act, with only a few differences.

These circumstances point strongly towards the legislative intention to eliminate, as far as possible, the differences between arbitration agreements in the two contexts, and to recognise their identical legal nature.

Perhaps as an unfortunate oversight, the Russian procedural codes continue, in some cases, to use the term '*treteyskoye soglashenie*'. One may hope, however, that this discrepancy will now only be of minor significance, and will be corrected at the first opportunity.

The further analysis in this chapter, unless otherwise specified, will apply equally to arbitration agreements in the domestic and international context.

[D] Definition of the Arbitration Agreement

Article 7(1) of the Arbitration Act 2015 defines arbitration agreement as an agreement by the parties to submit to arbitration all or certain disputes which have arisen or which may arise between them in respect of a defined legal relationship, whether contractual or not. An arbitration agreement may be in the form of an arbitration clause in a contract or a separate document.

This statutory text mirrors the Option I of the UNCITRAL Model Law Article 7(1). While amending the Model Law in 2006, the Commission put forward two alternative approaches. The first one followed the structure of the original 1985 text. Like the New York Convention, it required a written agreement but deemed the recording of its content in various additional ways acceptable to meet the requirement of writing. The broad wording of the Option I encompassed most electronic formats. In deviation from the New York Convention Article II(2), there was no need to establish an exchange of messages between the parties, as long as the content of the agreement was recorded in some form. The second approach (Option II) imposed no formal requirements on the arbitration agreement at all, leaving the matter to the contract law of the enacting State.[16]

The elements of this definition are uncontroversial and have been accepted in Russian law for a long time. It contains two essential components.

15. Kotelnikov A.G., *The Legal Nature and Effects of an Arbitration Agreement: An Abstract of a Doctor of Law Dissertation*, 11-13 (Ekaterinburg, 2008) [Kotelnikov A.G., Pravovaya priroda i poslyedstviya zaklyuchyeniya arbitrajnogo soglashyeniya: Avtoryef.diss...k.yu.n. - Ekaterinburg, 2008. S. 11-13].
16. *Explanatory Note by the UNCITRAL Secretariat on the Model Law on International Commercial Arbitration* 28, http://www.uncitral.org/pdf/english/texts/arbitration/ml-arb/07-86998_Ebook.pdf (accessed 14 June 2018).

First, Article 7(1) emphasises the need for a 'defined legal relationship' between the parties, thus avoiding any encroachment on the right of access to justice. A prominent Russian arbitration scholar A.I. Vitsin addressed the importance of this requirement as far back as in 1856. He argued against the suggestion that 'entire regions should sign arbitration compromises among themselves' because such an agreement would be nothing but an establishment of a court, which is only permissible by the authority of the government and not through private initiative.[17]

Second, the definition contains three broad permissions.

(1) The agreement may concern 'all or certain disputes' in respect of a legal relationship – for example, an arbitration clause in a contract may with equal legitimacy refer to 'all disputes that may arise out of this contract' or '*payment* disputes that may arise out of this contract'.
(2) The agreement may concern present or future disputes ('which have arisen or which may arise'); it will not affect the enforceability of the clause.[18]
(3) Finally, the nature of a dispute does not have to be contractual ('whether contractual or not'), as long as it is arbitrable as a matter of law. For example, it is perfectly acceptable for the parties to include into the purview of their arbitration agreement the disputes that arise from a non-contractual relationship, such as delict (tort) or unjust enrichment, whether on their own or in connection with an identified contract.

According to Article 7(12) of the Arbitration Act 2015, if an arbitration agreement refers to a set of arbitration rules, they become an inseparable part of the agreement. The previous Act contained the same provision (Article 7(3) of the Arbitration Act 2002), and the doctrine[19] and court practice[20] recognised its effects for a long time.

The new provision in the 2015 Act is the second sentence of Article 7(12), which stipulates that the rules of a permanent arbitral institution cannot include the terms that, according to this Act, only a direct agreement of the parties can bring into force. This provision introduced the important notion of a 'direct agreement'. Section §3.04 of this chapter will discuss this matter in more detail.

[E] Effects of the Arbitration Agreement

The Russian doctrine commonly considers the effects of an arbitration agreement in line with the classic René David's framework,[21] distinguishing between the positive

17. Vitsyn A.I., *On Arbitration in Russian Law*, 24 (Moscow, 1856) [Vitsyn A.I. O tryetyeiskih sudah po russkomu pravu. M., 1856. S. 24.].
18. For more details on this distinction, *see* below, §3.04[B].
19. Kurochkin S.A., *Domestic and International Commercial Arbitration*, 83 (Moscow, 2017) [Kurochkin S.A. Tryetyeiskoye razbiratyelstvo i myejdunarodnyi kommyerchyeskii arbitraj. M., 2017. S. 83].
20. *See*, e.g., the Ruling of the Supreme Commercial Court of the Russian Federation of 19 December 2011 No. 14325/11.
21. David R., *Arbitration in International Trade*, 232 (Springer, 1985).

(enabling) and negative (precluding) effects. Positive effects include the parties' obligation to refer their disputes to arbitration and the emergence of the tribunal's jurisdiction. Negative effects encompass the competent court's obligation to refer the relevant disputes to arbitration and the parties' obligation to refrain from starting an action in an otherwise competent national court.[22]

The central and most important effect of a valid arbitration agreement is the ousting of the courts' jurisdiction to hear the case. The Russian procedural law does not enable any court to compel arbitration.[23] However, the procedural codes stipulate that the statement of claim shall be left without consideration if there is an agreement between the parties to refer the dispute to arbitration, and one of the parties, no later than on the day of filing its first application on the merits of the dispute, raises an objection on this ground.[24] The court leaves the claim without consideration unless it finds that the agreement is null and void, inoperable, or incapable of being performed. This rule follows Article II of the New York Convention 1958 and Article 8 of the UNCITRAL Model Law.

In Russian civil procedure, leaving a claim without consideration is the 'soft' form of ending the court process, allowing the parties to commence the proceedings anew if the relevant grounds cease to exist.[25] Its 'hard' counterpart is the termination of proceedings where the repeated claim between the same persons on the same subject matter and the same grounds becomes barred. The court will terminate the proceedings, for example, if it finds that there is a judgment with a res judicata effect between the parties. Another ground for the termination of the proceedings is an award of an arbitration tribunal rendered in the dispute between the same parties, on the same subject matter and the same grounds, unless a competent court has earlier refused to enforce or has set aside the award.[26]

[F] Legal Nature of the Arbitration Agreement

The debates about the legal nature of the arbitration agreement in Russia traditionally revolve around the combination of substantive and procedural legal elements in it. It is common to proceed from the assumption that an arbitration agreement contains both aspects. It is contractual by genesis, and procedural in its jurisdictional character.[27] This 'mixed' (or sui generis)[28] theory does receive an occasional challenge. For example, some courts treat an arbitration agreement as a purely procedural mechanism

---

22. *Commentary to the Federal Law 'On Arbitration (Arbitral Proceedings) in the Russian Federation' (Clause-by-Clause, Academic and Practical Commentary)*, *supra* note 1, Commentary to Article 7, at §10-11.
23. Khodykin R., *Arbitration Law of Russia: Practice and Procedure*, 37 (Juris, 2013).
24. Article 148(1)(5) of the Commercial Procedure Code, Article 222 of the Civil Procedure Code.
25. Article 149 of the Commercial Procedure Code, Article 223 of the Civil Procedure Code.
26. Articles 150, 151 of the Commercial Procedure Code.
27. Lebedev S.N., *International Trade Arbitration*, 82 (Moscow, 1965) [Lebedev S.N. Myejdunarodnyi torgovyi arbitraj. M., 1965. S. 82].
28. Kostin A.A., Davydenko D.L., *Chapter 7: Russia*, in: *Law and Practice of International Arbitration in the CIS Region*, 259 (Hober K., Kryvoi Y., eds, Alhen aan den Rijn, The Netherlands, 2017).

and therefore refuse to apply any Civil Code rules to it.[29] However, the majority of experts agree that the 'mixed' theory describes the legal nature of arbitration most accurately. The Constitutional Court also confirmed the coexistence of substantive and procedural legal elements in an arbitration agreement in its Decree,[30] and courts often reference it to justify the application of the Civil Code rules to the invalidity of arbitration agreements.[31]

In particular, the following matters relevant to the agreement are thought to be substantive (contractual):

- Legal capacity of the parties
- The form of the arbitration agreement
- Validity and invalidity of the arbitration agreement.[32]

One aspect often classified as procedural is the prohibition of repudiating an arbitration agreement unilaterally.[33]

A practical consequence of this classification is that substantive legal matters, in case of a dispute about them, are resolved according to substantive law, and procedural matters according to procedural law. In turn, this affects the applicable law. If a matter is substantive, private international law rules determine which country's law governs any particular issue. It can be Russian substantive law, i.e., the relevant provisions of the Civil Code and other federal legislation. The conflict of law rules may also lead to the application of foreign law. But if any matter is procedural, the courts will always resolve it under Russian procedural law – the procedural codes, the Arbitration Act 2015, and, where applicable, the ICA Act 1993 – with no reference to foreign law.

§3.02 AUTONOMY OF THE ARBITRATION AGREEMENT

The statutory provisions on the autonomy of the arbitration agreement in Russian law follow the UNCITRAL Model Law approach, with some small differences. Article 16(1) of the Arbitration Act 2015 'Competence of arbitral tribunal to rule on its jurisdiction' contains the following rule:

> (1) The arbitral tribunal may rule on its own jurisdiction, including any objections with respect to the existence or validity of the arbitration agreement. An arbitration clause that forms part of a contract shall be treated as an agreement independent of the other terms of the contract. A decision by the arbitral

29. *See*, e.g., Decree of the Federal Commercial Court for the West-Siberian Circuit of 23 August 2002, case No. F04/3024-382/A75-2002; Decree of the Federal Commercial Court for the North-Western Circuit of 29 January 2004, case No. A42-914/03-9.
30. Decree of the RF Constitutional Court of 26 May 2011 N 10-П.
31. *See* below, §3.07.
32. Absalyamov A.V., Arsenov I.G., Vinogradova E.A., et al., *Commercial Court Procedure: The Textbook*, 627 (Yarkov V.V., ed., 4th ed., Moscow, 2010) [Arbitrajnyi procyess: uchyebnik / A.V. Absalyamov, I.G. Arsenov, E.A. Vinogradova i dr.; otv. ryed. V.V. Yarkov. 4-ye izd., pyeryerab. i dop. M.: Infotropik Myedia, 2010. C. 627].
33. *Ibid.*

> tribunal that the contract is null and void shall not in itself entail the invalidity of the arbitration agreement.[34]

Article 16(1) of the Arbitration Act 2015 is a mandatory rule, i.e., the parties cannot dispense with the autonomy of the arbitration agreement by their agreement. There appears to be no compelling reason for this, and indeed some national statutes do provide the parties with more flexibility. For example, section 7 of the English Arbitration Act 1996 stipulates that an arbitration agreement shall not be regarded as invalid, non-existent or ineffective because that main agreement is invalid, or did not come into existence or has become ineffective, and it shall for that purpose be treated as a distinct agreement, '*unless otherwise agreed by the parties*'. Arguably, the parties would rarely need to exclude the principle of autonomy by their agreement, but there appears to be no compelling reason to forbid it altogether.

In Russian law, 'autonomy' and 'separability' of an arbitration clause have the same meaning. The French concept of the agreement's independence of all national laws (asserting that the proper analysis of an arbitration agreement should proceed by universally accepted 'substantive rules' without reference to any particular national law)[35] was subject of some discussion in the literature.[36] However, it never received wide acceptance – neither as a theoretical matter nor in legal practice. The proper analysis of any issue about the arbitration agreement under Russian law should always begin with establishing the applicable law.

Although the preamble to the ICA Act 1993 (but not the Arbitration Act 2015) does acknowledge the role of the UNCITRAL Model Law and the importance of uniform regulation of arbitration in international trade, Russian legislator never implemented Article 2A of the Model Law ('International Origin and General Principles'). Therefore, the possibility of statutory interpretation with reference to the law's international origin and to the need to promote uniformity in its application remains questionable. Commentators often point out the Russian courts' cautious preference for the positivist and literal interpretation of the law.[37] Perhaps the higher courts could be more susceptible to the arguments based on the international practice where the law contains a genuine uncertainty, but the likelihood of success for such arguments would decrease in the lower courts. Under those circumstances, the adoption of this French doctrine calling for the application of loosely defined supranational principles governing the arbitration agreement would be premature in Russia – as well as in many other countries.

---

34. Hereafter in this chapter, the unofficial translations from Russian are by the author, Andrey Kotelnikov.
35. *Fouchard, Gaillard and Goldman on International Commercial Arbitration*, *supra* note 7, at 132.
36. *See*, e.g., Grigoriev T.Yu., Kolomiets A.I., *The Principle of Autonomy of an Arbitration Clause: The Review of Russian and Foreign Practice*, 2 Herald of Commercial Court Practice 5, 9 [Grigoriev T.Yu., Kolomiets A.I. Princip avtonomnosti arbitrajnoi ogovorki: obzor rossiiskoi i zarubyejnoi pravoprimyenityelnoi praktiki // Vyestnik arbitrajnoi praktiki. 2017. N 2. S. 9].
37. Sultanov A.R. *The Formalism of Civil Procedure and the Standards of Fair Trial*, 3 Herald of Civil Procedure 73, 73-93 (2012) [Sultanov A.R. Formalizm grajdanskogo procyessa i standarty spravyedlivogo pravosudiya // Vyestnik grajdanskogo procyessa. 2012. N 3. S. 73-93].

Unlike the previous Arbitration Act 2002 and the UNCITRAL Model Law, the current statutory text does not imply any close connection between the autonomy of an arbitration agreement and the principle of competence-competence. Article 16(1) of the UNCITRAL Model Law reads in relevant part:

> (1) The arbitral tribunal may rule on its own jurisdiction, including any objections with respect to the existence or validity of the arbitration agreement. *For that purpose*, an arbitration clause which forms part of a contract shall be treated as an agreement independent of the other terms of the contract (emphasis added).

There is indeed no direct logical connection between separability of an arbitration agreement and the competence-competence principle.[38] While the autonomy of an arbitration agreement can be instrumental in ascertaining the jurisdiction of the tribunal, it also has other effects. For example, the law applicable to the main contract and the arbitration clause could be different. Likewise, the tribunal could apply the principle of competence-competence without ever considering the arbitration agreement or its validity in any detail. For instance, this could happen where one of the parties challenges the arbitrability of the dispute. It is uncontroversial that the separability principle may have other consequences that go beyond jurisdictional issues.[39] Therefore, this deviation of the Russian statutory text from the Model law is a small but welcome development.

For many years, Russian courts consistently applied the principle of separability of an arbitration clause from other terms of the contract. For example, in *Oleg Troshkov v Zhemchuzhina Urala*,[40] the Supreme Commercial Court confirmed the reasoning of the lower courts that refused to declare a contract null and void due to the conflict of interest. The courts held that, in relation to the arbitration clause, a separate ground to refuse the lawsuit was its autonomy from the main contract. Since the clause was separable, the statutory rules of company law requiring an approval of transactions involving a conflict of interest did not apply.

In *GlavPromStroy v Avielen*, the Federal Commercial Court (FCC) for the North-Western Circuit went as far as to argue that the autonomy of an arbitration agreement is a universally recognised principle of both international and Russian law. According to Article 15 of the Russian Constitution, the universal principles and rules of international law and international treaties are an integral part of the Russian legal system.[41] This was merely an *obiter* remark because the literal interpretation of Russian statutory law led to the same conclusion. However, it was a welcome acknowledgement of the importance of separability principle for the Russian law.

38. Kurochkin S.A., *supra* note 19, at 76.
39. *UNCITRAL 2012 Digest of Case Law on the Model Law on International Commercial Arbitration* 76, http://www.uncitral.org/pdf/english/clout/MAL-digest-2012-e.pdf (accessed 22 June 2018).
40. Ruling of the Supreme Commercial Court of 30 July 2008 No. 9068/08, case No. A71-3873/2007.
41. Decree of the Federal Commercial Court for the North-Western Circuit of 23 October 2009, case No. A56-45732/2008.

The principle of separability will usually salvage an arbitration clause if the court declares the main contract is invalid, but not always. Some grounds for the invalidity will affect both the contract and the arbitration clause – for example, where the entire contract was a forgery.[42]

It is convenient to consider the principle of autonomy under the following three headings defining its most important practical effects.

First, invalidity or repudiation of the main contract, as well as the fact that it never came into existence,[43] as such do not affect the arbitration agreement. Conversely, defects of the arbitration agreement do not invalidate the main contract.

Second, with the expiry of the main contract, the arbitration agreement remains in force unless the parties agree otherwise.[44]

Third, the law applicable to the main contract and the arbitration agreement, as well as the choice of law rules, can differ.[45]

The Civil Code of Russia contains the choice of law rules for contracts and other substantive obligations. According to Article 1210(5) of the Civil Code, the parties may agree on the applicable law for the contract or any of its parts. However, if the parties' relationship only concerns one country, the mandatory rules of this country shall apply regardless of the parties' choice of law. For example, a contract between two Russian companies with no foreign investment, the performance of which takes place only in Russia, will be subject to mandatory rules of Russian law even if the parties were to stipulate that the English law governed the contract.

The choice of law rules for arbitration agreements, on the other hand, is contained in a different framework of rules, which includes the New York Convention 1958 and the European Convention on International Commercial Arbitration 1961 to which Russia is a party. The effect of these rules, at least in most cases, is that the law of the arbitral seat (*lex arbitri*) will govern the arbitration clause.[46] Thus in the example above, if the parties agree to arbitrate their disputes in London, English law will govern the arbitration clause without any reservations about the application of Russian mandatory rules.

Lately, there appears a tendency in the practice of commercial courts to apply a mechanism similar to Article 1210 of the Civil Code to arbitration agreements. In a case known as the *Russian-Singaporean Arbitration case,* two Russian parties in a purely

---

42. Ruling of the Supreme Court of 2 November 2016 N 306-ES16-4741, case No. N A65-19616/2015.
43. On the 'not concluded' contracts, *see* below, §3.07[D].
44. Information Letter No. 96 of the Presidium of the Supreme Commercial Court of the Russian Federation of 22 December 2005 'Review of Commercial Court Practice in Cases on Recognition and of Writs of Execution for the Enforcement of Arbitral Awards', section 22 [Informacionnoye pismo Pryezidiuma VAS RF ot 22.12.2005 N 96 'Obzor praktiki rassmotryeniya arbitrajnymi sudami dyel o priznanii i privyedyenii v ispolnyeniye ryeshyenii inostrannyh sudov, ob osparivanii ryeshyenii tryetyeiskih sudov i o vydachye ispolnityelnyh listov na prinudityelnoye ispolnyeniye ryeshyenii tryetyeiskih sudov' (p. 22)].
45. Kurochkin S.A., *supra* note 19, at 76.
46. Karabelnikov B.R., *Enforcement and Challenge of International Commercial Arbitration Awards. A Commentary to the New York Convention 1958 and Chapters 30 and 31 of the Commercial Procedure Code 2002* (3rd ed., Moscow, 2008) [Karabelnikov B.R. Ispolnyeniye i osparivaniye ryeshyenii myejdunarodnyh kommyerchyeskih arbitrajyei. Kommyentarii k Nyu-Iorkskoi konvyencii 1958 goda i glavam 30 i 31 APK RF 2002 goda. 3-ye izd., M., 2008].

domestic dispute attempted to bypass the requirement of the Arbitration Act 2015 to the operation of permanent arbitration institutions. The arbitration agreement provided for institutional arbitration in Singapore, although in fact Singapore only ever featured on paper in the resolution of the dispute. The sole Russian arbitrator rendered an award in Moscow, and no hearings ever took place outside of Russia. The courts refused the recognition of the arbitral award, holding that since the arbitration took place in Russia, this was effectively a Russian domestic arbitration, so the rules concerning the enforcement of foreign arbitral awards were inapplicable.[47] The experts criticised this approach for its lack of statutory basis and disregard of the distinction between the seat of arbitration and the hearing venue.[48] However, it remains likely that the courts might continue to interpret Russian mandatory rules in such a 'protectionist' way in the foreseeable future.

§3.03 THE FORM OF THE ARBITRATION AGREEMENT

Article II(2) of the New York Convention requires an arbitration agreement to be 'signed by the parties or contained in an exchange of letters or telegrams'. Since the Convention opened for signature in 1958, the use of technology in contracting has progressed significantly. The need to accommodate the new practices led, among other things, to the adoption of the UNCITRAL Recommendation regarding the interpretation of Article II of the Convention,[49] and the 2006 edition of the Model Law Article 7. These documents purported to respond to the new challenges by recognising new forms of contracting, in particular, the electronic commerce, in the context of arbitration agreements.

During the arbitration reform in 2015, the Russian legislature has partially followed the UNCITRAL Model Law Option I of Article 7. However, there were two important differences in the final text of the Russian statutes.

First, the Arbitration Act 2015 and the ICA Act 1993 both provide that the agreement must be in writing, but they are more conservative than Option I in recognising the various ways of concluding an arbitration agreement. They list fewer technological means of contracting than their UNCITRAL counterpart and refrain from any mention of a possibility of an oral arbitration agreement.

Second, the new statutes incorporated the additional methods of concluding an arbitration agreement, carrying out other objectives of the arbitration reform 2015. In particular, they make it possible to include arbitration agreements into the Rules of

47. Decree of the Federal Commercial Court for the Moscow Circuit of 14 March 2017 No. F05-2079/2017, case No. A40-219464/16.
48. Asoskov A.V., *Can Purely Domestic Disputes Without a Foreign Element Be Referred to Foreign Arbitration?*, 8 Zakon 115-123 (2017) [Asoskov A.V. Dopustimo li pyeryedavat chisto vnutryenniye spory byez inostrannogo elyemyenta na razryeshyeniye inostrannogo arbitraja? // Zakon. 2017. N 8. S. 115-123].
49. UNCITRAL Document A/6/17, adopted by the United Nations Commission on International Trade Law on 7 July 2006 at its thirty-ninth session Available at http://www.newyorkconvention.org/11165/web/files/document/1/5/15978.pdf (accessed 27 June 2018).

exchanges and clearing organisations, and into the articles of association of a Russian company.

As a result, there are now six distinct methods of concluding an arbitration agreement under the Arbitration Act 2015 and the ICA Act 1993.

[A] A Single Document

The traditional written form of a contract as a single paper document signed by the parties remains the 'golden standard' of business-to-business contracting in Russia, especially where significant sums are at stake. There are signs that the position might be changing. For example, in the sphere of public procurement where the sums involved are often considerable, there is now a legislative requirement to conduct the tenders via the Internet, and to sign many types of contracts in the electronic form,[50] However, outside the regulated areas and e-commerce as such, for now, there is a preference among Russian lawyers and business managers to err on the conservative and cautious side. With a contract as a single paper document with the signatures of both parties, there is hardly any risk of non-compliance with the formal requirements to the arbitration agreement.

[B] Exchange of Messages

With the exchange of messages, the statutory texts differ in the ICA Act 1993 (governing the international commercial arbitration), and the Arbitration Act 2015 (that regulates arbitration on all other categories of cases). How much do the textual differences reflect a substantive variation in legal requirements?

According to Article 7 of the ICA Act 1993:

> 3. An arbitration agreement complies with section 2 of this article [*requiring an arbitration agreement to be in writing*][51] if it is in a form that permits the recording of information contained therein or the accessibility of such information for subsequent use.
> 4. An arbitration agreement is concluded in the written form via electronic communications if the information contained therein is accessible for subsequent use and its conclusion complied with the law on contracting by an exchange of documents via electronic communications.

Article 7(3) above is very similar to the equivalent Article 7(3) of the Model Law, which provides:

> (3) An arbitration agreement is in writing if its content is recorded in any form, whether or not the arbitration agreement or contract has been concluded orally, by conduct, or by other means.

50. The Federal Law of 5 April 2013 N 44-FZ 'On the Contractual System in the Procurement of Goods, Works and Services for the State and Municipal Needs'.
51. Translator's note.

On comparing the two provisions, one may notice that, while the Russian statute does not specifically mention the exchange of messages, it omits any reference to the conclusion of an arbitration agreement orally or by conduct. As a matter of general Russian law, oral contracts (as well as the conclusion of oral contracts by conduct and the acceptance of a written offer by conduct) are permissible in principle.[52] However, Article 161 of the Civil Code makes the written form a mandatory requirement for all transactions between legal persons, legal persons and individuals, and between individuals where the value of the contract is above a modest monetary threshold.

Therefore, in the context of international commercial arbitration, a reference to the conclusion of an arbitration agreement orally or by conduct becomes unnecessary, because written contracts are standard practice in this sphere. At the same time, with this exclusion, it is hard to think of any other way to conclude an arbitration agreement that would not involve an exchange of messages.

Thus, the exchange of messages becomes a presumed requirement for the conclusion of a valid arbitration agreement under the ICA Act 1993. Article 7(4) reinforces this point by requiring an exchange of messages to conclude an agreement via electronic communications.

The position on the necessity of an exchange of messages is even more straightforward under the Arbitration Act 2015. According to its Article 7(3):

> 3. An arbitration agreement complies with section 2 of this article [*requiring an arbitration agreement to be in writing*][53] if it is concluded [...] by an exchange of letters, telegrams, telexes, telefaxes or other documents, including electronic documents transferred via the channels of communication, that permit the identification of the other party as the originator of the document.

Here, it is beyond doubt that the exchange of messages is required to conclude an arbitration agreement.

Unlike its UNCITRAL counterpart, the Arbitration Act 2015 does not mention electronic mail or electronic data interchange (EDI) as a legitimate means of concluding an arbitration agreement. The definition is broad enough to cover a wide range of electronic communications, including, for example, an exchange of messages via the companies' official email address. However, Russian practitioners remain cautious about this method, voicing their concern that in practice, only the encrypted documents with an electronic signature might fall under the definition of a 'communications that permit the identification of the other party as the originator of the document'.[54] The cases where courts had to consider cases involving an arbitration agreement concluded via the email are extremely rare. In one decision, the court did recognise the validity of such an agreement, but the parties, in that case, exchanged the paper

52. Articles 158(2), 159 and 438(3) of the Civil Code.
53. Translator's note.
54. Zhilina M., *From 1 September We Arbitrate by New Rules*, 143-154, 3 Arbitral Disputes (2016) [Zhilina M. 1 syentyabrya - v tryetyeiskii sud po novym pravilam // Informacionno-analitichyeskii jurnal 'Arbitrajnyye spory'. 2016. N 3. S. 143-154.]

versions of the contract after sending each other its scanned versions by email, which made the court's task easier.[55]

The Russian general law on contracting by an exchange of documents via electronic communications does contain the rule identical to the missing part of the UNCITRAL Model Law formula. According to Article 434(2) of the Civil Code, a contract may be concluded by an exchange of [...] electronic documents transferred via the channels of communication that permit the identification of the other party as the originator of the document. 'Electronic documents transferred via the channels of communication' means the information generated, sent, received or stored by electronic, magnetic, optical or similar means, *including electronic data interchange and electronic mail* [emphasis added].

It remains unclear why exactly the mention of EDI and email ended up in the Civil Code but not in the arbitration statutes. From a practical perspective, caution with concluding arbitration agreements via email and EDI remains justified until the relevant court practice emerges.

Only the exchange of documents with an electronic signature will quite certainly comply with the statutory requirements. By a direct legislative prescription, such documents are equivalent to paper versions in all contexts where the law requires a document to be in a 'written form'.[56] Electronic signatures are the basis of the developing electronic contracting and data exchange in Russia in many spheres, including public procurement. The conclusion of an arbitration agreement via the exchange of documents with a qualifying electronic signature is thus a safe method of observing the requirements of writing under Russian law.

This brief analysis shows, therefore, that the variation of wording in the Arbitration Act 2015 and the ICA Act 1993 does not lead to many significant differences in substance. In both cases, the exchange of messages is necessary. The more traditional telecommunication methods such as telegrams and telex will satisfy the requirement of writing, and so will the document exchange where both parties use a qualifying electronic signature. However, it remains best to be cautious with unencrypted EDI and email.

[C] The Exchange of Statements of Claim and Defence

The exchange of a statement of claim where one party asserts the existence of an arbitration agreement and the other party does not object is a well-known and uncontroversial way of agreeing to arbitrate. It has been part of Russian law for a long time, and the current arbitration statutes contain this important rule. The courts have often cited participation in arbitration without any objections as sufficient ground to confirm the existence of an agreement to arbitrate between the parties.[57]

55. Decree of the Federal Commercial Court for the Moscow Circuit of 5 September 2016 N F05-12307/2016, case No. A40-51713/16.
56. Article 6 of the Federal Law of 6 April 2011 N 63-FZ 'On Electronic Signature'.
57. Decree of the Presidium of the Supreme Commercial Court of 19 April 2006 N 15973/05, case No. A40-38205/05-68-272.

Russian arbitration statutes also incorporate the Model Law Article 4 on the waiver of right to object. According to this rule, a party who knows that any provision of this Law from which the parties may derogate [...] has not been complied with and yet proceeds with the arbitration without stating his objection [...] shall be deemed to have waived his right to object.

The provisions in the nature of estoppel, in various areas of law, have been subject of a discussion among legal experts in Russia in recent years. The principle of estoppel originates in the English law and describes a prohibition of acting inconsistently with one's previous behaviour, especially where such behaviour became a reason for some official decision. Estoppel is of particular relevance in civil procedural law where it is important to ensure consistency and sanction the parties' opportunistic behaviour.[58] While estoppel is still not a part of Russian law, estoppel-like legal provisions and reasoning are gaining popularity.

Article V of the European Convention 1961 establishes that the party which intends to raise a plea as to the arbitrator's jurisdiction based on the fact that the arbitration agreement was either non-existent or null and void or had lapsed, shall do so during the arbitration proceedings, not later than the delivery of its statement of claim or defence relating to the substance of the dispute. This rule comes into play where the Convention itself applies to arbitration proceedings, i.e., in proceedings between companies and individuals from Russia and another Contracting States of the Convention.[59]

With the adoption of the new legislation in 2015, this rule now became universal in Russian arbitration. Should a respondent participate in the proceedings and fail to raise a timely objection against the tribunal's jurisdiction, he will thereby conclude an arbitration agreement by an exchange of the statement of claim and defence.

[D] Reference to a Document Containing an Arbitration Clause

Reference in a contract to any document containing an arbitration clause constitutes an arbitration agreement in writing if the reference is such as to make that clause part of the contract.[60]

One example of such a document is the standard terms of a contract. Before the 2015 reform dramatically reduced the number of permanent arbitration centres in Russia,[61] many large corporations included an arbitration clause to their standard terms. For example, one of the Russian Railways' approved contractual schemes invited their clients to accept a public offer on their website. Such an acceptance referred to the approved form of the contract containing an arbitration clause in favour

58. Chernykh I.I., *Estoppel in Civil Procedure*, 12 Laws of Russia: Experience, Analysis, Practice 81-88 (2015) [Chernykh I.I. Estoppel v grajdanskom sudoproizvodstvye // Zakony Rossii: opyt, analiz, praktika. 2015. N 12. S. 81-88].
59. Article I of the Convention.
60. Article 7(5) of the Arbitration Act 2015, Article 7(6) of the ICA Act 1993.
61. *See* above, §1.03 of Chapter 1.

of a nominated arbitral institution.[62] After 2015, the use of such mechanisms became less frequent – although this effect might be only temporary.

Another example of a document the parties can incorporate by reference is a separate 'general' arbitration agreement between the parties covering their various legal relationships. Such an agreement can make sense if the parties periodically enter into the same type of contracts. In practice, this method of concluding an arbitration agreement is quite rare.

[E] Arbitration Clause in the Rules of Exchanges and Clearing Organisations

The rule allowing licensed commodity exchanges, stock exchanges, and clearing organisations to include arbitration agreements into their Rules first appeared in Russian legislation in 2011. The legislature recognised that arbitration, with its flexible procedure and availability of expert arbitrators, is uniquely suitable for the resolution of disputes in these fast-moving and specialised markets. This provision was also in keeping with the historical prominence of exchange arbitration in nineteenth-century Russia.[63]

The effect of such inclusion is that all the participants of trading are deemed to have agreed to arbitrate the disputes among themselves in the nominated arbitral institution.[64]

The exchanges and clearing organisations often do take advantage of this statutory provision. For example, the Trading Rules of the Moscow Exchange provide that all the disputes concerning the conclusion, amendment, and termination of transactions concluded under the Rules, as well as the disputes concerning the Rules themselves or their interpretation, shall be resolved by the Arbitration Centre at the Russian Union of Industrialists and Entrepreneurs.[65]

[F] Arbitration Clause in a Company's Articles of Association

Many novel provisions of the 2015 reform focus on the arbitration of corporate disputes. One of them concerns arbitration agreements.

An arbitration agreement can be included in the company's articles of association and cover all or certain disputes between the participants of the company and the legal entity itself. Any company can take advantage of this provision, except public joint-stock companies and joint-stock companies with more than a thousand voting

62. Administrative Order of Russian Railways JSC of 27 February 2014 N 529r 'On the approval of the standard form of the contract for the provision of services to optimise logistic schemes for carriage of railway cars'.
63. *See* above, §1.01 of Chapter 1.
64. Article 7(6) of the Arbitration Act 2015, Article 7(7) of the ICA Act 1993.
65. *FX and Precious Metals Market Trading Rules of the Moscow Exchange* (entering into force 2 July 2018) [*Pravila organizovannyh torgov PAO Moskovskaya Birja na valyutnom rynkye i rynkye dragocyennyh myetallov (vstupayut v silu s 02.07.2018)*], https://fs.moex.com/files/1498/28074 (accessed 29 June 2018).

shareholders. An important condition for the validity of this kind of arbitration agreement is the unanimous consent of all company members.[66] Such a corporate arbitration agreement can also extend to the disputes involving third persons, but only if they expressly agree to be thus bound.[67]

One principal limitation associated with the arbitration of corporate disputes is the impossibility of choosing the seat of arbitration. It is a mandatory requirement that arbitration under a corporate arbitration agreement must take place in the Russian Federation.[68] It means, in turn, that Russian courts will be competent to assist the ongoing arbitration and to hear applications to set aside the award.

The choice of foreign law to govern such corporate arbitration agreement would be invalid because of the mandatory requirements of 1202 of the Civil Code. This provision stipulates that the law of the country where the company is registered shall govern the relations between the company and its members. The national company law comprehensively regulates the content of the Russian companies' articles of association.

§3.04 TYPES OF ARBITRATION AGREEMENTS

Russian doctrinal sources, like some leading international texts,[69] commonly classify arbitration agreements according to their form, time of conclusion, and the type of arbitration they envision.[70] Additionally, there is a lot of normative material on the so-called direct (or express) arbitration agreements and alternative agreements.

[A] A Clause or a Separate Agreement

Depending on the form, one can distinguish an arbitration clause incorporated in a larger document (usually, a contract), and an arbitration agreement drafted as a separate document. For the former but not the latter, the principle of autonomy is important.

66. The requirements to arbitration agreements in articles of association are similar to those in Germany, so the German experience may have been influenced the new provisions. *See* Duve C., Wimalasena P., *Arbitration of Corporate Law Disputes in Germany*, in: Arbitration in Germany. The Model Law in Practice 934-936 (Nacimiento P., Kröll S., Bockstiegel K., eds, 2nd ed., Alphen aan den Rijn, The Netherlands, 2014).
67. *Commentary to the Federal Law 'On Arbitration (Arbitral Proceedings) in the Russian Federation' (Clause-by-Clause, Academic and Practical Commentary)*, *supra* note 1, Commentary to Article 7, at §33.
68. Article 7(7) of the Arbitration Act 2015, Article 7(8) of the ICA Act 1993.
69. *See*, e.g., Blackaby N., Partasides QC C., Redfern A., Hunter M., *Redfern and Hunter on International Arbitration*, §2.02 (6th ed., Oxford University Press, 2015).
70. Kurochkin S.A., *supra* note 19, at 72.

[B] Existing or Future Disputes

The time of conclusion, relative to the dispute, allows the classification of agreements into two categories: those relating to a dispute that might arise in the future, and those that refer an already existing one to arbitration (submission agreements). The status of the two categories in current law is equal, although there used to be one exception.

From 2002 to 2015, an arbitration clause contained in a contract where one of the parties produces its terms on a template or another standard form, and the other party has no choice but to accept it by acceding to the contract as a whole (accession contract), was void.[71]

The arbitration agreement for an accession contract would only be valid if concluded after the factual basis for the claim has arisen. This measure meant to protect a weaker party in the relationship, because when the dispute begins, the advantages and disadvantages of arbitration become clearer to both parties, thus making an informed and rational choice easier. However, the legislature soon had to make several exceptions to this rule, notably relating to arbitration clauses in the trading rules of exchanges and clearing organisations. The rule also came under severe criticism from the expert community for being too paternalistic, especially in contracts between entrepreneurs.[72] The courts applied it willingly enough in the consumer context[73] but were often reluctant to do so in commercial disputes.[74]

The new Arbitration Act 2015 eventually abandoned the rule. Thus, accession contracts can now validly include arbitration clauses, and the distinction between arbitration clauses for future disputes and submission agreements is now more theoretical than practical.

[C] Ad Hoc or Institutional Arbitration

The agreement may envision arbitration ad hoc; then the arbitral procedure will be based on the agreement itself and on the ad hoc rules the parties referenced (if any), such as the UNCITRAL Rules. Alternatively, it may envision arbitration at a permanent institution, in which case the institution's rules will govern the procedure. In the Arbitration Act 2015, the rules on ad hoc arbitration became more stringent, and the possibilities of court assistance decreased significantly compared to institutional

71. Article 5 of the Arbitration Act 2002; there was never an equivalent rule for international commercial arbitration in the ICA Act 1993.
72. Kuzmina A.V., *Arbitration Clauses in Accession Contracts: Problems of Reforming the Civil and Procedural Legislation*, 4 Zakon 121, 123-124 (2015) [Kuzmina A.V., Tryetyeiskiye ogovorki v dogovorah prisoyedinyeniya: problyemy ryeformirovaniya grajdanskogo i procyessualnogo zakonodatyelstva // Zakon, No. 4, Apryel 2015. S. 123-124].
73. Review of the Practice of the Supreme Court of Russian Federation in the Fourth Quarter of 2011 [Obzor sudyebnoi praktiki Vyerhovnogo Suda Rossiiskoi Fyedyeracii za chyetvyertyi kvartal 2011 goda].
74. *See*, e.g., Decree of the Presidium of the Supreme Commercial Court of 20 December 2011 N 12686/11, case No. N A65-5394/2011 (refusing to treat an energy supply contract between an individual entrepreneur and a provider as an accession contract despite the vast difference in bargaining power).

arbitration.[75] The parties that agree to ad hoc arbitration, therefore, limit the potential for court assistance and increase the amount of court supervision, in exchange for greater flexibility and confidentiality of the proceedings. The parties to an ad hoc agreement also have a smaller choice of direct (or express) agreements available to them.

[D] Direct Arbitration Agreements

A direct (or express) arbitration agreement is an important novel introduced into Russian law in 2015. According to Article 2(13) of the 2015 Act, the parties may conclude a direct agreement in the enumerated situations. Such an agreement has priority over the institutional rules of arbitration. The enumerated situations include the following:

(1) In case of a failure of the tribunal appointment procedure, any of the parties may petition the competent court to assist in overcoming this difficulty. However, the parties to an agreement that envisions arbitration at a permanent institution may by their direct agreement exclude any involvement of the court in this matter (Article 11(4) of the Arbitration Act 2015).

(2) Where an arbitrator challenge has been unsuccessful under the agreed procedure, a party may refer it to the competent court. Likewise, the parties to an agreement that envisions arbitration at a permanent institution may by their direct agreement exclude this possibility (Article 13(3) of the Arbitration Act 2015). The same rules apply in case of an arbitrator's failure or impossibility to act (Article 14(1) of the Arbitration Act 2015).

With the grounds (1) and (2) above, an interesting issue may arise with the International Commercial Arbitration Court at the Chamber of Commerce and Industry of the Russian Federation (ICAC at the RF CCI) – Russia's most prominent arbitration centre. According to section 11 of the ICAC Rules (Annex 1 to the ICA Act 1993), in ICAC arbitrations the President of CCI shall perform these functions instead of a competent court. At the same time, the relevant Articles 11(3), 11(4), 13(3) and 14 of the ICA Act 1993 do not mention the parties' right to exclude the involvement of the President of ICAC. It would be logical to interpret these rules as allowing such exclusion by the parties' direct agreement since the exclusion of the court's involvement is permissible. However, the courts are yet to test this interpretation.[76]

(3) Where an arbitral tribunal rules issues an interim award on a party's plea challenging its jurisdiction, this award can be subject to review in a competent court. However, the parties to an agreement that envisions arbitration at a

75. For more details, *see* below, Chapter 6, especially §6.06.

76. Muranov A.I., *The New Recommended Arbitration Agreements of ICAC at the RF CCI 2017: The Comprehensive Analysis of Their Positive and Negative Features, and the Unusual History of Their Publication. The Current 'Shining' of the Absence of an Equivalent Agreement for MAC at the RF CCI*, in: *V.A. Kabatov, S.N. Lebedev: In Memoriam. A Collection of Memories, Articles, Other Materials* 683, 701 (A.I. Muranov, O.N. Zimenkova, A.A. Kostin, eds, Moscow, 2017) [Muranov A.I. Novyye ryekomyenduyemyye arbitrajnyye soglashyeniya MKAS pri TPP RF 2017 g.: komplyeksnyi analiz ih plyusov, minusov, nyeobychnoi istorii ih opublikovaniya. Tyekushyeye 'blistaniye' otsutstviya analogichnogo soglashyeniya dlya MAK pri TPP RF // V.A. Kabatov, S.N. Lebedev: In Memoriam: Sbornik vospominanii, statyei, inyh matyerialov / Nauch. ryed.: A.I. Muranov, O.N. Zimenkova, A.A. Kostin; sost. A.I. Muranov. M., 2017. S. 701].

permanent institution may by their direct agreement exclude any involvement of the court in this matter (Article 16(3) of the Arbitration Act 2015).

(4) Subject to any contrary agreement by the parties, the arbitral tribunal shall decide whether to hold oral hearings or to conduct the proceedings solely by documents. However, the arbitral tribunal shall hold such hearings at an appropriate stage of the proceedings if so requested by a party, unless the parties have directly agreed that no hearings will take place (Article 27(1) of the Arbitration Act 2015). This direct agreement, unlike many others, is available in both ad hoc and institutional arbitration.

(5) The parties to an agreement that envisions arbitration at a permanent institution may by their direct agreement stipulate that the arbitral award shall be final as between the parties. The final arbitral award cannot be subject to an application for setting aside in a competent court (Article 40 of the Arbitration Act 2015).

(6) Unless the parties to an agreement that envisions arbitration at a permanent institution have directly agreed otherwise, an arbitral institution cannot make the appointment of arbitrators dependent on their belonging to any list of recommended arbitrators (Article 47(1) of the Arbitration Act 2015).

This statutory regulation of direct (express) arbitration agreements is, in itself, a positive development. It has a high potential as an instrument for resolving inconsistencies between institutional rules and the parties' agreements, setting up a clear hierarchy of rules. However, as currently implemented, the main effect of these provisions is increasing the attractiveness of institutional arbitration and decreasing the appeal of ad hoc arbitration in Russia. For example, the parties in institutional arbitration can exclude the possibility of setting an award aside, but the parties in ad hoc arbitration cannot do so. This speaks of a distrust of the Russian legislature to ad hoc arbitration and a preference towards institutional arbitration. Leaving aside the question of whether this preference is justified, one could only point out that the mechanism of a direct (express) agreement could be useful in other contexts as well.

[E] Alternative Arbitration Agreements

An alternative arbitration agreement provides one or both parties, when a dispute arises, with a choice between initiating a case in arbitration or a competent national court. Another kind of an alternative arbitration agreement provides one or both parties with a choice between two or more arbitral institutions enumerated in the agreement.

One could argue that alternative agreements represent a fair and sensible option in some industries and some types of contracts. An obvious example are commercial loan agreements where the lender who extends credit facilities to a borrower ought to be able, in case of default, to select the most appropriate forum to recover the debt depending on the location of the debtor's assets. In some of the more 'liberal' jurisdictions such as England, virtually all types of alternative clauses are valid.[77]

77. NB Three Shipping Ltd v Harebell Shipping Ltd [2004] EWHC 2001 (Comm), Deutsche Bank Ag v Tongkah Harbour Public Company Ltd [2011] EWHC 2251 (Comm), Law Debenture Trust Corporation plc v Elektrim Finance BV and others [2005] EWHC 1412 (Ch).

However, the drafters of alternative arbitration agreements should exercise caution if the matter may end up in front of a Russian court.

One type of alternative agreements names several arbitral institutions on an alternative basis, giving the claimant the right to select one of them. There is at least one reported ICAC case where the tribunal assumed jurisdiction under such a clause.[78] Some experts consider such clauses as perfectly valid and enforceable.[79] Others caution that they may fall prey to the position of the Supreme Commercial Court[80] requiring the arbitration clause, in case of institutional arbitration, to name a particular arbitral institution at the risk of invalidity.[81]

Another type of alternative arbitration agreement envisions a party choosing, when a dispute arises, between arbitration and a competent national court. Such clauses are sometimes termed hybrid, or optional, dispute resolution clauses.[82] Depending on whether this choice belongs to one or both (all) parties to the agreement, hybrid clauses can be either symmetrical or asymmetrical.

Symmetrical alternative arbitration agreements are perfectly enforceable in Russia. In *Katren v Surgutfarmaciya*, the Presidium of the Supreme Commercial Court confirmed the validity of an agreement that gave the claimant a choice between the Siberian Arbitration Centre and the relevant competent Commercial Court. The court explained this conclusion by the freedom of contract, the entitlement of both parties to make a choice, and the absence of any statutory restriction for such agreements.[83]

However, several months later, in the famous *Sony Ericsson case*, the Supreme Commercial Court held that asymmetrical arbitration clauses were unenforceable in Russia. The sales agreement between Sony Ericsson and its Russian distributor contained an International Chamber of Commerce (ICC) arbitration clause, which, in addition to the conventional provisions about resolving all disputes in arbitration, gave Sony Ericsson the right to recover any debt via the court of competent jurisdiction. The Russian distributor sought a remedy against Sony Ericsson in the Commercial Court of the City of Moscow, but the court declined to hear the case because there was a valid arbitration agreement between the parties. When the case reached the Supreme Commercial Court, it held as follows:

> Thus, a dispute settlement agreement cannot confer the right to apply to the competent court only on one party of a contract (seller) and deprive the other party (buyer) of such a right. Such an agreement is invalid because it violates the balance of rights between the parties. Therefore, a party whose right has been infringed by such a dispute resolution agreement is also entitled to apply to the

78. ICAC Award of 29 October 1996, case No. 441/1996.
79. Nosyreva E.I., *The Consequences of Alternative Arbitration Agreements*, 10-14, 20 Yurist (2013) [Nosyreva E.I. Poslyedstviya zaklyuchyeniya altyernativnyh arbitrajnyh (tryetyeiskih) ogovorok // Yurist. 2013. N 20. S. 10-14].
80. Decree of the Presidium of the Supreme Commercial Court of 27 February 1996 N 5278/95.
81. Kurochkin S.A., *supra* note 19, at 73.
82. Andrews N., *Arbitration and Contract Law: Common Law Perspectives*, 19 (Switzerland, 2016).
83. Decree of the Presidium of the Supreme Commercial Court of 14 February 2012 N 11196/11, case No. A75-1836/2011.

> competent state court, thus realising its guaranteed right of access to justice on an equal footing with its counterparty.[84]

One could criticise the decision on several grounds, in particular for the lack of clarity on the law applicable to the arbitration clause in question.[85] However, the excerpt above shows that the Supreme Commercial Court adopted an interesting solution. Instead of invalidating the arbitration agreement in its entirety, the court decided to remedy the then-invalid clause without striking it down. The decision effectively grants both parties the same rights and access to their preferred method of dispute resolution, be it ICC arbitration or litigation before the competent court.[86]

Arguably, this represents a more nuanced solution than the one that the French *Cour de Cassation* adopted in *Madame X v Banque Privie Edmond de Rothschild.*[87] The French court considered a similar clause in a case involving a bank customer attempting to close her accounts in a local branch of the bank. The court found the entire dispute resolution clause invalid on the grounds of unconscionability – which may have been justified given the different facts and context. The underlying rationale based on procedural equality of the parties, however, is very similar.

§3.05 INTERPRETATION OF THE ARBITRATION AGREEMENT

One positive development in the Arbitration Act 2015 was the introduction of statutory rules on the interpretation of an arbitration agreement. Those rules will be considered below.

[A] Doubts as to the Agreement's Validity and Enforceability

According to Article 7(8) of the Arbitration Act 2015, 'when interpreting an arbitration agreement, any doubt must be construed in favour of its validity and enforceability'.[88] This provision is absent from the UNCITRAL Model Law on International Commercial Arbitration, and its precise reach and significance for the Russian law are yet to be determined in the court practice.

This provision appears to draw inspiration in the method of 'effective interpretation', which is indeed a universally recognised rule of interpretation. This method can be traced back to Article 1157 of the French Civil Code, which provided that 'where a clause can be interpreted in two different ways, the interpretation enabling the clause to be effective should be adopted in preference to that which prevents the clause from

84. Decree of the Presidium of the Supreme Commercial Court of 19 June 2012 N 1831/12, case No. A40-49223/11-112-401.
85. Khodykin R., *supra* note 23, 28-29.
86. Miller L.D., *Is the Unilateral Jurisdiction Clause No Longer an Option: Examining Courts' Justifications for Upholding or Invalidating Asymmetrical or Unilateral Jurisdiction Clauses*, 51 Texas International Law Journal 321, 331 (2016).
87. *Cour de cassation [Cass.] Paris, Ass. plen., Sept. 26, 2012, Bulletin des arrets de la Cour de cassation, Chambres Civiles 2012, 983, M. Charruault.*
88. Article 7(9) of the ICA Act 1993 contains the identical rule.

being effective'. This provision has been contained in the French Civil Code since 1804 and is now incorporated in the law of many jurisdictions.[89] The UNIDROIT Principles of International Commercial Contracts include the same rule in Article 4.5 (All terms must be given effect). When applied to an arbitration agreement, this principle leads to the assumption that the parties could not knowingly intend to include a pathological agreement into their contract.

The method of effective interpretation must not be confused with interpretation *in favorem validatis*, which requires an extensive interpretation of an arbitration agreement, thus giving preference to arbitration over litigation in a competent state court. Thus worded, the principle becomes more questionable, especially when it is applied to the matter of the very existence of an arbitration agreement between the parties. Indeed, a mere allegation that the agreement to arbitrate exists should not raise a presumption that such an allegation is true.[90]

[B] The Default Scope of an Arbitration Agreement

The range of disputes that may arise in any given relationship is impossible to predict with any certainty. Would a disagreement arise during the performance of a contract? Perhaps one of the parties might attempt to obtain a decision declaring some provisions of the contract null and void? Anticipating all the possibilities might be difficult even for an experienced transactional lawyer, let alone an ordinary commercial party acting without legal advice.

This problem does not only affect arbitration in Russia. Courts in many jurisdictions regularly interpret the scope of arbitration agreements, trying to ascertain the parties' intentions. For example, in *Fiona Trust & Holding Corporation v Privalov*,[91] the UK House of Lords had to strike down the distinction the English courts previously drew between 'narrow' arbitration agreements covering only disputes 'out of the contract' and 'wide' clauses that encompassed disputes out of the contract as well as those 'in connection' with the contract.[92] Lord Hoffman held that construction of an arbitration clause should start from the assumption that the parties, as rational businessmen, are likely to have intended any dispute arising out of their relationship to be decided by the same tribunal.

The prevailing opinion in Germany and Switzerland favours a broad interpretation of arbitration clauses supporting an all-encompassing jurisdiction of the arbitral tribunal.[93] Courts in other countries, such as the US, continue to uphold the distinction between wide and narrow clauses.[94] For instance, in *Cape Flattery Ltd v Titan Maritime*

89. *Fouchard, Gaillard and Goldman on International Commercial Arbitration*, *supra* note 7, at 258-259.
90. *Ibid.* at 262.
91. Fiona Trust & Holding Corporation v Privalov (2007) UKHL 40.
92. Welser I., Molitoris S., *The Scope of Arbitration Clauses – Or 'All Disputes Arising out of or in Connection with This Contract ...'*, 17 Austrian Yearbook on International Arbitration 19, 20 (2012).
93. *Ibid.* at 19.
94. *Ibid.* at 21.

LLC, the US Court of Appeals for the Ninth Circuit held that the distinction is long-standing; therefore, the parties are entitled to rely on it when they conclude their agreements.[95]

Under the previous legislation, Russian courts often assumed narrow and literal interpretation of arbitration agreements. The new arbitral legislation introduced two connected rules to remedy the situation.

First, unless the parties agreed otherwise, an arbitration agreement covering disputes arising from a contract, or in connection therewith, extends to any transactions between the parties aimed at the performance, amendment, or termination of said contract.[96]

Second, an arbitration agreement contained in a contract extends to any disputes in connection with the conclusion of the said contract, its entry into force, amendment, termination, or validity. It also extends to the disputes arising in connection with an obligation to return everything performed under a contract if it is declared void or not concluded. This rule applies if it does not follow otherwise from the arbitration agreement itself.[97] The courts have interpreted it, for example, to apply to unjust enrichment obligations connected with the contract.[98]

The approach of the Arbitration Act 2015 thus makes the distinction between wide and narrow agreements virtually non-existent and creates the prerequisites for a more favourable judicial approach to the scope of arbitration agreements.

§3.06 ASSIGNMENT AND SUCCESSION IN ARBITRATION AGREEMENTS

The question whether or not the arbitral clause should follow the fate of the main obligation under the contract, e.g. a monetary debt when it is assigned to a third person, has been contentious in Russia for a long time.[99]

The Civil Code does not require a debtor to agree to the assignment unless the obligation is 'inseparable' from the personality of the creditor. Therefore, a creditor can usually assign a debt without asking the debtor's opinion.[100] On the other hand, a debtor cannot legally substitute himself with the new debtor (this is known as a substitution of a debtor or a transfer of the debt to another person) without the creditor's agreement.[101] Transfer of an arbitration clause to a new creditor without the debtor's consent also puts into question the voluntary nature of arbitration, which the highest courts of Russia hold in utmost regard.

---

95. Cape Flattery Ltd v Titan Maritime, LLC (U.S. Court of Appeals, 9th Circuit 2011).
96. Article 7(9) of the Arbitration Act 2015, Article 7(10) of the ICA Act 1993.
97. Article 7(11) of the Arbitration Act 2015, Article 7(12) of the ICA Act 1993.
98. Decree of the Ninth Commercial Appeal Court of 23 January 2017 N 09AP-66804/2016, case No. A40-122354/16-34-1071.
99. *See* Khodykin R., *supra* note 23, at 33-34.
100. Article 388 of the Civil Code.
101. Article 391 of the Civil Code.

Before the 2015 reform, scholarly opinion was divided. Some commentators argued that the arbitral agreement has a procedural nature distinct from the substantive obligation, and the voluntariness of arbitration should be of paramount importance. Therefore, since the debtor never expressly agreed to arbitrate with the new creditor, the arbitration agreement should become void on assignment. Others pointed out that the method of dispute resolution is but a component of a contractual obligation, and the separation of debts from the method of their recovery is both unnecessary and undesirable. The court practice on this issue was also inconsistent.[102]

Article 12(10) of the Arbitration Act 2015 attempts to put an end to the debate. It provides that if a creditor or a debtor changes in a relationship covered by an arbitration agreement, it remains valid for both old and new debtor, as well as for both old and new creditor.[103] This is a welcome solution for the assignment of commercial debts because the need to obtain the debtor's agreement would impede the liquidity on the market and make investments riskier and thus more costly. On the other hand, it is a far-reaching mandatory rule, covering both assignments of debts and substitutions of debtors in obligations; both contractual and statutory mechanisms, such as company reorganisation and succession; applicable both in commercial and non-commercial relations. In some contexts, one could doubt whether such a firm connection between a substantive obligation and the arbitration agreement is desirable. However, in light of the previous debates and inconsistency, the certainty of this rule is a positive factor.

A related matter is the transfer of rights and liabilities from one permanent arbitral institution to another. This question may arise, for example, if an arbitral institution merges with another or splits into two new institutions. Some arbitration agreements concluded before the event would still reference the institution's old name – do they become inoperable?

The court practice treats the name and identity of a permanent institution as a necessary term of an arbitration agreement. Therefore, attempts of reorganised institutions to apply the usual rules of succession to the arbitral agreements have generally failed.

For example, in 2007, in the course of the ongoing energy reform, RAO Unified Energy Systems of Russia (RAO UES) – the umbrella holding company acting as a semi-governmental regulator for the state-owned energy companies – was merged with another company and ceased to exist. This meant that its permanent arbitral institution, the RAO UES Arbitration Centre, could no longer exist either. Meanwhile, over the years companies in the sector concluded many contracts with arbitral clauses in their favour. In one of its last documents, RAO UES informed the energy companies that their arbitral clauses remained valid, and the disputes under them should be referred to the new centre. Inevitably, some of the respondents later objected to the jurisdiction of the new centre. In a series of cases, commercial courts upheld these objections of the reluctant respondents. They held that RAO UES was attempting to unilaterally impose

102. For a review of the main arguments, *see* Bevzenko R.S., *Does the Arbitration Clause Survive an Assignment?*, 11 Corporate Lawyer (2007) [Bevzenko R.S., Sohranyayetsya li tryetyeiskaya ogovorka pri ustupkye tryebovaniya? // Korporativnyi yurist, No. 11, 2007].
103. Article 7(10) of the Arbitration Act 2015, Article 7(11) of the ICA Act 1993.

its will upon the energy companies that freely agreed to the jurisdiction of the RAO UES Arbitration Centre before, but never consented to arbitrate under the auspices of its successor. The courts did not consider it relevant that some arbitral agreements expressly gave RAO UES the right to reorganise the Arbitration Centre or to determine its successor.[104]

After this series of cases, succession between arbitral institutions in Russia became virtually impossible, except in cases where both parties expressly consented to the successor's jurisdiction. The newly created 'successors' of the reorganised arbitral centres thus have to start anew, building their own 'client base' from scratch, and the arbitration agreements in favour of the reorganised centres become inoperable. This remains the position until this day, with only two known exceptions.

One exception is ICAC at the RF CCI, which 'inherited' the arbitration agreements from its predecessor, the Foreign Trade Arbitration Commission (FTAC), by a statutory rule which expressly confirmed the succession in 1993.[105]

The second, more recent exception, deals with the situation where a permanent arbitral centre fails to obtain the necessary government permit required after the 2015 reform.[106] To avoid making the arbitration agreements inoperable, the law allows such defunct centres to determine their successors from among the arbitral institutions that have successfully obtained a permit.[107]

§3.07 DEFECTS OF AN ARBITRATION AGREEMENT

The description of possible defects of an arbitration agreement in the Arbitration Act 2015 and the Russian procedural codes follow the wording of Articles II and V of the New York Convention 1958. The courts will give an effect to an arbitration agreement or to an award stemming from an agreement unless they find that the agreement is null and void, inoperative, or incapable of being performed. The first of those three categories (nullity or invalidity) corresponds to the approach of the Civil Code to the invalidity of contracts generally and therefore is a familiar notion for Russian civil lawyers. The other two, however, are otherwise unknown in Russian legal system and their use is confined to arbitration law. Under the Civil Code, arbitral agreements in Russian law can also be 'not concluded'. This section will proceed to consider each category in turn.

[A] Invalid Agreements

There are two categories of grounds for invalidity of an arbitration agreement: those resulting from the non-compliance of an agreement to the dedicated requirements of

104. Decree of the Presidium of the Supreme Commercial Court of 23 June 2009 N 1434/09, case No. A55-10329/2008.
105. Annex I to the ICA Act 1993 – the Statute of ICAC.
106. *See* above Chapter 1 for more details.
107. Article 52(6) of the Arbitration Act 2015.

the Arbitration Act 2015 and the procedural codes; and those based on the general rules of the Civil Code.

From a doctrinal point of view, this division corresponds to the two positions in court practice. Some judges treat an arbitration agreement as a purely procedural agreement, therefore deeming it impossible to apply the rules of the Civil Code. Those judges will only apply the rules on the invalidity of an arbitration agreement contained in arbitration and procedural law. The others (a majority) believe that there are substantive legal elements in an agreement to arbitrate, and therefore apply the general Civil Code rules to its validity or invalidity.[108]

The non-compliance of an agreement to the Arbitration Act 2015 may be formal or substantive. For example, an oral agreement would be void because it contravenes the requirements to its form.[109] Likewise, an arbitration clause in the public joint-stock company's articles of association would be invalid as directly contradicting Article 7(7) of the 2015 Act.[110]

Procedural codes define the categories of non-arbitrable disputes, such as those arising from privatisation of state and municipal property, public procurement, or damage to the environment.[111] Other federal laws can also occasionally contain the rules on arbitrability, e.g. the Federal Law 'On bankruptcy (insolvency)'.[112] An agreement purporting to refer a non-arbitrable dispute to arbitration will also be null and void.[113]

The general grounds for invalidity of contracts are set out in Chapter 9 (Articles 166-181) of the Civil Code. Instead of 'invalidity of a contract', the Code operates with the term 'invalidity of a transaction', defining a transaction as 'any action of an individual or legal person directed at the creation, amendment or termination of civil rights and obligations'.[114] The Code uses the term 'transaction' because, in addition to bilateral and multilateral transactions (i.e., contracts) it also includes any unilateral acts.[115]

Perhaps the most 'popular' ground for invalidity of transactions in the Civil Code that may apply to arbitration agreements is the contravention of the law or other legal acts (Article 168). Unless a court treats an arbitration agreement merely as a procedural

108. *See* above, §3.01[F]. *See also* Bevzenko R.S., Zainullin S.B., Kurskova O.N., et al., *The Academic and Practical Commentary to the Federal Law 'On Arbitration in Russian Federation' with a Review of Commercial Court Practice (Clause-by-Clause)*, 84 (A.N. Lysenko, A.A. Khorosheva, eds, Moscow, 2011) [*Nauchno-praktichyeskii kommyentarii k Fyedyeralnomu zakonu 'O tryetyeiskih sudah v Rossiiskoi Fyedyeracii' s obzorom sudyebno-arbitrajnoi praktiki (postatyeinyi) / R.S. Bevzenko, S.B. Zainullin, O.N. Kurskova i dr.;* pod ryed. A.N. Lysenko, A.A. Khorosheva. M., 2011].
109. *See* above, §3.03[B].
110. *See* above, §3.03[F].
111. Article 33 of the Commercial Procedure Code, Article 22.1 of the Civil Procedural Code.
112. For more details on arbitrability, *see* below, Chapter 7.
113. The Review of the Supreme Court Practice No. 2 (2015), approved by the Presidium of the Supreme Court of Russian Federation on 26 June 2015 [Obzor sudyebnoi praktiki Vyerhovnogo Suda Rossiiskoi Fyedyeracii N 2 (2015) (utv. Pryezidiumom Vyerhovnogo Suda Rossiiskoi Fyedyeracii 26.06.2015)].
114. Article 153 of the Civil Code.
115. Article 154 of the Civil Code.

mechanism without any substantive (contractual) elements, a reference to this article often supplements the reasoning grounded in the requirements of the arbitration and procedural law. For example, one court used Article 168 to strike down an overly broad clause that failed to specify a particular legal relationship between the parties and the range of disputes to which it applied.[116] An agreement relating to a non-arbitrable matter also can be declared invalid under Article 168 of the Civil Code in conjunction with the relevant article of a procedural code or another federal law.[117]

Russian courts sometimes adopt a more creative stance on Article 168, applying it in conjunction with Article 10 of the Civil Code (misuse of civil rights). This approach allows them to strike down transactions that do not contradict the literal meaning of legal rules but make improper use of otherwise lawful instruments. For example, in one case the court declared invalid an arbitration clause concluded for the use in bankruptcy proceedings and solely aimed at defrauding creditors of an insolvent company.[118]

The next category is transactions with the aims that contradict the basic notions of law and order, or morality (Article 169 of the Civil Code). The standard for the application of this article is high, and the mere contradiction to the law is insufficient. Along with Article 168, a reference to this article allowed courts to formulate the present requirement that parties in an arbitration agreement cannot nominate a permanent arbitral institution if the institution is affiliated with, and financed by, one of them. Such an agreement would be invalid because it contravenes the law's basic requirement of independence and impartiality in arbitration.[119]

Another significant group of grounds includes transactions resulting from a material error (Article 178), deception, coercion, threats, or duress (Article 179). Claimants under these two articles sometimes allege collusion or conspiracy between the managers who signed an agreement, or between their legal advisors. The burden of proof for such allegations is high, so claims of this kind are rarely successful.[120]

[B] Agreements Incapable of Being Performed

An arbitration agreement may become 'incapable of being performed' where the arbitral institution agreed by the parties ceased to exist or never existed, e.g., because of being inaccurately named.[121] Likewise, severe defects in the agreed procedure of the

116. Ruling of the Supreme Court of 27 March 2017 N 309-ES17-2079, case No. A50-11392/2016.
117. The Review of the Supreme Court Practice No. 2 (2015), *supra* note 113.
118. Decree of the Federal Commercial Court for the West-Siberian Circuit of 26 October 2012, case No. A67-9053/2006.
119. Ruling of the Supreme Commercial Court of 18 April 2013 N VAS-18412/12 and Decree of the Presidium of the Supreme Commercial Court of 9 July 2013 N 18412/12, case No. A73-5201/2011; Decree of the Presidium of the Supreme Commercial Court of 28 June 2011 N 1308/11, case No. A40-15962/10-104-120; Ruling of the Supreme Court of 26 October 2015 N 305- ES15-4679, case No. A40-91439/2014.
120. *See*, e.g., Ruling of the Supreme Court of 16 June 2017 N 305- ES17-2959, case No. A40-66494/16; Decree of the Federal Commercial Court for the Moscow Circuit of 2 February 2010 N KG-A40/14840-09, case No. 40-48635/09-132-423.
121. Khodykin R., *supra* note 23, at 25.

tribunal formation, which the parties cannot remedy through the usual legal means, will also render the agreement incapable of being performed. It is common in Russian doctrinal sources to equate pathological arbitration agreements with the agreements incapable of being performed.[122]

[C] Inoperable Agreements

This exception encompasses withdrawal of a consent to arbitrate, cessation or repudiation of an arbitration agreement. An agreement ceases to be operable for a given dispute where an arbitral tribunal has already resolved an identical dispute between the same parties and rendered an award. The arbitral agreement also ceases to be operable where it was contractually limited in time, and the time limit has expired.[123]

[D] Not Concluded Agreements

According to Article 7(11) of the Arbitration Act 2015, in addition to invalidity and other 'conventional' defects of an arbitral agreement, it could also be 'not concluded'. This notion is a result of the treatment of an arbitration agreement as yet another transaction governed by the Civil Code.

According to Article 432 of the Civil Code, a contract is concluded when the parties reached an agreement on all its necessary terms, in the form required by the law for this type of contracts. The necessary terms are those that the law names as such, and those on which, according to one party's declaration, the parties must agree for the contract to come into existence.

Many rules in the Civil Code and other federal laws name the specific terms that are necessary for the particular categories of contract. For example, a contract for the sale of a plot of land must include the detailed description of the plot with reference to the cadastre (land register), its price, information about any servitudes, and so on.[124] If any of those terms is absent from the contact, it does not become invalid – it never even comes into existence. It is, in other words, merely a 'not concluded' contract.

The same consequence will ensue if the parties' exchange of an offer and acceptance was defective, for example, where acceptance never reached the offeror. Some contracts only become concluded when the property changes hands (e.g., in a loan agreement between private individuals),[125] or when a competent authority registers the contract (e.g., in real property transactions).[126]

For all those cases, Russian law developed a specific remedy – a judicial declaration that a contract is 'not concluded', which is a distinct remedy from declaring a contract null and void. The courts cannot apply the Civil Code rules on the invalidity

122. *Ibid.*
123. *Ibid.* at 95-96.
124. Articles 555-557 of the Civil Code, Article 37 of the Land Code.
125. Article 807 of the Civil Code.
126. Articles 609 and 651 of the Civil Code. This applies to the real property contracts concluded before 2015; since then, the law has changed.

of transactions to contracts that never came into existence in the first place, so their approach to 'not concluded' contracts is somewhat different.[127]

This distinction between void and 'not concluded' contracts also holds in the context of arbitration agreements. A 'not concluded' arbitration agreement is unenforceable, cannot endow a tribunal with jurisdiction to hear a dispute, and an award rendered on the basis of such an agreement is at risk of being set aside. Thus, the effects of an arbitration agreement being invalid and 'not concluded' are very similar. Sometimes, the two categories get mixed in court practice.[128]

[E] Declaring an Arbitration Agreement Invalid

Until recently, it used to be a contentious issue whether a separate court action to declare an arbitration agreement invalid (or not concluded) was admissible in principle. Some courts[129] and commentators[130] argued that, since an arbitration agreement is not a civil contract but a purely procedural agreement, the parties could not challenge it on its own using a separate court claim. The courts could only assess the validity of an arbitration agreement in the proceedings designed explicitly for arbitration, e.g., when they dealt with enforcement or setting aside applications.

However, just like the procedural theory of an arbitration agreement, this view proved unpopular. The majority of courts accepted and heard separate claims seeking to declare an arbitration agreement invalid,[131] and the commentators in the recent years supported this position.[132] It seems to be a settled practice now that such claims are admissible, and courts can assess the validity of arbitration agreements in separate proceedings as well as while dealing with enforcement and setting aside applications.

127. Information Letter No. 165 of the Supreme Commercial Court of the Russian Federation of 25 February 2014 'Review of Commercial Court Practice in Cases Concerning the Declaration of Contracts Not Concluded'.
128. For example, in the Ruling of the Supreme Commercial Court of 28 August 2008 N 8711/08, case No. A67-438/08, the court said 'the arbitration agreement is not concluded, and therefore invalid'.
129. Decree of the Ninth Commercial Court of Appeal of 26 September 2014 N 09 AP-28440/2014, case No. A40-106363/11 (vacated on further appeal).
130. Kholodenko Yu.V., Andryukova E.V. *Challenging an Arbitration Agreement: The Need for a Single Approach in the Application of the Law,* 4 Treteysky Sud 93-93 (2014) [Kholodenko Yu.V., Andryukova E.V. Osparivaniye tryetyeiskogo soglashyeniya: nyeobhodimost yedinyh podhodov v procyessye pravoprimyenyeniya // Tryetyeiskii sud. 2014. N 4. S. 93-96]; Kostin A.A., Davydenko D.L., *supra* note 28, at 271.
131. *See*, e.g., Decree of the Federal Commercial Court for the North-Western Circuit of 25 July 2008, case No. A56-17133/2007; Decree of the Federal Commercial Court for the North-Western Circuit of 3 September 2012, cases No. A42-7229/2011 and A42-7231/2011, Ruling of the Supreme Court of 2 December 2015 N 308-ES15-10232.
132. Chernikova I.V., *Court Practice in Cases of the Declaration of Arbitration Agreements Invalid*, 1 Arbitral Disputes, 68-74 (2017) [Chernikova I.V. Sudyebnaya praktika rassmotryeniya iskov o priznanii tryetyeiskih soglashyenii nyedyeistvityelnymi // Arbitrajnyye spory. 2017. N 1. S. 68-74].

One exception to this rule concerns the clauses specifying that disputes on their validity shall be resolved in arbitration. In such cases, the courts will usually leave the claim without consideration according to the general rules.[133]

The application of the Civil Code to the invalidity of arbitration agreements also means that the regular statute of limitation applies to claims seeking to declare an arbitration agreement invalid. If a claimant misses the statutory limit, this circumstance alone will be a sufficient ground to refuse the declaration.[134] In the absence of exceptional circumstances, the general statute of limitation in Russia is three years since the day the claimant found out or should have found out about the agreement.[135]

133. Ruling of the Supreme Court of 3 August 2017 N 305-ES17-9577, case No. A41-70451/2016.
134. Ruling of the Supreme Court of 1 February 2016 N 307-ES15-18382, case No. A42-8843/2013.
135. Articles 196 and 200 of the Civil Code.

CHAPTER 4
Arbitrators

§4.01 LEGAL STATUS OF THE ARBITRATORS AND THEIR AUTHORITY

In Russia, the legal status of an arbitrator in domestic arbitration is determined by the provisions of the Federal law 'On Arbitration in the Russian Federation' (the Arbitration Act 2015), the status of an arbitrator in international commercial arbitration – by *lex arbitri* (in Russia – the Law of the Russian Federation 'On International Commercial Arbitration', hereinafter 'the ICA Act 1993'). An arbitrator is an individual selected (appointed) by the parties or in accordance with the procedure established by law to resolve a dispute as a sole arbitrator or as part of a panel of arbitrators.

The main duty of the arbitrators is to resolve the case. In the course of the proceedings, the arbitrators must ensure fair consideration of the circumstances of the parties' dispute, remain independent and impartial, provide the parties with equal opportunities to present their position, protect their rights and interests, devote the necessary time and due attention to the proceedings, and observe confidentiality. Arbitration is a procedure involving the enforcement of the law, so the Russian legislature provided the arbitrators with a number of procedural powers. These powers concern the conduct of the proceedings. Thus, the arbitral tribunal may, if it considers the evidence to be insufficient, invite the parties to submit additional documents, appoint an expert, or request assistance in obtaining evidence from a competent court. The arbitral tribunal may order that any written evidence be accompanied by a translation into the languages agreed by the parties or determined by the arbitral tribunal.

The law requires the arbitrators to make their award legally enforceable. At the same time, the arbitrators can also contribute to the subsequent execution of the award. At the request of any party, the arbitral tribunal may order a party to adopt an interim measure it deems necessary and require any party to provide appropriate security in connection with the said measure.

A set of legal safeguards ensures that the arbitrators exercise their authority in a proper manner. Thus, an arbitrator cannot be examined as a witness about the facts that became known to him during the proceedings. In addition, arbitrators, on their own initiative and without the consent of the parties, may not disclose information they learned in the course of the arbitration.

Arbitrators have the right to demand payment of the fee, compensation of the expenses incurred in connection with their participation in arbitration, with inspection of goods and documents at their location, expenses for travel to the hearing venue. In administered arbitration, the rules of the permanent arbitral institution determine the arbitrators' fees. In ad hoc arbitration, the fees of the arbitrators are determined by agreement of the parties. In the absence of such agreement, the arbitral tribunal determines its own fees taking into account the sums in dispute, the complexity of the case, the time spent by the arbitrators in conducting the arbitration and any other relevant circumstances.

§4.02 REQUIREMENTS TO THE ARBITRATORS

Russian law imposes different requirements on arbitrators in international commercial arbitration and in domestic arbitration. The ICA Act 1993 is an example of an extremely liberal approach and does not contain other conditions for participation of a person in the proceedings as an arbitrator, except for his independence and impartiality. Otherwise, the parties are free to agree on the requirements to arbitrators, including the requirements as to their qualification. Thus, in international commercial arbitration any individual independent of the parties, capable of providing an impartial resolution of the dispute, and having the qualifications stipulated by an agreement of the parties may be selected (appointed) to the tribunal.

The main requirements to arbitrators in disputes without a foreign element are defined in Article 11 of the Arbitration Act 2015. A person may be selected (appointed) as an arbitrator if he or she is independent of the parties, has given consent to perform the duties of an arbitrator, is capable of providing an impartial resolution of the parties' dispute in the absence of a direct or indirect interest in the outcome of the case. The law does not preclude foreign citizens and stateless persons from acting as arbitrators.

The Arbitration Act 2015 defines the minimum requirements to the person and qualifications of a candidate to the arbitral tribunal. The parties may agree on additional requirements to arbitrators, including requirements for their qualification, or agree that a particular arbitrator or arbitrators shall resolve their dispute.

[A] Basic Personal Requirements

Only the individuals who have reached the age of twenty-five years may be selected (appointed) as arbitrators. An arbitrator may not be a person who, in accordance with their status determined by federal law, cannot be selected (appointed) as an arbitrator. An individual cannot be selected (appointed) as an arbitrator because of their official status or public functions as defined by federal legislation. The implementation and preservation of special status are ensured by the prohibition to engage in any other activity, except scientific, teaching, and other creative pursuits. The systemic interpretation of the legislative provisions allows one to conclude that the arbitrators cannot be:

(1) judges of the courts of general jurisdiction or commercial ('arbitrazh') courts;
(2) judges of the Constitutional Court of the Russian Federation and regional constitutional tribunals;
(3) magistrates;
(4) employees of law enforcement authorities;
(5) officials of the prosecuting authorities;
(6) officials of the investigating agencies;
(7) notaries;
(8) members of the Council of Federation, as well as deputies of the State Duma of the Federal Assembly of the Russian Federation;
(9) the Chairman and vice-chairmen, all auditors of the Accounts Chamber of the Russian Federation;
(10) members of regional parliaments, elected officials of regional governmental bodies (only where the respective position is their full-time job);
(11) members of local (municipal) parliaments, elected officials of different institutions within local governments (only where the respective position is their full-time job);
(12) leading municipal officials;
(13) military men;
(14) customs officials;
(15) Federal Courier Agency officials.

The individuals who, in accordance with their status as defined by federal law, cannot be appointed as an arbitrator in domestic arbitration, cannot participate as an arbitrator in international commercial arbitration either. The preservation of a special status in the categories listed above is ensured, first of all, by the sectoral legislation, and only then by the arbitral legislation.

Russian legislation does not prevent state civil servants and municipal employees from acting as arbitrators, as long as it does not lead to a conflict of interest and entail no violation of express legislative prohibitions or non-performance of their duties established by anti-corruption legislation. The legislation permits an appointment of an advocate to the arbitral tribunal as an arbitrator, provided that there are no attorney-client relations between the advocate and either of the parties in the arbitration proceedings and the advocate has no other interest in the case. At present, the practice of appointing advocates as arbitrators is widespread in the Russian Federation.

An arbitrator may not be an individual who has an unexpunged or outstanding criminal conviction. An arbitrator may not be a person whose powers as a judge, advocate, notary, investigator, public prosecutor, or other law enforcement officer have been terminated in the Russian Federation in the prescribed manner for misconduct incompatible with their professional activities. The grounds for termination of these powers are provided for by Russian legislation on the status of judges, on advocacy, on the notaries, on the Prosecutor's office of the Russian Federation, on the Investigative Committee of the Russian Federation, etc.[1]

Neither the parties nor the permanent arbitral institutions have the ability to verify information that prevents the selection (appointment) of an individual as an arbitrator. The guarantee of compliance with the personal requirements can be found in Article 12 of the Arbitration Act 2015 and Article 12 of the ICA Act 1993. According to these legislative provisions, any person approached in connection with his possible selection (appointment) as an arbitrator shall inform the parties in writing of any circumstances likely to give rise to justifiable doubts as to his impartiality or independence in the resolution of the respective dispute. The said person shall inform the parties in writing of the circumstances that, in accordance with the federal law, prevent their appointment as an arbitrator.

[B] Qualification Requirements

Arbitration is a jurisdictional activity. Compliance with the mandatory standards of this activity requires the arbitral tribunal to have in-depth professional knowledge and practical skills in the application of legal rules. For this reason, the Russian legislation established a qualification requirement for the sole arbitrator to have a legal education, confirmed by a diploma of the established format issued in the territory of the Russian Federation or documents of foreign states duly recognised in the territory of the Russian Federation. In case of collegial resolution of a dispute, the chairperson of the arbitral tribunal shall have a legal education, but the parties may agree that the chairperson of the arbitral tribunal shall be exempt from these requirements, provided that the arbitral tribunal shall include one arbitrator with legal education.

The parties may agree on additional requirements to the qualification of arbitrators. Provisions on arbitrator qualifications and other requirements to arbitrators in an arbitration administered by a permanent arbitral institution shall be included in the rules of such a permanent arbitral institution. Arbitrators may be challenged if they do not possess qualifications agreed by the parties.

Special qualification requirements are provided by the legislation dealing with the formation of permanent arbitral institutions' recommended lists of arbitrators (the Arbitration Act 2015, Article 47). In each list, no less than a third of arbitrators shall have a degree awarded in the territory of the Russian Federation in a certain scientific speciality, and no less than a half of arbitrators shall have experience of resolution of civil disputes. Such experience may be in a capacity of arbitrators or as judges of federal

1. The above grounds are established by the following laws: Law of the Russian Federation of 26 June 1992 No. 3132-1 'On the Status of Judges in the Russian Federation' (Article 14), Federal Law of 31 May 2002 No. 63-FZ 'On Advocacy in the Russian Federation' (Article 17), Fundamentals of Legislation of the Russian Federation on Notaries (Article 12), Federal Law of 17 January 1992 No. 2202-1 'On the Prosecutor's Office of the Russian Federation' (Article 43), Federal Law of 28 December 2010 No. 403-FZ 'On the Investigative Committee of the Russian Federation' (Article 30), etc.

courts, regional constitutional tribunals, or magistrates. Such experience must also be within ten years preceding date of inclusion in the list of arbitrators.

§4.03 IMPARTIALITY AND INDEPENDENCE OF THE ARBITRATORS

In Russia, any person who meets the requirements established by law may be selected (appointed) as an arbitrator. However, under certain conditions, in order to ensure the fair procedure, the participation of particular persons in the resolution of the dispute is limited. This is due to the assumption of their inability to provide an impartial resolution of the dispute of the parties under the influence of a number of factors, the presence of direct or indirect interest in the outcome of the case, or the lack of independence from the parties.

In assessing the impartiality of an arbitrator in Russia, one must take into account both his personal position in a particular case and the objective criterion. The objective criterion denotes the existence of the arbitrator's connections with one of the parties as a circumstance that allows one to contest his independence or doubt whether sufficient guarantees were in place excluding the possibility of any bias against the other party. The Supreme Court of the Russian Federation noted that the impartiality of an arbitral tribunal is ensured through the impartiality of each individual member of the tribunal – which is assumed until proven otherwise. The arbitral tribunal's equal connection to both parties guarantees its impartiality; each party can select its arbitrator from the list or submit its arbitrator from outside the list, or the parties could agree on a single arbitrator whom they both trust.[2]

Independence and impartiality is a mandatory condition for the exercise by the arbitrators of their authority to resolve the dispute. The arbitrator shall be impartial and independent from the moment of acceptance of the appointment and throughout the entire arbitral proceedings. From the time of his appointment and throughout the arbitral proceedings, an arbitrator shall without delay disclose any such circumstances to the parties unless they have already been informed of them by the arbitrator.

The Rules on the Impartiality and Independence of Arbitrators approved by the Chamber of Commerce and Industry of the Russian Federation in 2010 (RF CCI Rules on Impartiality) are a practical guide for arbitrators and arbitration institutions, which are designed to resolve various issues dealing with the challenge of arbitrators and termination of their mandate. The rules are advisory in nature, but they are highly regarded by Russian courts in cases on setting aside of the awards, as well as cases on the issuance of a writ of execution for the enforcement of arbitral awards. The Rules set out requirements for the impartiality and independence of arbitrators and can be used by permanent arbitral institutions.

The general requirements for the impartiality and independence of arbitrators are as follows. Arbitrators shall be considered impartial if they are not directly or indirectly interested in the outcome of the case and have no pre-existing preferences or other prejudices against a particular party, its representative, expert, consultant, or witness.

2. Ruling of the SC RF dated 24 February 2015 N 304-ES14-495, case No. A67-1587/2014.

Arbitrators are independent if there is no such relationship between them and the parties, their representatives, experts, consultants, witnesses who are able to influence the position of the arbitrator in the case.

The law requires a person approached in connection with a possible selection (appointment) as an arbitrator to refuse the appointment, and if already appointed, to refuse to continue exercising them any further and to recuse oneself if the arbitrator does not consider himself or herself to be impartial or independent. Justifiable doubts as to impartiality and independence may arise from a property, business, professional or personal relationship which, in the course of or in the reasonable time preceding the arbitration, links the arbitrator to the party, its representative, expert, consultant or witness, as well as to a marital relationship, a relationship of official dependence which, during the course of the arbitration, links the arbitrator to other arbitrators of the same panel.

The RF CCI Rules on Impartiality define three groups of circumstances that are relevant to the assessment of the impartiality and independence: circumstances that clearly preclude the exercise of the powers of an arbitrator; circumstances that require disclosure; and circumstances that do not require disclosure. The following circumstances clearly demonstrate a lack of impartiality or independence and make the exercise of the powers of the arbitrator impossible:

(1) the arbitrator, his/her spouse or close relative acts or have acted previously in the case in question as a party, its representative, expert, consultant or witness;
(2) the arbitrator, his/her spouse or a close relative has a significant share in the charter capital or is a member of the executive body, the supervisory board or other body of the legal entity acting as a party to the arbitration, or representing a parent or subsidiary in relation to the party or its representative (the share of participation is recognised as significant if the arbitrator, his/her spouse or a close relative individually or jointly own a share in the amount of more than 5% of the charter capital));
(3) the arbitrator is the spouse or a close relative of the arbitrator of the same arbitral tribunal;
(4) the arbitrator is in an employment relationship with the party or its representative, or receives remuneration from them under civil-law contracts, or represents the interests of the party to the arbitration in another case not related to the dispute, or acts in it as its expert or consultant;
(5) the arbitrator has previously made public statements in relation to the case in question, in particular by giving a public legal assessment of the case.

The impartiality may be compromised by a non-procedural contact of the future arbitrator with one of the parties in the absence of the other party (*ex parte*) concerning the dispute. Such contact may consist in the provision of documents and evidence to the arbitrator, examination, and examination of goods in their location without the knowledge of the other party, discussion of the case outside the agreed procedure. The rules on the impartiality and independence of arbitrators establish the procedure for the communication of prospective arbitrators with the parties and their representatives. The arbitrator, as well as a person considering an offer to exercise the powers of an arbitrator, shall not be entitled to discuss any issues related to the case with the parties, their representatives, experts, consultants, witnesses outside the established framework of the proceedings. Violation of the limits of the discussion of matters relating to arbitration is a circumstance that may give rise to justifiable doubt as to the impartiality or independence of the arbitrator.

Before deciding on the person who will be invited to act as an arbitrator, the party or its representative may invite a possible candidate to interview them in a prescribed manner. Such an interview shall be conducted solely to confirm that there is no justifiable doubt as to the impartiality and independence of the candidate, to determine whether the candidate meets the professional qualifications and experience required to exercise the powers of the arbitrator, and to determine whether the candidate has sufficient time to participate in arbitration. The interview may concern the following questions: the names of the parties and their representatives, the names of the main and subsidiary companies in relation to the parties and their representatives, the names of third parties who are or may be involved in arbitration, the names of other selected or appointed arbitrators on the same tribunal, as well as the names of experts, consultants and witnesses involved. During the interview with the party or its representative, a candidate may discuss general nature of the dispute, type of claim, language of arbitration, applicable law, seat of arbitration and applicable arbitration rules, the anticipated duration of the arbitration, the prospective arbitrator's professional qualifications and experience, brief biographical information about the arbitrator, including information about education, current and past professional activities.

A candidate's interview with a party or its representative in compliance with these provisions shall not be regarded as a circumstance that may give rise to justifiable doubts as to the impartiality or independence of the arbitrator, and shall not require further disclosure. During the interview the candidate should not discuss the actual circumstances on which the claim is based, legal positions and arguments of the parties, the calculation of the amounts of claims, evidence that a party has submitted or intends to submit in the arbitration, special conditions for payment of the arbitration fee, fees or any costs of the arbitrator, and other issues the discussion of which involves the expression of the candidate's opinion on the dispute.

Without giving reasons, a candidate may refuse or terminate the interview at any time. Such refusal or termination of an interview also shall not be considered as a circumstance that may give rise to justifiable doubts as to the impartiality or independence of the arbitrator and shall not require disclosure.

§4.04 DISCLOSURE OF INFORMATION ABOUT ARBITRATORS

When a person is approached in connection with a possible appointment as an arbitrator, he or she shall inform the parties in writing of any circumstances likely to give rise to justifiable doubts as to his or her impartiality or independence in the proceedings of the relevant dispute. From the time of the appointment and throughout the arbitral proceedings, an arbitrator shall without delay disclose any such circumstances to the parties unless they have already been informed of them by the arbitrator (Article 12 of the Arbitration Act 2015, Article 12 of the ICA Act 1993).

RF CCI Rules on Impartiality define circumstances that require and do not require disclosure. The arbitrator shall disclose any circumstances that, from a reasonable and informed person's point of view, may give rise to justifiable doubt as to his or her impartiality or independence in the proceedings dealing with the dispute in question. Any doubts shall be interpreted in favour of the disclosure of the relevant circumstances. In particular, the following circumstances are subject to disclosure:

(1) the arbitrator during the three years preceding the commencement of the arbitration was in an employment relationship with a party or its representative or received remuneration from them under civil-law contracts;
(2) the arbitrator, during the three years preceding the commencement of the arbitration, represented the interests of any of the parties in another case unrelated to the dispute or acted in another case involving one of the parties as a representative, expert or consultant;
(3) the arbitrator is in an employment relationship with the organisation, or earns income from the organisation under civil-law contracts, or is the organisation's lawyer, if such organisation or legal entity provides or provided, within three years preceding the commencement of arbitration, legal assistance (legal services) to one of the parties or its parent or subsidiary company, whether in the current dispute or in another unrelated matter;
(4) the arbitrator and the representative or expert or consultant of one of the parties are or had been in an employment relationship with the same organisation during the three years preceding the commencement of the arbitration;
(5) the arbitrator is or had been in a relationship of official dependence with the arbitrator on the same tribunal during three years prior to the commencement of the arbitration;
(6) the arbitrator, his / her spouse or close relative shall have a share in the chartered capital of the party or its principal or subsidiary, and the amount of such share is not significant;
(7) the arbitrator was previously selected by a party (its parent or subsidiary company) as an arbitrator in another case or was otherwise selected (appointed) as an arbitrator in another case involving a party in the arbitration, provided that the other case is related to the current dispute and has not been initiated simultaneously with the arbitration at hand;
(8) there had been a discussion between the arbitrator and a party (its representative) of the issues related to the arbitration outside the established procedure;
(9) the arbitrator acts or during the three years preceding the commencement of the arbitration, acted as an academic supervisor or adviser in the preparation of the dissertation by a party's representative in the case, or a

representative of the party in the case acts or during the three years preceding the commencement of arbitration acted as an academic supervisor or adviser in the preparation of the arbitrator's dissertation;

(10) there are close relations of friendship between the arbitrator and the representative of one of the parties, in particular, the arbitrator and the representative of the party on a regular basis devote considerable time to personal communication unrelated to their professional activities or participation in the work of professional or public associations.

The disclosure by the arbitrator of the circumstances that may lead to justifiable doubts regarding his impartiality or independence, in itself, does not preclude the acceptance of the arbitral mandate and does not oblige the competent authority to grant an application challenging the appointment of such arbitrator.

In Russia, an arbitrator is under no obligation to disclose circumstances that do not give rise to justifiable doubts about their impartiality or independence. The following circumstances are not subject to disclosure:

(1) the arbitrator, in the press or in a public lecture, expressed, without regard to the present dispute, general opinion on the legal question that arose in the present case;
(2) the representative of the party in the case receives or has received in the past education in the educational institution in which the arbitrator teaches or has taught in the past;
(3) the arbitrator is or has been a member of the same chamber of advocates, another professional association or public association with a representative of the party in the case, an expert, a consultant, a witness or other arbitrators of the same arbitral tribunal;
(4) several arbitrators from the same arbitral tribunal work or have worked in the past for the same company (provided that such arbitrators are not and within three years prior to the commencement of the arbitration had not been in a relationship of official dependence);
(5) several members of the tribunal are acting or previously acted together as arbitrators on the same or another arbitral tribunal;
(6) an arbitrator and a representative of a party, an expert, a consultant, a witness are or had previously been members of another arbitral tribunal together, provided that such other arbitral tribunal was constituted to deal with a case unrelated to the dispute under consideration;
(7) the arbitrator was selected by the same party or by its principal or subsidiary company as an arbitrator in another case or was otherwise appointed as an arbitrator in another case involving a party in the arbitration, if that another case, by the nature of the claims, is not related to the dispute under consideration, or such other case, which, by the nature of the claims, is unrelated to the dispute under consideration, or was initiated simultaneously with the arbitral proceedings at hand;

(8) the arbitrator took part in public events (conferences, seminars, presentations, etc.) to which the party or its representative provided financial or organisational support if the arbitrator did not receive remuneration from that party or its representative;

(9) the arbitrator and the representative of the party are or previously had been included in the same recommended list of arbitrators or conciliators used by a permanent arbitral institution or other alternative dispute resolution body;

(10) the arbitrator is or had been in the past a consumer of the goods (works, services) of the party or its main or subsidiary company, provided that the conditions of the arbitrator's acquisition of such goods (works, services) are similar to the conditions under which the goods (works, services) are purchased by other consumers.

It should be noted that general standards relating to impartiality, independence and disclosure contained in the updated IBA Guidelines on Conflicts of Interest in International Arbitration 2014 are applied for international commercial arbitration seated in Russia. This guide reflects typical situations arising in modern arbitration practice; it contains instructions to the parties, arbitrators, arbitral institutions, and state courts as to the circumstances that lead or do not lead to a conflict of interest and are subject or not subject to disclosure.

§4.05 LIABILITY OF ARBITRATORS

In international practice, arbitrators shall not be liable to any party in a dispute for any act or omission in connection with the arbitration, unless such act or omission is intentional or grossly negligent. The relevant provisions are reflected in the rules of the major arbitration institutions to the extent that applicable law does not prohibit such limitation of liability. In Russia, as a matter of civil law, the arbitrator cannot be held liable to the parties in arbitration, as well as to a permanent arbitral institution in connection with non-performance or improper performance of the functions of an arbitrator and in connection with the arbitration. An exception from this rule is a liability in a civil suit within a criminal case, which may be filed against an arbitrator in accordance with the criminal procedural legislation of the Russian Federation in order to compensate for damages caused by a crime of which the arbitrator was found guilty in accordance with the procedure established by law. At the same time, the rules of a permanent arbitral institution may provide for a possibility of reducing the arbitrators' fees in the event of non-performance or improper performance of their functions.

Chapter 5
Constitution of the Arbitral Tribunal

§5.01 MAIN APPROACHES TO THE COMPOSITION OF THE ARBITRAL TRIBUNAL

Formation of the arbitral tribunal is one of the main procedures of arbitration. The purpose of implementing the rules established by law for the constitution of the arbitral tribunal, including the procedure for the removal of arbitrators, is to ensure the necessary conditions for a fair trial, one of which is the lack of prejudice and partiality on the part of the arbitrator. The Constitutional Court of the Russian Federation drew attention to this fact.[1]

The arbitral tribunal is a panel of arbitrators formed in accordance with the law and the agreement of the parties or the sole arbitrator selected (appointed) in accordance with the established procedure, authorised to resolve the dispute. In Russia, the parties are free to determine its composition and may agree at their discretion on the procedure for the selection (appointment) of an arbitrator or arbitrators. At the same time, there are conditions based on the requirements of the *ordre public* that limit parties' autonomy to form the arbitral tribunal. In the Russian Federation, these requirements are enshrined in Article 11 of the Federal law 'On Arbitration in the Russian Federation' (the Arbitration Act 2015) and Article 11 of the Law 'On International Commercial Arbitration' (the ICA Act 1993). As professor Born remarks, most national laws impose a limited range of restrictions on the parties' autonomy to select an arbitral tribunal. These limitations include: (a) prohibitions against unduly one-sided mechanisms for selecting arbitrators, (b) prohibitions against arbitrators who lack impartiality and/or independence, (c) requirements for minimum qualifications (e.g., legal capacity) and (d) more controversially, requirements with regard to nationality and religion.[2] In Russia, failure to comply with the first three of

1. Decree of the Constitutional Court of the Russian Federation of 18 November 2014 No. 30-P.
2. Born G., *International Commercial Arbitration*, 1381-1382 (The Hague, 2009).

these restrictions may result in setting aside of the arbitral award or refusal to recognise and enforce it. No requirements with regard to nationality, religion, membership in political parties or public associations can restrict the parties' autonomy to select an arbitral tribunal in Russia.

The parties shall determine the procedure for the selection (appointment) of an arbitrator or arbitrators. Parties whose arbitration agreement provides administering of arbitration by a permanent arbitral institution, as a rule, use the procedure established by the rules of this institution. In accordance with the provisions of the Arbitration Act 2015, each permanent arbitral institution shall form a list of arbitrators recommended by it, consisting of at least thirty persons. This list includes persons who may be selected by the parties to resolve a particular case. It is known that lists by their nature may be recommended or mandatory. In the Russian Federation, the lists of arbitrators are not compulsory. The law prohibits making the selection of arbitrators by the parties to the arbitration conditional on their belonging to a list of recommended arbitrators. A rule stipulating otherwise must be expressly agreed by the parties. These provisions do not apply to the appointment of arbitrators by a permanent arbitral institution in accordance with its rules.

The parties intending to resolve their dispute in the ad hoc arbitration shall determine the procedure for selection (appointment) of arbitrators by their agreement, including an express contract clause or a reference to the applicable arbitration rules. For these purposes, Russian parties often choose the UNCITRAL Arbitration Rules.[3]

In Russia, parties in domestic arbitration are free to determine the number of arbitrators, but it shall be odd. The provisions of the Arbitration Act 2015 are similar to the legislation of Italy, Belgium, the Netherlands, and many other countries. The appointment of an odd number of arbitrators is intended to ensure that the dispute is resolved regardless of the arbitrators' potential differences. The form of the document in which the parties record the agreement on the number of arbitrators is not regulated by the Arbitration Act 2015. In administered arbitration, the number of arbitrators shall be determined by the rules of the permanent arbitral institution. Often they allow the resolution of disputes with a small value of the claim by a sole arbitrator. A panel of three arbitrators usually resolves complex disputes. If the parties fail to determine the number of arbitrators, three arbitrators shall be appointed.

§5.02 METHODS OF APPOINTING ARBITRATORS

The variety of ways to form an arbitral tribunal is one of the advantages of arbitration. It allows taking into account the peculiarities of the parties' relationship, to ensure the implementation of the arbitration procedure. In Russia, the following methods are used for this purpose:

3. References to such arbitrations are often found in judicial acts – e.g., Decree of the Supreme Court of the Russian Federation dated 25 March 2016, case No. N 305-ES16-1103; Resolution of the Presidium of the Supreme Commercial Court of the Russian Federation dated 12 December 2005 No. 9982/05, etc.

(1) selection of arbitrators by the parties;
(2) appointment of arbitrators by other arbitrators;
(3) appointment of arbitrators by arbitral institutions (ICAC, MAC);
(4) appointment of arbitrators by organisations in which arbitral institutions have been established or by other competent authorities;
(5) hybrid methods combining the above elements;
(6) appointment of arbitrators by state courts.

Russian scholars consider the selection of arbitrators as a procedure in which the arbitrator acquires its status as a result of the direct expression of parties' will. The appointment is considered to be either a procedure compensating for the lack of an expressed will of the parties (for instance, in case of a failure to participate) or an exercise of the authority to select arbitrators delegated by the parties (in order to simplify and accelerate the formation of the panel).

§5.03 BASIC RULES OF THE CONSTITUTION OF THE ARBITRAL TRIBUNAL

General rules for the constitution of the arbitral tribunal in domestic arbitration are defined by Article 11 of the Arbitration Act 2015. The panel of arbitrators shall be formed via selection by the parties themselves or via appointment by persons (bodies) to whom such right has been delegated by parties' agreement.

The parties may agree on the procedure for the selection (appointment) of an arbitrator or arbitrators, subject to the provisions of the law. Failing such agreement, in arbitration with three arbitrators, each party shall appoint one arbitrator, and the two arbitrators thus appointed shall appoint the presiding arbitrator. If a party fails to appoint the arbitrator within one month of receipt of a request to do so from the other party, or if the two arbitrators fail to agree on the third arbitrator within one month of their appointment, the appointment shall be made, upon the request of a party, by the competent court. In an arbitration with a sole arbitrator, if the parties are unable to agree on the arbitrator, he shall be appointed, upon the request of any party, by the court. This procedure for the formation of the arbitral tribunal shall be applied both in the administered arbitration and in the ad hoc arbitration.

If one of the parties fails to comply with the agreed procedure for the selection (appointment) of arbitrators, either the parties or the two arbitrators are unable to reach an agreement in accordance with such procedure, or a third party, including a permanent arbitral institution, fails to perform, in accordance with the rules of arbitration, any function assigned to it under such procedure, any party may request the court to take the necessary measures (unless the agreement of the parties provides for other means). The parties whose arbitration agreement provides administering of arbitration by a permanent arbitral institution may exclude by their direct agreement the possibility of resolving this issue by the court (if the parties have excluded such a possibility the arbitration shall be terminated and this dispute may be referred to the competent court).

In international commercial arbitration seated in Russia, the parties are free to agree on a procedure of appointing the arbitrator or arbitrators. This is often done by reference to the applicable arbitration rules. For instance, all cases with a sole arbitrator in ICAC are to be resolved by an arbitrator appointed by the ICAC's Nomination Committee from the List of Arbitrators. The following procedure applies in cases where an arbitral tribunal is to be composed of three arbitrators. First, the claimant shall inform the ICAC about the arbitrator appointed by him (within fifteen days after receipt of a notice from the Secretariat). Otherwise, the Nomination Committee will appoint an arbitrator for claimant from the ICAC's List of Arbitrators. Second, the respondent shall give the Secretariat notice of the arbitrator chosen by him (within fifteen days after receipt of a notice from the Secretariat that an arbitrator has been chosen or appointed by the claimant). Likewise, failing such a notice, the Nomination Committee will appoint an arbitrator for him from the ICAC's List of Arbitrators. The presiding arbitrator shall be appointed by the Nomination Committee from the ICAC's List of Arbitrators. In cases of multiple parties, the multiple claimants and the multiple respondents shall each appoint one arbitrator upon agreement between themselves. If they have failed to reach an agreement, again the Nomination Committee shall appoint an arbitrator for the respective party from the ICAC's List of Arbitrators. It is easy to notice that ICAC's procedure for the formation of the arbitral tribunal is similar to the ICC rules.

According to the MAC Rules, an arbitral tribunal shall consist of two arbitrators, unless the Appointing Committee decides, in its own discretion, in view of the complexity of the case, the total amount of the claims filed in due time, and other circumstances, that the case shall be settled by a sole arbitrator. Where an arbitral tribunal is to be composed of two arbitrators, the claimant shall give MAC notice of the arbitrator appointed by him within fifteen days. The respondent shall give MAC notice of the arbitrator chosen by him within fifteen days after receipt of a notice from MAC Secretariat that an arbitrator has been chosen or appointed by the claimant. If the claimant or the respondent does not choose an arbitrator, the Appointing Committee shall appoint an arbitrator for them. Where two arbitrators have not reached an agreement as to the dispute resolution, the Appointing Committee shall appoint the presiding arbitrator, as a rule, from the List of Arbitrators. The Appointing Committee may authorise MAC Chairman to appoint an arbitrator.

In the absence of an agreement on the procedure for the selection of arbitrators, the provisions of the ICA Act 2015 are in force to regulate the process. Thus, in arbitration with a sole arbitrator, if the parties do not agree on the selection of an arbitrator, the appointment shall be made by a competent court upon the request of any party. In an arbitration with three arbitrators, each party shall appoint one arbitrator and the two arbitrators so appointed shall appoint a third arbitrator. If a party fails to appoint an arbitrator within thirty days of receipt of the request, or if two arbitrators fail to agree on the appointment of a third arbitrator within thirty days of their appointment, the appointment shall be made by a competent court upon the request of either party. In appointing an arbitrator, the competent court shall take into account any requirements imposed on the arbitrator by parties' agreement and such considerations that may ensure the appointment of an independent and impartial arbitrator.

If one of the parties fails to comply with the agreed procedure for the selection (appointment) of arbitrators, either the parties or the two arbitrators are unable to reach agreement under such procedure, or a third party, including a permanent arbitral institution, fails to perform any function assigned to it under such procedure, any party may request the competent court to take the necessary measures. Such measures of assistance shall be taken by the court that takes into account the procedure of selection (appointment) of arbitrators agreed by the parties (except if the agreement on such procedure of selection (appointment) does not provide for other ways of ensuring the appointment). For arbitration administered by a permanent arbitral institution, parties via a direct agreement may exclude the possibility of resolving this issue by a state court. In this case, if the above circumstances arise, the arbitration shall be terminated and the dispute may be referred to the competent court.

Court proceedings in cases related to the performance of the functions of assistance in respect of arbitration by courts are determined by Russian procedural legislation. The court shall consider the appointment of arbitrators upon an application filed by a person or persons participating in the arbitration. Such an application shall be submitted to the court at the seat of arbitration within a period not exceeding one month from the date when the applicant became aware or should have become aware of the circumstances that form the basis for filing the application. The applicant must pay the state fee in the amount equal to the fee designated for claims of non-proprietary nature. The application can also be submitted by filling in the form on the court's official website. The application is resolved by a sole judge according to the procedural rules applicable in the court of the first instance within one month from the date of receipt. The parties shall be notified by the court of the time and place of the court session, their absence is not an obstacle to resolving the case. The court will appoint an arbitrator if it is satisfied that the conditions agreed by the parties are complied with or the court has the power to do so according to the statutory requirements. Having considered the application for assistance, the court makes an order that cannot be appealed.

Russian arbitration law does not mention substitute arbitrators, but the rules of some arbitral institutions allow for their appointment. For example, in the ICAC or in the MAC a substitute (reserve) arbitrator may be appointed if the mandate of an arbitrator terminates because of his withdrawal for any other reason or because of the revocation of his mandate by parties' understanding or in any other case of termination of his mandate. Such appointment shall be made according to the rules that were applicable to the appointment of the arbitrator being replaced.

§5.04 ORIGIN AND TERMINATION OF ARBITRATOR'S POWERS

In Russia, the powers, or the mandate, of arbitrators arise from the date when all the actions defined by the law, the agreement of the parties and the rules of the permanent arbitral institution are performed. Such actions include the completion of the procedure for the formation of the arbitral tribunal, as a result of the direct expression of the parties' will (a selection), or other bodies to whom the parties have delegated the right to choose arbitrators (an appointment). The arbitrator shall give his or her consent to perform the relevant functions. The agreement is often drawn up by an 'arbitral contract' signed by the arbitrators and the parties, an act on the authorities of the arbitrators, a memorandum, terms of reference, etc.

As a rule, the powers of arbitrators are terminated after they render an award in a particular case due to the *functus officio* doctrine. The grounds and procedure for termination of the arbitrators' powers are defined at Article 14 of the Arbitration Act 2015 and Article 14 of the ICA Act 2015. The grounds for early termination of powers may be:

(1) arbitrator's self-recusal;
(2) parties' agreement to terminate the arbitrator's mandate;
(3) a court order in the case of the performance of the functions of assistance in respect of the arbitration made on the application for termination of the arbitrator's powers.

If an arbitrator becomes de jure or de facto unable to perform his functions or for other reasons fails to act without undue delay, his mandate terminates if he withdraws or if the parties agree on the termination. If an arbitrator withdraws or a party agrees to the termination of the arbitrator's mandate, this does not imply acceptance of the validity of any ground for withdrawal or challenge. Otherwise, if a controversy remains concerning any of these grounds, any party may request the court to decide on the termination of the mandate. In arbitration administered by a permanent arbitral institution, the parties may agree to a different procedure for termination and replacement of the arbitrator or, by their direct agreement, may exclude recourse to the court.

The application for termination of the arbitrator's powers shall be satisfied by the court where the procedure of termination of the arbitrator's powers was agreed by the parties or established by law (in accordance with which the issue of termination of powers is referred to the court). Law establishes grounds for termination of the arbitrator's powers. Court's decision shall be subject to no appeal.

In case of premature termination of powers, including due to the fact that the arbitrator declares self-withdrawal, or due to the cancellation of his powers by parties' agreement, as well as in any other case of termination of his powers, the new arbitrator shall be appointed in accordance with the rules that applied to the appointment of the replaced arbitrator.

§5.05 GROUNDS FOR CHALLENGE OF ARBITRATORS

Arbitration law provides only two grounds for challenge, both for domestic and international commercial arbitration. An arbitrator may be challenged only: (a) if circumstances exist that give rise to justifiable doubts to his impartiality or independence or (b) if he does not meet requirements specified by law or does not possess qualifications agreed by the parties. A party may challenge an arbitrator appointed by him, or in whose appointment this party has participated, only for reasons of which he becomes aware after the appointment has been made. As regards the substance for the challenges, Russian law distinguishes between the principles of objective impartiality (i.e., independence of an arbitral institution from the parties) and subjective impartiality (i.e., impartiality of particular arbitrators).[4]

The effectiveness of the relevant rules is ensured by the obligation of persons whom the parties contact in connection with his or her possible selection (appointment) as an arbitrator, to disclose any circumstances that may raise justifiable doubts about his or her impartiality or independence in the arbitral proceedings. When a person is approached in connection with a possible appointment as an arbitrator, he or she shall disclose any circumstances likely to give rise to justifiable doubts as to his or her impartiality or independence. An arbitrator, from the time of an appointment and throughout the arbitral proceedings, shall without delay disclose any such circumstances to the parties unless they have already been informed of them by him. In order to perform the duty to disclose certain circumstances, arbitrators must take into account all information available to them, as well as conduct a reasonable check of the information available. Any doubts should be interpreted in favour of the disclosure of the relevant circumstances.

In international commercial arbitration, the challenge procedure also applies in cases of the arbitrator's failure to act, intentional breach of the agreement of the parties or the rules of arbitration, or his or her de jure or de facto inability to perform his or her functions.

In Russia, experts and interpreters may be challenged on these grounds. Thus, in the International Commercial Arbitration Court, the reasons mentioned above may be cited to challenge an expert or an interpreter participating in the proceedings. In this case, the decision on the release from the appointment shall be made by the arbitral tribunal.

§5.06 CHALLENGE PROCEDURE

In Russia, the parties are free to agree on a challenge (disqualification) procedure. Failing such agreement, compensatory provisions of Article 12 of the Arbitration Act 2015 (for domestic arbitration) or Article 13 of the ICA Act 2015 (for international arbitration) are to be applied. A party who intends to challenge an arbitrator shall, within fifteen days after becoming aware of the constitution of the arbitral tribunal or after becoming aware of any circumstance relating to arbitrator's impartiality or independence, shall send a written statement of the reasons for the challenge (the notice of challenge) to the arbitral tribunal. Unless the challenged arbitrator withdraws or the other party agrees to the challenge, the arbitral tribunal shall decide on the challenge. The notice of challenge made by a party does not suspend or terminate powers of an arbitrator. If one party has challenged the arbitrator, the other party may agree to challenge the arbitrator. Such consent is not regarded as recognition of the

4. *Dispute Resolution in Russia: The Essentials (Collection of Articles)*, 318 (Dedov D., Molotnikov A., eds, Moscow, 2019).

validity of the grounds for challenge. Before considering an application for a challenge on the merits, the arbitrator, the other party, and any other members of the arbitral tribunal shall be given the opportunity to comment, which shall be communicated to all parties and arbitrators.

The challenge procedure in an arbitration administered by a permanent arbitral institution may differ. For instance, in the ICAC's arbitration, a party may send a written notice of challenge stating the reasons therefor to the special Nomination Committee within fifteen days after being notified of the constitution of the arbitral tribunal or having become aware of circumstances that can serve as a ground for challenge. For international commercial disputes, the Nomination Committee may consider the merits of the notice of challenge filed after the deadline taking account of the reasons for the late filing and the nature of grounds for challenge indicated by the party. If the challenged arbitrator does not withdraw voluntarily or if the other party does not agree to the challenge, the decision on the release of the arbitrator from his appointment shall be made by the Nomination Committee. It decides on the challenge of the arbitrator for the reasons mentioned above.

If a challenge under any procedure, either statutory or agreed upon by the parties, is not successful, the challenging party may request, within one month after having received notice of the decision rejecting the challenge, the court to decide on the challenge. While such a request is pending, the arbitral tribunal, including the challenged arbitrator, may continue the arbitral proceedings and render an award. Court's decision on the challenge is a subject to no appeal. By direct agreement, the parties whose arbitration agreement provides for administering the arbitration by a permanent arbitral institution may exclude the possibility of resolving this issue by the court.

Disqualification of an arbitrator can be granted by the court only if: (a) there is the applicable procedure for challenging an arbitrator agreed by the parties or set by the legislation, in accordance with which the challenge of an arbitrator has been referred to the resolution of the court and (b) there are statutory grounds for disqualification. Granting the challenge, the court shall determine whether the circumstances demonstrate a justifiable doubt to the impartiality or independence of the arbitrator. At the same time, the impartiality and independence of the arbitrator shall be assessed from the point of view of a neutral and reasonable person who has full information about all relevant circumstances.

§5.07 CONSEQUENCES OF FAILURE TO OBSERVE THE ARBITRAL TRIBUNAL CONSTITUTION RULES

Failure to comply with the procedure for the formation of the arbitral tribunal is the basis for setting aside of the final award or refusal to issue a writ of execution for its enforcement. In Russia, dispute resolution by arbitrators appointed with violations of the agreed procedure entails a refusal to recognise the final award.[5]

5. Decree of the Federal Commercial Court for the North-Western Circuit dated 1 October 2008, case No. A56-14453/2008.

CHAPTER 6

Establishment and Functioning of Arbitral Institutions

§6.01 ESTABLISHMENT OF A PERMANENT ARBITRAL INSTITUTION

Under the current Russian legislation, a *permanent arbitral institution* is a *subdivision of a* non-profit organisation that performs on a permanent basis the functions of administering the arbitration. The legislator proceeds from the premise that a permanent arbitral institution *cannot be an independent legal entity*. In the Russian doctrine, there were some discussions about the possibility of endowing arbitral institutions with legal personality.[1] Nevertheless, the current law has refused to do so. Only the organisation that acts as the founder of the arbitral institution has separate legal personality.

The excessively liberal approach to regulating arbitration that was dominant in Russia during the period from 1993 to 2016 allowed a wide range of stakeholders to set up an arbitral institution. These included not only chambers of commerce, exchanges, public associations of entrepreneurs and consumers, but also commercial organisations and public authorities, including federal ministries and local municipal bodies.

1. Kandybka A.I., *What an Arbitral Institution Should Be (Comments on Certain Provisions of the Draft Federal Law 'On Arbitration in the Russian Federation')*, 2 Treteysky Sud, 13-14 (2001) [*Kandybka A.I. Kakim byt tryetyeiskomu sudu (kommyentarii k nyekotorym polojyeniyam proyekta Fyedyeralnogo zakona 'O tryetyeiskih sudah v Rossiiskoi Fyedyeracii'.* // Treteysky Sud. 2001. No. 2. S. 13-14]; Commercial Law: Textbook. Volume 1, 606-607 (V.F. Popondopoulo, V.F. Yakovleva, eds, 3rd ed., Moscow, 2002) (author of the chapter - K.K. Lebedev) [Kommyerchyeskoye pravo: Uchyebnik. V 2 ch. CH. 1. / Pod ryed. V.F. Popondopulo, V.F. Yakovlevoi. 3-ye izd.,pyeryerab. i dop. – M., 2002. S. 606-607 (avtor glavy – K.K. Lebedev)], Volosov D.A., Does an Arbitral Institution Need Legal Personality?, 1 Treteysky Sud, 87 (2013) [*Volosov D.A. Nyeobhodimo li yuridichyeskoye lico tryetyeiskomu sudu?* // Treteysky Sud. *2013. No. 1. S.87*]; Morozov M.E., Volosov D.A., Five Questions about the Arbitration Reform, 2/3 Treteysky Sud, 202 (2014) [*Morozov M.E., Volosov D.A. Pyat voprosov k ryeformye tryetyeiskih sudov. //* Treteysky Sud. *2014. No. 2/3. S 202*].

Currently, the legislator narrowed the circle, only permitting non-profit organisations to act as founders of arbitral institutions.

For some entities, there is a direct prohibition to set up arbitral institutions. These include federal government agencies, regional authorities, local government bodies, state and municipal institutions, state corporations, state companies, political parties, and religious organisations, as well as chambers of lawyers (advocates) and notaries.

Thus, if the previous legislation relied on a *notification* procedure for the creation of permanent arbitral centres, the current law introduced a *licensing* system for their establishment.

The technicalities of setting up an arbitral institution require that the non-commercial organisation wishing to establish one must undergo a number of mandatory procedures to:

- draft arbitration rules for a permanent arbitral institution;
- adopt a list of recommended arbitrators;
- obtain a recommendation from the Council for the Improvement of Arbitration under the relevant executive agency (the Ministry of Justice);
- publish the deposited arbitration rules on its website on the Internet;
- obtain the permission to act as a permanent arbitral institution[2] (the two exceptions are the International Commercial Arbitration Court and the Maritime Arbitration Commission at the Russian Federation CCI, which according to the law are not required to obtain an appropriate permit).

In the initial years following the 2015 arbitration reform, the Government of the Russian Federation was the final authority granting or refusing a permission to act as a permanent arbitral institution to the applicant. Since March 2019, those functions had been transferred to the Ministry of Justice.[3]

In making a decision whether to grant the right to act as a permanent arbitral institution to the applicant, the licensing authorities consider the reputation of a non-profit organisation; the scale and nature of its activities, taking into account that of its members; its ability (including the financial ability) to ensure a high level of organisation in a permanent arbitral institution, as well as the organisation's contribution to the development of arbitration in the Russian Federation.

As of 21 December 2017, the Ministry of Justice received the applications for a permit to exercise the functions of a permanent arbitral institution from about fifty non-profit organisations located on the territory of the Russian Federation. In total, there were eighty-eight applications because some non-profit organisations applied several times. In most cases, applications and supporting documents were returned to applicants due to the discovery of inaccurate information in them.

2. This right is granted in accordance with the Decree of the Government of the Russian Federation of 25 June 2016 No. 577 'On Approval of the Rules for Granting the Right to Perform the Functions of a Permanent Arbitral Institution and Regulations on the Deposit of Rules of a Permanent Arbitration Institution.'
3. For more details, see §1.03 of this book.

The refusal to grant a non-profit organisation the right to exercise the functions of a permanently arbitral institution may be appealed to the competent court.

The Council for the Improvement of Arbitration under the Ministry of Justice, which issues recommendations to the Government of the Russian Federation, plays an essential role in the establishment of arbitral institutions.[4] There are fifty members in the Council, including its chairman and deputies. Members of the Council participate in its work on a voluntary basis (*pro bono*).

The Council includes holders of public offices and civil servants who cannot constitute more than one-third of its total membership. The Council also includes two representatives from all-Russian associations of entrepreneurs and two representatives from chambers of commerce and industry, as well as representatives of the legal, academic and business community and other members from various walks of life. At least half of the total membership of the Council must have academic degrees in the legal sciences. The composition of the Council shall be rotated by at least one-third once every three years.

The main task of the Council is to establish favourable conditions for the development of independent and professional arbitration in the Russian Federation. To this end, the Council performs the following functions:

- it participates in the identification, analysis, dissemination, and support of the best Russian and international practices in the field of arbitration;
- it provides information and expert assistance to the Ministry of Justice in the exercise of its powers to regulate in the field of arbitration and participates in the monitoring of the legal practice;
- it considers the drafts of normative legal acts related to arbitration and submits proposals to the Ministry of Justice concerning the drafting of such acts;
- it prepares recommendations to the Government of the Russian Federation on granting or refusing to grant non-profit organisations and foreign arbitral institutions the right to exercise the functions of a permanent arbitral institution;
- it submits recommendations to the Ministry of Justice concerning the list of specialities in which at least one-third of the arbitrators included in the list of recommended arbitrators of a permanent arbitral institution must have academic degrees;
- it assists the Ministry of Justice in dealing with requests from arbitral institutions and other persons on the application of arbitral legislation;
- it submits recommendations to the Ministry of Justice on whether to issue a non-profit organisation or a foreign arbitration institution that has obtained the right to exercise the functions of a permanent arbitral institution an order to take a decision to cease operating as a permanent arbitration institution in the territory of Russia;

4. The Council acts on the basis of the Ministry of Justice's Order No. 165 of 13 July 2016 'On the Council for the Improvement of Arbitration.'

- it reviews the practice of the Council reviewing documents from the applicants seeking a recommendation to the Government of the Russian Federation on granting the right to exercise the functions of a permanent acting arbitration institution;
- it reviews the practice of the application of arbitral legislation.

§6.02 FUNCTIONING OF PERMANENT ARBITRAL INSTITUTIONS

The modern regulation of commercial arbitration in Russia distinguishes between, on the one hand, the arbitration (resolution) of disputes and, on the other hand, the administration of arbitration, i.e., the administrative assistance to the tribunal.

The Arbitration Act 2015 defines *administration of arbitration* by listing the following functions of a permanent arbitral institution:

- the organisation of the arbitration, including the arrangement of selection, appointment, and challenge of the arbitrators;
- records management;
- collection and distribution of arbitral fees.

The functions of an arbitral tribunal concerned directly with the resolution of a dispute fall outside this definition.

A permanent arbitral institution acts in accordance with its Rules of Arbitration, which it should post on its website and deposit with an authorised federal agency.[5] These rules are facilitative to the openness of arbitration and the wider availability of information about its activities.

If any provisions in the Rules of a permanent arbitral institution are contrary to the Arbitration Act 2015, such provisions are void. In turn, this can become a basis for setting aside of arbitral awards rendered by such Rules or refusal to enforce them where the contradiction is such that it has triggered one of the grounds for setting aside under the procedural law.

The Rules of Arbitration of a permanent arbitral institution must be approved by the relevant governing body of its founding non-profit organisation. The law does not specify which governing body it should be, and the non-profit organisation is free to regulate this issue independently. The non-profit organisation's Charter (Articles of Association) should specify the responsibilities of its governing bodies and, in particular, determine which body is competent to adopt the arbitration rules of a permanent arbitral institution. In practice, such documents are usually subject to the approval of the highest governing body in a non-profit organisation, the general meeting of its members. However, it is possible that a permanent collegial body of a non-profit organisation (the board of directors or the supervisory board) might be competent to perform this function.

5. *See* the Regulations on the Deposit of a Permanent Arbitration Institution's Rules, approved by Decree of the Government of the Russian Federation No. 577 of 25 June 2016.

If the Rules of a permanent arbitral institution provide for the administration of international commercial arbitration, such an institution may maintain a single list of recommended arbitrators or separate lists of recommended arbitrators for domestic and international commercial arbitration. In every recommended list of arbitrators of a permanent arbitration institution, at least one-third of the arbitrators must have an academic degree awarded on the territory of the Russian Federation in the speciality included in the list approved by the authorised federal executive agency on the basis of the recommendation of the Council for the Improvement of Arbitration. At least half of the arbitrators should have experience in resolving civil disputes in the capacity of arbitrators or judges of a federal court, constitutional court of a region of Russia, or as justices of the peace for at least ten years preceding the date of inclusion in the recommended list of arbitrators. The same person cannot be included in the recommended lists of arbitrators of more than three permanent arbitral institutions.

After the 2015 reform, the number of cases resolved by the arbitration fell sharply. However, the most authoritative arbitration institution, the ICAC at the RF CCI, mostly retained its caseload. Since the entry into force of the Arbitration Act 2015 until 15 December 2017, ICAC considered 279 cases by way of international commercial arbitration, and from 27 January 2017 to 15 December 2017, it considered 51 domestic arbitration case. During this period, 110 out of 152 arbitrators from the recommended list participated in the resolution of international commercial arbitration disputes, and 54 out of 101 arbitrators from the equivalent list took part in the resolution of domestic disputes.

MAC at the RF CCI considered 15 cases from 1 September 2016 to 15 December 2017.

From the moment it received the right to administer arbitration (1 July 2017) until 29 December 2017, the Arbitration Center at the Russian Union of Industrialists and Entrepreneurs received 75 requests for arbitration, including 4 counterclaims, and also continued to administer the affairs of the predecessor institutions that were not resolved by 1 July 2017. During this period, the arbitration proceedings were completed in 6 cases. In total, in 2017, the Arbitration Center at the Russian Union of Industrialists and Entrepreneurs (RSPP) and its predecessor institutions received 157 requests for arbitration, including 5 counterclaims. In the second half of 2017, out of 96 arbitrators included in the recommended list, 55 arbitrators were elected or appointed as members of arbitral tribunals in the Arbitration Center at the RSPP.

In the Institute of Modern Arbitration, since the moment it obtained the right to administer arbitration, has had 10 arbitration cases, the proceedings in which have not yet been completed.[6]

6. Report on the activities of the Council for the Improvement of Arbitration for the year 2017. Prepared by the Ministry of Justice of the Russian Federation (as of 24 June 2018).

§6.03 THE PROHIBITION OF A CONFLICT OF INTEREST IN AN ARBITRAL INSTITUTION

The law devotes particular attention to the conflict of interests in arbitration, in particular in a permanent arbitral institution.

A *conflict of interest* is a situation where a permanent arbitral institution administers an arbitration where one of the parties is:

(1) the non-profit organisation that established this permanent arbitral institution;
(2) a member of the non-profit organisation that established this permanent arbitral institution (except for non-profit organisations with more than one hundred participants) or a person who is in effect able to determine the actions of this non-profit organisation;
(3) a person competent to resolve questions related to the appointment, challenge or removal of arbitrators, or his close relatives, as well as any organisation where this person has the right, directly or indirectly, to command more than 50% of the votes in the supreme governing body of that organisation or the power to appoint (elect) a chief executive officer and (or) more than 50% of the membership of the collegial body of this organisation.

The law does not define a conflict of interest; the legislator chose instead to list the cases where a conflict of interest is deemed to exist. At the same time, an analysis of the circumstances of the above situations makes it possible for the courts to interpret them broadly. For example, if the court comes to the conclusion that the person who is in effect able to determine the actions of the non-profit organisation, this circumstance can be the basis for concluding that affiliation and, therefore, the conflict of interests exist.

The law allows permanent arbitral institutions to expand the range of situations leading to a conflict of interest in its Rules. For example, the Rules of Arbitration may deem it a conflict of interest if a party to a dispute or its representative have family ties with a member of the secretariat or a person assisting the arbitration. Conflict of interest can take place where the founding non-profit organisation has a commercial relationship with the participant of a dispute referred to this arbitral institution.

In itself, a conflict of interest does not yet constitute a basis for the conclusion that the arbitral award is unlawful, that is, it cannot serve as the basis for the setting aside of the arbitral award or for the refusal to enforce it. This position follows from the premise that the guarantees of independence in arbitration mainly focus on the impartiality of the arbitral tribunal hearing each particular case, which is presumed unless there is evidence to the contrary.

The Arbitration Act 2015 contains some requirements to the internal arrangements within a permanent arbitral institution. A collegial body, the Nominating Committee, should handle all matters relating to the appointment, challenges, and removal of arbitrators. This is a default rule, i.e., it can be altered by the institution's

Rules of Arbitration. If the Rules of a permanent arbitral institution delegate the resolution of such questions to one of its officers acting alone, the Rules must give the parties a right to appeal this officer's decision before the Nominating Committee.

At least two-thirds of the Nominating Committee shall be elected by a vote of the persons included in the recommended list of arbitrators. This decision requires a simple majority of the total number of persons on the list. This is also a default rule because the law allows the Rules of a permanent arbitral institution to stipulate a different procedure for the selection of one-third of the Nominating Committee. At least one-third of the Nominating Committee must have a degree in Law. The Rules of a permanent arbitral institution may establish additional requirements to the members of the Nominating Committee.

There must be a mandatory rotation of membership in the Nominating Committee so that at least one-third of its composition renews every three years, and the same person is unable to serve on the Nominating Committee for three years after stepping down. The membership of the Committee cannot be terminated prematurely, except where the members make this decision of their own accord, or in the case of factual or legal impossibility of continuing to serve on the Nominating Committee.

To minimise conflicts of interest, the legislator established additional rules for the membership in the Council for the Improvement of Arbitration. The following persons cannot be members of the Council:

- officers of permanent arbitral institutions (e.g., a chairman or another official) who can unilaterally take any decision on behalf of the institution when it administers an arbitration, or in connection therewith;
- members, employees or officers of commercial organisations that previously had permanent arbitration centres in their structure;
- members, employees or officers of commercial organisations that belong to the same group of persons as the founding organisation of an arbitral institution (i.e., affiliated with it in any way).

§6.04 TERMINATION OF A PERMANENT ARBITRAL INSTITUTION

An arbitral institution may cease to operate voluntarily if its founder so decides, or its activities may be discontinued by order of the authorised federal executive agency, the Ministry of Justice.

The grounds for termination of the permanent arbitral institution are:

(1) decision of the founding non-profit organisation;
(2) decision of the competent state court.

If the Ministry of Justice of the Russian Federation finds an irregularity in the activities of a permanent arbitral institution, it can issue an order for the non-profit organisation to make a decision to discontinue the operation of the relevant institution. The Arbitration Act 2015 contains two grounds for making such an order:

(1) discovery of severe, repeated violations of the Arbitration Act, which caused considerable damage to the rights and legitimate interests of the parties in arbitration and other persons;
(2) discovery of the permanent arbitral institution's non-conformity to the requirements of the Arbitration Act:
   - non-conformity of the Rules of a permanent arbitral institution to the requirements of the Arbitration Act;
   - lack of a recommended list of arbitrators that conforms to the requirements of the Arbitration Act;
   - provision of inaccurate information about the founding non-profit organisation and its members.

Within one month from the date of the Ministry of Justice's order, the non-profit organisation must adopt a decision to discontinue the operation of its permanent arbitral institution. If the non-profit organisation fails to comply within the time limit, the Ministry of Justice (its respective regional branch) shall apply to the competent commercial court of the first instance, to obtain a court order terminating of the permanent arbitral institution.

The Arbitration Act 2015 sets out the legal consequences of termination of the permanent arbitral institution. Arbitral awards rendered in the proceedings administered by this institution remain binding on the parties. In itself, the termination of the permanent arbitral institution does not constitute a ground for setting aside or refusing to enforce an arbitral award.

If a case began prior to the date of termination of the arbitral institution and the proceedings have not been completed by this date, it remains possible for the parties and the tribunal to proceed with the resolution of the dispute. In this case, the tribunal must consider any administrative assistance from the institution as if parties agreed from the start to refer their dispute to ad hoc arbitration.

§6.05 LIABILITY OF THE ORGANISATION THAT ESTABLISHED A PERMANENT ARBITRAL INSTITUTION

Since it lacks separate legal personality, a permanent arbitration institution is a subdivision of a non-profit organisation and therefore cannot have any liabilities of its own. Accordingly, the legislator made the non-profit organisation liable instead, limiting the forms of liability to a recovery of damages. The law directly stipulates that such liability is of a civil-law nature.

At the same time, non-profit organisations can increase the extent of their liability.

Civil liability of a non-profit organisation for the actions of a permanent arbitral institution can arise under the following circumstances:

(1) the permanent arbitral institution has not fulfilled or improperly fulfilled its obligations in the administration of arbitration;

(2) the actions of the permanent arbitral institution were intentional or grossly negligent.

Recovery from the permanent arbitration institutions must comply with the rules contained in Article 15 of the Civil Code, which establishes the general principles for this type of action. For the recovery of damages under Article 15, the plaintiff needs to prove that the defendant's actions were illegal, the very fact of incurring a loss, the amount of this loss, and the causal link between the defendant's actions and the adverse effects for the plaintiff.

One must bear in mind that the law distinguishes between the liability of the non-profit organisation and the liability of arbitrators. A non-profit organisation is not responsible for the consequences of wrongful acts or omissions by the arbitrators.

Matters of civil responsibility of the permanent arbitral institutions become most pertinent where the plaintiff seeks to recover the arbitral fees because the tribunal failed to resolve a case without an appropriate legal ground for this failure, thus putting into question the entitlement of a permanent arbitral to withhold the fees.[7]

With regard to the liability of arbitrators, the pre-existing law did not regulate the matter. The current Arbitration Act introduced the institution of arbitrator immunity.[8] At the heart of the arbitrator immunity doctrine is the postulate of functional similarity between the activities of a state judge and an arbitrator. Hence, the state, giving them the authority, must ensure that they perform their functions without fear of incurring liability for mistakes. The arbitrator immunity can be absolute or limited (relative). The absolute immunity implies that the arbitrator is not subject to any liability for their actions. Relative immunity means that the arbitrator shall only be liable in cases established by law. Russian law chose the latter approach, i.e., the limited immunity. The general rule is that an arbitrator cannot be held liable by the parties or by the permanent arbitral institution (i.e., its founding non-profit organisation) in connection with the failure to perform or the improper performance of arbitral functions. However, this rule has exceptions. First, an arbitrator can be held liable in a civil action within a criminal case that aims to recover damages caused by a crime. Such liability is only possible if the arbitrator was found guilty of a crime that led to the loss. Second, arbitrators can be liable in the event of failure to perform or the improper performance of their functions. Such liability is only possible where the institutional Rules of Arbitration provide so. The liability takes the form of the reduction of fees for arbitrators. Thus, in this case, the arbitrator is liable to the arbitral institution that administered the dispute.

---

7. *See*, e.g., the Decree of the Presidium of the Supreme Commercial Court of 23 June 2009 No. 1434/09; the Decrees of the Federal Commercial Court for the Moscow Circuit of 3 February 2011, case No. A40-33705/10-68-311; of 4 September 2009, case No. A40-94467/08-68-802; of 28 May 2012, case No. A40-73886/11-52-601.
8. *See Commentary to the Federal Law 'On Arbitration in the Russian Federation' (Clause-by-Clause. Academic and Practical)*, 324-325 (O.Yu. Skvortsov and M.Y. Savransky, eds, Moscow. Statute, 2016) (author of the commentary - RR Miftakhov) [*Kommyentarii k Fyedyeralnomu zakonu «Ob arbitrajye (tryetyeiskom razbiratyelstvye) v Rossiiskoi Fyedyeracii (postatyeinyi, nauchno-praktichyeskii). / Pod ryed. prof. O.Yu. Skvortsova i prof. M.Yu. Savranskogo* – M. Statut, 2016. S. 324-325 *(avtor kommyentariya – R.R. Miftakhov)*].

§6.06 ESTABLISHMENT AND FUNCTIONING OF AN AD HOC ARBITRATION

Ad hoc arbitration denotes a tribunal constituted by the parties to settle a particular dispute. In other words, it is the kind of arbitration that acts in the absence of administration by a permanent arbitral institution (except where the latter performs individual functions related to the administration of a particular dispute if the arbitration agreement so provides – Article 2(17) of the Arbitration Act 2015). Upon the completion of the arbitration proceedings and the rendering of the award, the ad hoc tribunal ceases to operate.

The new Arbitration Act, unlike the previous legislation, has established different legal regimes for permanent arbitral institutions and ad hoc arbitration. The powers of ad hoc arbitration are much less extensive than the powers of a permanent arbitral institution.

Procedures for the establishment and functioning of ad hoc arbitration, in turn, vary depending on whether or not it is administered by a permanent arbitral institution.

The permanent arbitral institution can assist the tribunals in ad hoc arbitration. Such administrative assistance may include the selection and appointment of arbitrators, resolving challenges to arbitrators, termination of their mandate. Also, an institution can yield organisational and technical assistance: to provide premises and personnel, to facilitate the dispatch of documents to the arbitrators and the parties, to receive an advance on arbitration fees and redistribute it according to the instructions from the parties and the tribunal, and so on. A permanent arbitral institution can only do those things if its Rules stipulate that it can assist in ad hoc arbitration. The Rules should list specifically all those functions that the institution can perform for ad hoc arbitration.

It is a condition for obtaining the assistance from a permanent arbitral institution that the parties in their agreement should provide that they will apply to a particular institution for assistance in organising their ad hoc arbitration. For the arbitral institution, this activity is similar to the administration of disputes under the institution's own Rules.

The Act specifically notes that the institution's performance of individual administrative functions for ad hoc arbitration does not make it 'administered' by a permanent arbitral institution.

Some administrative functions for ad hoc arbitration can only be performed by a permanent arbitral institution. Those organisations that have not obtained the right to operate as a permanent arbitral institution cannot perform these functions.

If an ad hoc arbitration does not resort to the assistance of a permanent arbitral institution, the burden of organising the proceedings lies with the parties or the arbitral tribunal.

There are significant limitations for the activity of ad hoc arbitration. In particular, ad hoc arbitration cannot request assistance from a competent state court in obtaining evidence; ad hoc arbitration may not resolve corporate disputes. Some procedures in ad hoc arbitration have their specific features – for example, filing a claim and the exchange of documents. Arbitration fees are also determined differently.

Restrictions for ad hoc arbitration also concern its competence. In particular, ad hoc arbitration is not entitled to deal with disputes arising from corporate relations. Only the permanent arbitral institutions have the right to settle corporate disputes, and only under certain conditions stipulated by the law.

Another limitation is that the parties cannot enter into agreements that provide for the finality of awards in ad hoc arbitration. As a result, those awards can be set aside on broader grounds than the awards of institutional arbitration.

Thus, the current regulation provides institutional arbitration with a much broader range of powers and opportunities than ad hoc arbitration.

The ad hoc arbitral tribunal, being created to resolve a particular dispute, does not have a specific location. Its juridical seat, as well as the venue of arbitral hearings, is determined by agreement of the parties or the arbitral tribunal, taking into account the convenience of the parties and other circumstances relevant for the fast, efficient, and cost-effective dispute resolution. Thus, unlike in institutional arbitration where the difference between the seat of arbitration and the venue of arbitral hearings is crucial, for ad hoc arbitration this distinction is less significant. This changes the situation with setting aside and enforcement of ad hoc arbitration awards because an award can be challenged at the seat of arbitration.

It has been pointed out that the international trend of convergence between institutional arbitration and ad hoc arbitration is noticeable in Russia as well.[9] This trend seems to be, to some extent, objectively predetermined – although, in the end, it does not erase the demarcation line that separates the two forms of arbitration. This is due to the different opportunities that the two forms of dispute resolution can offer to the parties. At the same time, one way of supporting ad hoc arbitration is the development of arbitration rules tailored for this kind of arbitration. This approach is embodied in the arbitration rules developed under the auspices of the UN: (1) The Arbitration Rules of the United Nations Economic Commission for Europe (January 1966); (2) The Rules for International Commercial Arbitration of the United Nations Economic Commission for Asia and the Far East (April 1966); (3) The Arbitration Rules of the United Nations Commission on International Trade Law (UNCITRAL Arbitration Rules 1976).[10]

The practice of international ad hoc tribunals could be useful for their Russian counterparts. In particular, there is a large body of experience generated by the

9. Boguslavsky M.M., *Contemporary Trend of Broadening the Applications of Institutional Arbitration*, in: *Topical Questions in International Commercial Arbitration*, 50 (Komarov A.S., ed., Moscow, 2002) [*Boguslavsky M.M. Sovryemyennyye tyendyencii rasshiryeniya sfyery dyeistviya institucionnyh arbitrajnyh sudov. // Aktualnyye voprosy myejdunarodnogo kommyerchyeskogo arbitraja. / Otv. ryed. A.S. Komarov* - M., 2002. S. 50].

10. Lebedev S.N., *The Selected Papers on International Commercial Arbitration, International Trade Law, Private International Law, Private Law of the Sea*, 294 (Compiled by A.I. Muranov, Moscow, 2009) [Lebedev S.N. Izbrannyye trudy po myejdunarodnomu kommyerchyeskomu arbitraju, pravu myejdunarodnoi torgovli, myejdunarodnomu chastnomu pravu, chastnomu morskomu pravu. / Sost. A.I. Muranov. – M., 2009. S. 294].

international ad hoc tribunals acting under the UNCITRAL Arbitration Rules, adopted by the United Nations Commission on International Trade Law in 1976 (revised in 2010).[11] These Rules contribute to a quicker resolution of disputes and provide a way out of the impasse for the event that the respondent fails to appoint its arbitrator or where the two arbitrators cannot reach an agreement on the presiding arbitrator.[12] As it has been pointed out, these Rules 'provide the combination of predictability in the resolution of procedural issues that are characteristic to institutional arbitration, with the organisational autonomy and flexibility of ad hoc arbitration'.[13]

§6.07 THE LEGAL STATUS OF FOREIGN ARBITRAL INSTITUTIONS OPERATING IN RUSSIA

A foreign arbitral institution is an organisation established outside the Russian Federation and performing on a regular basis the functions of arbitral administration, regardless of whether or not it has a separate legal personality (Article 2(5) of the Arbitration Act 2015).

Foreign arbitration institutions with widely recognised international reputation can more easily obtain the right to exercise the functions of a permanent arbitral institution. Such foreign institutions do not have to provide their Rules and the list of arbitrators.

A foreign arbitral institution can operate in two legal modes: as a permanent arbitral institution and as an ad hoc arbitration.

An arbitral institution established in a foreign country can apply for a permit to operate on the Russian territory. If such permission is granted, the foreign arbitral institution acquires the legal status of a permanent arbitral institution.

If the Ministry of Justice does not grant a permit to operate on the Russian territory, the awards of such foreign institution shall be treated as ad hoc arbitral awards.

The provision of more favourable conditions for foreign arbitral institutions has been criticised in Russian literature.[14] This criticism is due to the inherent ambiguity of

---

11. For the drafting history of the UNCITRAL Arbitration Rules and the commentary thereto, *see* Nikiforov I.V., *UNCITRAL Arbitration Rules 2010 (with New Article, Paragraph 4, as Adopted in 2013: A Workbook* (Moscow, 2015) [*Nikiforov I.V. Arbitrajnyi ryeglamyent UNSITRAL 2010 goda (s novym punktom 4 stati 1, prinyatym v 2013 godu. Rabochaya tyetrad. – M., 2015*].
12. Shmittgoff K.M., *Ad Hoc Arbitration and Institutional Arbitration*, in: *Export Law and Practice of International Trade* 345 (Komarov A.S., ed., Moscow, 1993) [*Shmittgoff K.M. Arbitraj ad hoc i institucionnyi arbitraj. // Eksport: pravo i praktika myejdunarodnoi torgovli. / Otv. ryed. A.S. Komarov*. – M., 1993. S. 345].
13. Karabelnikov B.R., *Recognition and Enforcement of Foreign Arbitral Awards: Academic and Practical Commentary to the New York Convention 1958*, 22 (Moscow, Yustitsinform, 2001) [*Karabelnikov B.R. Priznaniye i privyedyeniye v ispolnyeniye inostrannyh arbitrajnyh ryeshyenii: Nauchno-praktichyeskii kommyentarii k Nyu-Iorkskoi konvyencii 1958 goda. - M.: ZAO 'Yuridichyeskii dom "Yusticinform"', 2001. S.22*].
14. *See Commentary to the Federal Law 'On Arbitration in the Russian Federation' (Clause-by-Clause. Academic and Practical)*, 266-267 (O.Yu. Skvortsov and M.Y. Savransky, eds, Moscow. Statute, 2016) (author of the commentary – K.K. Lebedev) [*Kommyentarii k Fyedyeralnomu zakonu «Ob arbitrajye (tryetyeiskom razbiratyelstvye) v Rossiiskoi Fyedyeracii (postatyeinyi,*

the notion of 'widely recognised reputation', which makes the foreign institution exempt from the procedures that the other arbitral institutions must undergo.

nauchno-praktichyeskii). / Pod ryed. prof. O.Yu. Skvortsova i prof. M.Yu. Savranskogo – M. Statut, 2016. S. 266-267 *(avtor kommyentariya – K.K. Lebedev)*].

CHAPTER 7
Arbitrability

§7.01 DETERMINING THE ARBITRAL COMPETENCE

Before proceeding to the merits of a dispute, an arbitral tribunal must determine the scope of its powers in respect of the dispute referred to it. The competence of the arbitrators is a set of their powers for resolving the dispute on the merits, as well as the powers for conducting the proceedings in a manner that guarantees a fair resolution of the case.

Any jurisdictional activity involves a relation of power. The competence to resolve certain categories of civil disputes is delegated to arbitral tribunal by the State. It is the State that either transfers the powers to arbitral tribunals within its sovereign territory or recognises their authority to render arbitral awards outside its borders. By agreeing to arbitrate, the parties engage the legal rules governing the arbitrator's competence – the authority to resolve the dispute and render a binding award. The origins of the arbitrators' competence lie in the law applicable to the arbitration agreement, *lex arbitri* and the law of the state in which the award is recognised and enforced.

The main source of arbitral competence in each particular case is the arbitration agreement. The scope of competence of the arbitral tribunal (the set of its powers) is derived from the scope of the arbitration agreement. Arbitral tribunals have the right to consider cases arising from a specific legal relationship defined by the arbitration agreement, so the award made in a dispute that goes beyond it cannot give rise to any legal consequences. Exceeding the powers of arbitrators in resolving the dispute (*extra petita*) will entail either the setting aside of the arbitral award or the refusal to recognise and enforce it.

Russian arbitration reform removed from the legislative agenda a number of problems related to the interpretation of the scope of the arbitration agreement. At present, an arbitration agreement covering disputes arising from a contract or in connection therewith extends to any transactions between the parties aimed at the performance, amendment, or termination of said contract. In addition, an arbitration agreement contained in a contract extends to any disputes in connection with the conclusion of the said contract, its entry into force, amendment, termination, or validity. It also extends to the disputes arising in connection with an obligation to return everything performed under a contract if it is declared void or not concluded unless it follows otherwise from the arbitration agreement itself.

Arbitral competence, as well as the conditions and procedure for conducting the procedure in arbitration, are set forth in the applicable legal sources of arbitration, and, above all, in national legislation. In addition, provisions defining the scope and content of the powers of an arbitral tribunal are contained in rules of permanent arbitral institutions and ad hoc rules of arbitration. Procedural actions of the arbitrators are in themselves legal facts that may lead to emergence, modification, or termination of the respective rights and obligations. The arbitration agreement is also a source of arbitral competence; it is the basis for granting the arbitrators an authority to resolve a particular civil dispute. One should note, however, that the parties are free to grant the arbitrators rights and impose on them obligations only as long as such rights and obligations do not contradict the mandatory rules of law. Only the parties themselves can agree to the proceedings solely by documents (i.e., without a hearing), the finality of award (i.e., the exclusion of the possibility of its challenge), the application of interim measures in respect of the subject matter of the dispute, etc. This defines the role of the arbitration agreement and the rules of arbitration in determining the competence of the arbitral tribunal.

Among the sources of arbitral competence, Russian commentators often name an arbitral contract – the agreement between the parties and the arbitrators regarding the resolution of a dispute. It binds the parties and the arbitrators and constitutes the basis for reimbursement of the costs incurred by arbitrators in connection with the resolution of the case. The arbitral contract is not made in writing as a separate document, but it does not entail its invalidity.

In assessing the competence of arbitral tribunals, it is necessary to take into account the contractual nature of the parties' subordination to the authority of arbitrators and, accordingly, the contractual nature of the method for determining the scope of such competence. The scope of arbitral competence (powers) follows from the scope of the arbitration agreement. This fact is extremely important for the application of the respective legal rules, including the arbitrators' ruling on their own competence and for the control functions of state courts.

[A] Bodies Authorised to Decide on Arbitral Competence

The question of the arbitral competence may be the subject to determination by three different bodies. First, a permanent arbitral institution makes a decision as to the absence of obvious obstacles to the adoption of the dispute for the administering, on the appointment of arbitrators, on the determination of the amount of the advance to cover the arbitration costs. This concept is called *prima facie competence*, or competence 'at first glance', i.e., the resolution of the issue of competence without a full assessment of the case materials and positions of the parties. Further, after the transfer of a case to the arbitral tribunal, the latter is authorised to decide whether it has jurisdiction to resolve the dispute. Third, the question of competence may be decided by the relevant state court at the seat of arbitration.[1] In Russia, the central issue is the right of the arbitral tribunal to rule on its competence.

[B] Types of Arbitral Competence

Russian commentators distinguish two forms of arbitral tribunal's competence – objective and subjective. The objective competence determines whether a dispute may be a subject of arbitral proceedings, in other words, whether such dispute is arbitrable. Subjective competence lies in the presence and scope of the powers of the arbitral tribunal in respect of a particular dispute referred to it. The subjective competence of arbitration relies on the determination of four key components: competence in relation to the subject matter of the dispute (the object of the dispute); competence in relation to the parties to the arbitration agreement (subjects of dispute); competence in relation to the organisation of the arbitration process; competence in relation to the determination of remedies the tribunal can award to the parties in the dispute.[2]

Russian scholars further distinguish the substantive and functional powers of arbitral tribunals. Since the purpose of arbitration is to resolve disputes about the law, the arbitrators are vested with powers for its implementation, the totality of which constitutes the functional competence of the arbitrators. The content of the functional competence includes the power to accept the statement of claim for consideration, to demand from the respondent a statement of defence, the power to conduct the proceedings, the powers to take interim measures, the powers to render an award, etc. The powers of the arbitrators to perform their functions in respect of a certain range of subject matter (disputes of a civil nature in respect of which there is a valid arbitration agreement) constitute their substantive competence.

Substantive competence of arbitral tribunals (jurisdiction) is the relationship between the powers of arbitrators and the object of their activities. Taken in isolation from other legal mechanisms, this relationship does not allow one to draw an unambiguous conclusion about the suitability of a legal case to arbitration. Arbitration is an element of a complex single system of dispute resolution, an important component in the system of civil jurisdiction. That is why the institute of *subject-matter jurisdiction* (*'podvedomstvennost'*) acting across and influencing various areas of law is used to regulate the relations arising in connection with the referral of disputes to arbitration. As noted by Professor Osipov, the institute of subject-matter jurisdiction in the legal regulation of societal relations plays the role of a distributive mechanism through which the state ensures the direction of various legal cases to the appropriate

1. Zykov R., *International Arbitration in Sweden: Law and Practice*, 105 (Moscow, 2014) [Zykov R.O. Myejdunarodnyi arbitraj v Shvyecii. M., 2014. S. 105].
2. *Ibid*. 112.

forms of their resolution in accordance with the nature of those social relations from which such cases arise.[3]

The subject-matter jurisdiction of arbitration is the range of legal disputes the resolution of which is the responsibility of arbitral tribunals. As O. Skvortsov correctly pointed out, since arbitration is included in the jurisdictional system of the Russian Federation as a mechanism of protecting individual rights, one of the main institutes of law apportioning and defining the competence of arbitral tribunals in resolving civil disputes is the institute of subject-matter jurisdiction. In a complex structured system where different bodies resolve disputes of the same nature (civil-law disputes), a single procedural institution is needed that would ensure the distribution of cases between various parts of such a system and would prevent duplication of functions.[4] We are convinced that the institute of subject-matter jurisdiction acting across the different areas of law can and should be utilised to distribute cases to their correct procedural paths, including arbitration.

In practical terms, what is the relationship between the categories of 'competence of arbitration' and 'subject-matter jurisdiction of arbitration'? The main difference is that competence and subject-matter jurisdiction characterise the relationship between the power to handle disputes and its object in different ways. If the objective competence describes this relationship from the point of view of a subject wielding the relevant powers, subject-matter jurisdiction deals with the position of their object.[5] Thus, the objective competence characterises the relationship between the arbitral authority and the object of their activities from the point of view of its subject (the arbitral tribunal), and subject-matter jurisdiction – from the vantage point of its object (cases transferred to the arbitration in a prescribed manner).

The subject-matter jurisdiction is one of the juridical conditions necessary for the right to initiate arbitration to exist. Unlike subject-matter jurisdiction, arbitrability is not an independent condition that leads to the emergence of a right to submit a dispute to arbitration, and only as an integral element of subject-matter jurisdiction, it becomes a legal fact in a particular legal structure. In the system of the current legal regulation in Russia, arbitrability (as legal suitability of disputes for arbitration) can only be considered as an element of the mechanism of subject-matter jurisdiction.

As a legal mechanism, subject-matter jurisdiction is a system of rules with a single purpose and functional integrity that specifies the algorithm for the determination of authorities competent to resolve legal cases. The purpose of the institution of subject-matter jurisdiction is to distribute cases between jurisdictional bodies and to establish the order and conditions of such distribution. In this sense, subject-matter jurisdiction is a purely practical and functionally integrated institution. The public nature of subject-matter jurisdiction largely derives from its application across the different areas of law.

3. Osipov Yu., *Jurisdiction of Legal Affairs*, 121 (Sverdlovsk, 1973) [Osipov Yu.K. Podvyedomstvyennost yuridichyeskih dyel. Svyerdlovsk, 1973. S. 121].
4. Skvortsov O.Yu., *Arbitration of Commercial Disputes in Russia: Problems, Trends, Prospectives*, 382 (Moscow, 2005) [Skvortsov O.Yu. Tryetyeiskoye razbiratyelstvo pryedprinimatyelskih sporov v Rossii: problyemy, tyendyencii, pyerspyektivy. M., 2005. S. 382].
5. Osipov Yu., *supra* note 3, 7-18.

The subject-matter jurisdiction of both domestic and international arbitration is largely determined by *lex arbitri*. The system of legal rules governing the subject-matter jurisdiction forms the basis for the arbitral tribunal's competence to resolve disputes. Arbitral subject-matter jurisdiction denotes the range of legal disputes that the current legislation allows the parties to refer to arbitrators.

[C] Rules Governing the Subject-Matter Jurisdiction of Arbitration

The determination of the competence of arbitral tribunals to deal with particular categories of disputes is carried out by the legal rules comprising the institute of subject-matter jurisdiction, which ensures the integrity of the civil jurisdiction system. This mechanism operates by specifying certain criteria, depending on which particular cases are submitted for the resolution by certain jurisdictional authorities. In order to distribute civil cases between state courts and arbitral tribunals in a correct manner, one must ensure the coordinated, comprehensive application of the criteria.

In Russia, the competence of a domestic or international arbitral tribunal arises if the following criteria are present simultaneously:

(1) admissibility of referring the dispute to arbitration based on the nature of the disputed legal relationship;
(2) admissibility of referring the dispute to arbitration based on the identity of the participants in the case;
(3) the existence of a valid arbitration agreement;
(4) controversial nature of the case (only disputes may be referred to arbitration).

The first of these criteria is the admissibility of referring the dispute to arbitration based on the nature of the disputed legal relationship. This criterion is often helpful in distributing cases between arbitral tribunals and state courts. The admissibility of submitting the case to arbitration, based on the nature of the disputed legal relationship is the so-called objective arbitrability. For instance, the parties may agree to refer to international commercial arbitration the disputes between the parties arising out of civil-law relationships in the course of carrying out foreign trade and other types of international economic relations, if the place of business of at least one of the parties is abroad, or any place where a substantial part of the obligations out of the relationship of the parties is to be performed or the place with which the subject matter of the dispute is most closely connected are located abroad.

The reference to the civil nature of the dispute as a criterion determining the availability of arbitration as a method of its resolution means that the current legal regulation does not allow the parties the submit to arbitration the disputes arising from administrative and other public legal relations. Likewise, cases considered within a special procedure and lacking the traditional features of a legal dispute (such as the cases on the establishment of legally significant facts) are unsuitable for arbitration.[6]

Federal laws limit the range of disputes that may be submitted to arbitration. Disputes related to the protection of intellectual property, some categories of disputes arising on the securities markets, bankruptcy cases cannot be resolved by arbitration. Thus, the legislation excludes certain types of disputes arising from civil-law relations from the jurisdiction of arbitration.

The second criterion necessary for the case to become subject to arbitration is the admissibility of referring the dispute to arbitration based on the identity of the participants in the case. For instance, disputes may be referred to international commercial arbitration if at least one party's place of business is located abroad.

The validity of a dispute's transfer to arbitration, as derived from the legal status of the parties, is the subjective arbitrability. As Professor Yerpyleva rightly observed, subjective arbitrability is a product of both substantive and procedural legal capacity of a person.[7] It is often on this basis that cases are distinguished between arbitral tribunals and state courts, as well as between domestic and international commercial arbitration.

In Russia, as in many other countries, the law determines all the conditions for admissibility of cases for arbitration depending on the subject composition of the participants. E.g., economic disputes about the use and protection of natural medicinal resources, therapeutic areas, and resorts, as well as disputes related to compensation for damage caused to natural medicinal resources, therapeutic areas, and resorts, when the parties to the dispute are organisations and citizens-entrepreneurs, may be submitted to arbitration.

The second criterion applies only in conjunction with the objective arbitrability. It is fair to conclude that, as a rule, arbitrability is unaffected by the legal status of the participants in the proceedings, provided that the substantive relations between them are of a civil nature.[8]

Disputes may be submitted to arbitration only by agreement of the parties. The existence of a valid arbitration agreement between the parties is the main criterion determining the jurisdiction of the arbitral tribunal. It defines whether the case should be heard in arbitration or in state courts. Only a valid and enforceable arbitration agreement may be the basis for referring the case to arbitral jurisdiction.

And finally, the last criterion for the arbitral jurisdiction is the controversial nature of a case. Only disputed cases may be submitted to arbitration – disputes between the parties arising from civil-law relations, in the implementation of foreign trade and other types of international economic relations, disputes arising in connection with the implementation of foreign investments within the territory of the Russian

6. Ruling of the Constitutional Court of the Russian Federation of 26 May 2011 No. 10-P.
7. Yerpyleva N., *International Arbitration Agreements: Concept, Types and Grounds of Validity*, 2 Lawyer, 60 (2010) [Yerpyleva N.YU., Myejdunarodnyye arbitrajnyye soglashyeniya: ponyatiye, vidy i osnovaniya dyeistvityelnosti // Yurist. 2010. N 2. S. 60].
8. Skvortsov O., *Public Element to the Dispute and the Arbitrability*, 4 Treteysky Sud, 82-83 (2014) [Skvortsov O.Yu. Publichnyi elyemyent v sporye i arbitrabilnost // Treteysky Sud 2014. N 4. S. 82-83].

Federation or Russian investments abroad. Non-contentious cases, including cases on establishing facts of legal significance, cannot be resolved by arbitrators.

Thus, in Russia, for the purposes of the arbitration of internal disputes, arbitral tribunals have jurisdiction over disputes between legal entities and (or) citizens arising from civil legal relations in respect of which there is a valid and enforceable arbitration agreement, with the exceptions established by federal laws. International commercial arbitration may be used in cases in respect of which there is a valid and enforceable arbitration agreement between the parties arising from civil-law relations in the implementation of foreign trade and other types of international economic relations, if the commercial enterprise of at least one party is located abroad or if any place where a significant part of the obligations arising from the relations of the parties, or the place with which the subject of the dispute is most closely connected, is abroad, as well as disputes arising in connection with the implementation of foreign investments within the territory of the Russian Federation or Russian investments abroad.

§7.02 COMPETENCE OF THE ARBITRAL TRIBUNAL TO RULE ON ITS JURISDICTION

In Russia, the arbitral tribunal may rule on its own jurisdiction, including any objections with respect to the existence or validity of the arbitration agreement (Article 16 of the Federal law 'On Arbitration in the Russian Federation', Article 16 of the Law 'On International Commercial Arbitration'). This rule is known as the competence-competence principle (*Kompetenz-Kompetenz)*. The essence of the doctrine of *Kompetenz-Kompetenz* is as follows. The arbitral tribunal shall decide on its own whether or not it has jurisdiction to hear the dispute between the parties and may itself decide on the matter, including any objections to the existence or validity of the arbitration agreement.

The competence-competence principle limits the state's intervention in arbitration, prevents the courts from considering the issue of the competence of arbitration until it is resolved by the arbitrators themselves. The competence-competence principle is the rule of chronological priority. The arbitrators shall not be regarded as the sole but as the first persons to rule on the competence of the arbitral tribunal to deal with the parties' dispute.

In Russia, the right of the arbitral tribunal to rule on its jurisdiction is based on the legislative provisions, which gives arbitrators the opportunity to overcome pleas of invalidity of the arbitration agreement. The basic meaning of the competence-competence principle is that it allows the arbitral tribunal to continue its consideration of the merits of the case even when one of the parties has disputed the existence and validity of the arbitration agreement (as a basis for arbitral jurisdiction to resolve the dispute). The competence-competence principle has become an effective tool in the hands of arbitrators to counter ungrounded attempts to sabotage the proceedings. In the Russian Federation, the principle under consideration is consistently applied by state courts.[9] The rules of law and the algorithm of the conduct of arbitration participants in cases where they contest the competence of the arbitral tribunal have repeatedly been the subject of interpretation and explanation of the Russian higher courts.[10]

In general, a plea that the arbitral tribunal does not have jurisdiction shall be raised not later than the submission of the statement of defence. A party is not precluded from raising such a plea by the fact that it has appointed, or participated in the appointment of, an arbitrator. A plea that the arbitral tribunal is exceeding the scope of its authority shall be raised as soon as the matter alleged to be beyond the scope of its authority is raised during the arbitral proceedings. The arbitral tribunal may, in either case, admit a later plea if it considers the delay justified.

In Russia, the arbitral tribunal may rule on a plea that the arbitral tribunal does not have jurisdiction either as a preliminary matter or in a final award. If the arbitral tribunal rules as a preliminary question that it has jurisdiction, any party may request, within one month after having received notice of that ruling, the court to resolve the matter. A challenge of the decision that the tribunal has no jurisdiction is not allowed, and the parties have no judicial recourse against such rulings.[11] The parties whose arbitration agreement provides for the administering of arbitration by a permanent arbitration institution may exclude a possibility of judicial review of such decisions altogether by their direct agreement. While the jurisdictional challenge is pending before the court, the arbitral tribunal may continue the proceedings and render an award.

The competence-competence principle has two consequences, which are usually called positive and negative effects in the doctrine. 'The positive effect of the competence-competence principle is to enable the arbitrators to rule on their jurisdiction, as is widely recognised by international conventions and by recent statutes on international arbitration. However, the negative effect is equally important. It is to allow the arbitrators to be not the sole judges, but the first judges of their jurisdiction.'[12]

The right of arbitrators to rule on their competence is not absolute. It is obvious that granting of such a right by the state requires monitoring of its implementation. The bodies exercising such control are the courts. In no legal system is the right of arbitrators to determine their own competence outside the limits of judicial control. In common law countries, the arbitral tribunal's decision on its own powers may be subject to judicial review at any time after its issuance. In French law, judicial review of the arbitral award on its own jurisdiction is postponed until the final decision is

9. The Decree of the Commercial Court of the Moscow Circuit of 4 October 2018, case No. A40-74151/2018; the Decree of the Commercial Court of the Ural Circuit of 19 October 2017, case No. A50-3705/2017; the Decree of the Federal Commercial Court of the North-Western Circuit of 6 December 2012, case No. A56-57378/2011; etc.
10. The Decree of the Presidium of the Supreme Commercial Court of the Russian Federation of 3 November 2009 N 8879/09, case No. A40-47188/08-63-503; the decisions of the Supreme Court of the Russian Federation of 24 February 2015, 4 September 2017, 21 September 2018, etc.
11. The Decree of Commercial Court of the Moscow Circuit of 06 October 2017, case No. A40-62892/17.
12. Fouchard P., Gaillard E., Goldman B., *On International Commercial Arbitration*, 401 (The Hague, 1999).

rendered, which, in many respects, reflects the global trend of shifting the control of the court gradually to a later stage, to ensure the effectiveness of arbitration. In the Russian Federation, judicial control of the jurisdiction of the arbitral tribunal is also generally exercised in the proceedings for recourse against the final award or for the issue of a writ of execution for its enforcement.

In some countries, arbitrators are not granted the right to resolve the issues of its competence. Such a decision has to be made by the state courts before the commencement of the arbitration. This design allows for the implementation of the mechanism of preliminary control over the arbitration proceedings, which was not perceived in Russia. The protracted multistage procedure, focused on the involvement of state bodies, calls into question all the advantages of arbitration, and, above all, those related to efficiency and confidentiality.

§7.03 RUSSIAN CONCEPT OF ARBITRABILITY

Arbitration is a private method of dispute resolution by its genesis. At the same time, the right of the State to determine which cases can and cannot become the subject of arbitration on its territory is self-evident. The broad wording of the rules of law demands that courts and scholars create a legal mechanism to solve the issue of the admissibility of arbitral competence in each particular category of disputes.

Arbitrability can be considered a cornerstone of Russian arbitration practice. It gained prominence in the Russian legal doctrine during the last two decades. Its necessity for defining the objective competence of arbitral tribunals was explained by Professor O. Skvortsov. In his opinion, arbitrability is a narrower concept than subject-matter jurisdiction (*'podvedomstvennost'*); a legal mechanism that does not compete with its parent institution and is only one of the elements of the institution of subject-matter jurisdiction, ensuring the distribution of cases between different jurisdictional authorities (in our case, in the presence of certain conditions, holding that some categories of disputes belong to the jurisdiction of arbitration tribunals).[13] Modern Russian authors continue their research in this area.[14]

Arbitrability is the admissibility of the dispute's referral to arbitration. On the one hand, arbitrability is an opportunity, on the other hand, a limitation. Arbitrability is legal permission, a legal construct that provides freedom of action to participants of civil turnover to submit their dispute to arbitration for final resolution. Scholars usually start from the opposite end in the description of arbitrability – from the indication of which cases cannot be submitted to arbitration, i.e., which cases are non-arbitrable. The search for arbitrability goes as follows: from the general range of cases allowed to be submitted to arbitration (as a rule, these are economic disputes of a civil nature), for reasons of public order, disputes in which there is a 'sensitive' element for society are cut off. In common law countries, courts generally recognise certain categories of

13. Skvortsov O.Yu., *supra* note 4, at 386.
14. *See*, e.g., Minina A., *Arbitrability: Theory and Practice of International Commercial Arbitration*, (Moscow, 2014) [Minina A.I. Arbitrabilnost: tyeoriya i praktika myejdunarodnogo kommyerchyeskogo arbitraja. M., 2014].

disputes as non-arbitrable. In civil-law countries, exceptions from the scope arbitrability cases are usually fixed in the legislation.

The range of cases allowed for submission to arbitration is the result of coordinating private and public interests. Regardless of the country, arbitrable disputes always relate only to those rights that the parties are free to dispose of, so cases concerning the protection of inalienable rights cannot be submitted to arbitration.

It is obvious that the European and American approaches to arbitrability differ somewhat. In the European tradition, the arbitrability rules are a set of rules of national law based on public policy considerations that determine the admissibility for disputes to be resolved through arbitration. American experts traditionally rely on the non-arbitrability doctrine, which can be seen as an analogue to the legal construct of objective arbitrability. Thus, the non-arbitrability doctrine contemplates a peculiar, and limited, type of unenforceability of valid arbitration agreements. When an arbitration agreement is invalid for lack of consent, non-compliance with form requirements, duress, or mistake, then the agreement is invalid: the agreement is not binding or enforceable upon the parties in any circumstances. In contrast, the non-arbitrability doctrine provides that an otherwise valid arbitration agreement may not be given effect as applied to a particular 'dispute' or 'subject matter'.[15] In this sense, arbitrability is considered to be an external factor limiting the effectiveness of the arbitration agreement. Note that some scholars even consider arbitrability to be an element of the valid arbitration agreement.

Based on the subject matter of a legal case, arbitrability is legal permission that determines the possibility of its resolution by the arbitrators, as well as a general condition for recognising the competence of the arbitral tribunal to consider a dispute of a certain category. Arbitrability reflects the consent of the state to recognise the results of arbitration, which is formalised either by the legislator or by the courts. In this sense, arbitrability is a product of national law. Modern scholars put the question more broadly. 'It follows that arbitrability is a multi-faceted and multi-purpose concept which despite national origins has an international dynamic. It defines the classes of disputes that *may* be removed from the scope of arbitral reference and placed at the exclusive jurisdiction of given national courts.'[16]

In Russia, as in France, Belgium, Spain, many countries of Middle East, Africa, and Latin America, states that have adopted the UNCITRAL Model law, disputes are clearly divided into arbitrable and non-arbitrable. The touchstone in this legislation is often the distinction between claims that are, and those that are not, within the free disposition of the parties; or, in other words, between cases in which society's (the state's) interest in achieving a certain result is such that the rules established to advance this purpose cannot be overridden by an agreement between the parties (cases regulated by mandatory law), and those in which the state does not impose mandatory

15. Born G., *International Commercial Arbitration*, 769 (The Hague, 2009).
16. Mistelis L., *Arbitrability – International and Comparative Perspectives. Is Arbitrability a National or an International Law Issue?* 7, in: Arbitrability: International & Comparative Perspectives (L.Mistelis and S.Brekoulakis, eds, Alphen aan den Rijn, 2009).

rules.[17] It should be noted that the vague rules of law that allow arbitrating the disputes in respect of which the parties may conclude an agreement (such as in Belgium) or use other conciliation procedures, is not always convenient for practical usage.

Although not every legal system has stated in general terms that all disputes involving an economic interest are arbitrable, it is clear that matters which do not involve an economic interest are non-arbitrable.[18] The limitations of arbitrability primarily relate to the issues of implementation by the subjects of legal relations of rights that they cannot freely dispose of, as a rule, in cases arising in the areas 'sensitive' for the society (for example, at the sphere of antitrust regulation, intellectual property and corporate governance, bankruptcy).

It has been observed that 'restriction on party autonomy may be justified in *exceptional* cases and must not be the norm'.[19] At the same time, the right of the national legislature to outline the range of arbitrable, excluding disputes that affect the interests of the whole society and are 'sensitive' for the public order, should not be considered as the voluntary restriction of the parties' autonomy. It is in such cases that the will of the parties of the legal relationship is no longer absolute. The freedom of participants in civil turnover to choose a method of resolving their dispute ends where the freedom of others begins.

The admissibility of submitting certain disputes to arbitration, and, as a consequence, the recognition of the final arbitral awards in such disputes is primarily a decision of the national legislator, which is made taking into account the economic, political and social priorities of the State. As the Constitutional Court of the Russian Federation rightly pointed out, the implementation of the principle of autonomy of the parties (principle of dispositivity) does not affect the right of the federal legislator to determine – based on the need to ensure a balance between private and public interests – a list of types of disputes that can be submitted to arbitration, depending on their social significance, the current stage in the development of civil turnover and the socio-economic system as a whole, the maturity of the legal principles of market economy, legal culture and other factors, and to make changes to that list.[20]

It is evident that the purpose of limiting the range of arbitrable disputes is the protection of the public interest. The concept of arbitrability finds its origins in the mandatory rules of law that form the fundamental legal principles of highest imperativity, universality, social and public importance. They form the basis of the economic, political, legal system of the State, i.e., constitute the public order of the State.[21] In this aspect, arbitrability is a legal mechanism that ensures the protection of public interests both at the stage of the parties' choice of forum to protect their rights and legitimate

17. Varady T., Barcelo J., von Mehren A., *International Commercial Arbitration: A Transnational Perspective*, 220 (St. Paul, 1999).
18. Fouchard P., Gaillard E., Goldman B., *supra* note 12, at 339.
19. Mistelis L., *supra* note 16, at 4.
20. Ruling of the Constitutional Court of the Russian Federation of 25 May 2011 No. 10-P.
21. Kudelich E., *Arbitrability: Looking for a Balance Between Private Autonomy and Public Order*, 4 Zakon, 94 (2014) [Kudelich E.A. Arbitrabilnost: v poiskah balansa myejdu chastnoi avtonomiyei i publichnym poryadkom // Zakon. 2014. N 4. S. 94].

interests and at the stage of the decision about the inclusion of the final award into the national legal order.

In Russia, it is common to distinguish between objective and subjective arbitrability. Objective arbitrability relates to the nature of the dispute, determining the admissibility of resolving certain categories of cases through arbitration. Subjective arbitrability determines the possibility of concluding an arbitration agreement by some participants of civil legal relations. Some Russian authors also understand objective arbitrability as the possibility of concluding an arbitration agreement with respect to the subject matter of the dispute, and subjective arbitrability – as the ability of a party to conclude an arbitration agreement (which is considered to be an analogue of the procedural legal capacity).[22]

As well as in the rest of the world, arbitrability in a broad and narrow sense is distinguished in Russia. In a narrow sense, this term refers to the categories of disputes that can be submitted to arbitration. In a broad sense, the term 'arbitrability' refers to issues related to the existence and validity of the arbitration agreement, as well as the competence of the arbitral tribunal based on it. It should be noted that the broad meaning of the concept of arbitrability does not find many supporters among Russian lawyers and had been criticised.

Among other things, the mechanism that allows one to decide on the suitability of a particular dispute for arbitration is also a purely practical tool. Who and how determines the arbitrability of the dispute? First of all, it is the arbitrators resolving the dispute. They are the first to assess the arbitrability of the case taking into account the applicable law agreed by the parties. It is obvious that arbitrators must also take into account the rules on the arbitrability at the seat of arbitration (otherwise the award may be set aside by a local court), as well as the state in which the award is to be enforced. Recall that the purpose of the arbitrators is to make a valid and legally enforceable decision. The arbitrability of the dispute is also assessed by the courts. At the seat of arbitration, the courts shall examine whether a dispute may be the subject of arbitration when one of the parties to the arbitration applies to the court in spite of the arbitration agreement, when assisting the arbitral tribunal, as well as when considering applications for setting aside of arbitral awards. The arbitrability is also assessed by the courts when considering applications for recognition and enforcement of arbitral awards. Although the rules on arbitrability are addressed to arbitrators and courts, such rules should be taken into account primarily by the parties of a dispute when concluding an arbitration agreement.

Summarising the above, we must note that the arbitrability as defined by the subject matter of a legal case is legal permission that determines the possibility of its submission for the resolution to arbitration, as well as a general condition for the recognition of the arbitral tribunal's competence to resolve a dispute of a certain category. The arbitrability rules are a set of legal rules based on public policy

22. Yerpyleva N., *International Commercial Arbitration: Institutional and Regulatory Mechanism of Legal Regulation*, 1 Zakonodatielstvo i Economica, 42 (2011) [Yerpylyeva N.Yu. Myejdunarodnyi kommyerchyeskii arbitraj: institucionno-normativnyi myehanizm pravovogo ryegulirovaniya // Zakonodatyelstvo i ekonomika. 2011. N 1. S. 42].

considerations that determine the admissibility of a resolution of certain categories of disputes by an arbitral tribunal.

§7.04 DISPUTES TRANSFERABLE TO ARBITRATION

It can hardly be doubted that the substantial clarification of the arbitrability provisions is one of the most significant results of the Russian arbitration reform. The Federal law 'On Arbitration in the Russian Federation' (the Arbitration Act 2015) determines that only disputes between parties of civil legal relationships may be submitted to arbitration pursuant to the parties' agreement. Disputes which have arisen or which may arise out of administrative or public relationships, as well as non-contentious matters (e.g., the judicial establishment of facts) which do not satisfy the conventional attributes of a civil dispute and may not be submitted to arbitration.

Today in Russia, disputes arising from civil-law relations, falling within the jurisdiction of state commercial courts (in Russian transliteration, '*arbitrazh*' courts) and courts of general jurisdiction, in the presence of a valid arbitration agreement between the parties to the dispute, may be referred to arbitration. The determination of the range of cases suitable for resolution by arbitral tribunals in the Russian legislation is based mainly on the nature of the dispute (objective arbitrability).

Prior to the reform, both in theory and in practice, questions repeatedly arose about the correlation between the range of disputes the parties could submit to international commercial arbitration and to domestic arbitration. Currently, disputes between the parties to civil-law relations within the jurisdiction of commercial courts and courts of general jurisdiction may be submitted to arbitration, if there is a valid arbitration agreement between the parties of the dispute. Based on the nature of the disputed legal relationship, the general rules determining the admissibility of disputes for a referral to domestic arbitration and international commercial arbitration have become uniform. In Russia, the rules of objective arbitrability are the same for domestic arbitration and international commercial arbitration.

The Arbitration Act 2015 provides that disputes between the parties to civil relations may be submitted to arbitration by their agreement. According to the assessment of the Constitutional Court of the Russian Federation, 'the reference to the civil nature of the dispute as a criterion determining the availability of arbitration as a method of its resolution means that the current legal regulation does not allow the parties the submit to arbitration the disputes arising from administrative and other public legal relations. Likewise, cases considered within a special procedure and lacking the traditional features of a legal dispute (such as the cases on the establishment of legally significant facts) are unsuitable for arbitration. This limitation of the scope of jurisdiction of arbitral tribunals is related to the nature of civil relations, which is based on the recognition of equality of participants, inviolability of property, freedom of contract, inadmissibility of interference in private affairs, the need for unhindered exercise of civil rights, ensuring the restoration of infringed rights, their judicial protection'.[23] In addition, a number of federal laws specify the scope of arbitrable cases.

In determining the range of cases suitable for submission to international commercial arbitration, the legislator used the mechanisms of both objective and subjective arbitrability. Currently, the parties can refer to international commercial arbitration:

- disputes of the parties arising from civil-law relations in the course of foreign trade and other types of international economic relations, if the commercial enterprise of at least one party is located abroad or if any place where a significant part of the obligations arising from the relations of the parties, or the place with which the subject of the dispute is most closely connected, is abroad;
- disputes arising in connection with foreign investments in the territory of the Russian Federation or Russian investments abroad.

Civil-law relations the disputes out of which may be referred to international commercial arbitration include, in particular, relations on supply and exchange of goods, performance of works, rendering of services, carriage of goods and passengers, commercial representation, rent (leasing), sale of intellectual property rights or means of individualisation, construction of industrial and other facilities, licensing operations, investment, credit operations, insurance, joint ventures and other forms of industrial and entrepreneurial cooperation.

In cases provided for by international treaties of the Russian Federation and federal laws, disputes involving a foreign investor in connection with investments in the territory of the Russian Federation or Russian investments abroad may be submitted to international commercial arbitration. For example, disputes between the State and the investor related to the execution, termination, and invalidity of production sharing agreements may be submitted to arbitration (Federal law of 30.12.1995 No. 225-FZ 'On Production Sharing Agreements', Article 22). The Rules of the Maritime Arbitration Commission define a whole group of arbitrable disputes arising from contractual and other civil relations in the sphere of commercial navigation, regardless of whether the parties to such relations are subjects domiciled in Russia or abroad.

§7.05 LIMITS ON THE ARBITRABILITY OF CERTAIN DISPUTES

In Russia, federal laws may impose restrictions on submitting certain categories of disputes to arbitration. Non-arbitrability of disputes, as a rule, results from the specific features of the legal nature of the relations underlying them, the presence of public interest in them.

The Arbitration Act 2015 amended general provisions on arbitrability in order to define disputes capable of being referred to arbitration. Today all exceptions are

23. Ruling of the Constitutional Court of the Russian Federation of 25 May 2011 No. 10-P.

indicated with the utmost clarity at the procedural legislation. The cases listed below may not be submitted to arbitration:

(1) insolvency cases (bankruptcy cases);
(2) disputes on the protection of intellectual property rights with the participation of organisations carrying out the joint management of copyright and related rights, and disputes within the jurisdiction of the Intellectual Property Rights Court;
(3) cases arising from administrative and other public relations;
(4) cases concerning the refusal of official registration or evading the official registration of legal entities and individual entrepreneurs;
(5) cases concerning the establishment of legally significant facts;
(6) cases on compensation claims for a violation of the right to a fair trial within a reasonable time or the right to enforcement of a court decision within a reasonable period;
(7) cases on the protection of rights and legitimate interests of a group of persons (the Russian analogue of class actions);
(8) enumerated corporate disputes;
(9) cases relating to the privatisation of state or municipal property;
(10) disputes arising from relations of procurement of goods and services for state and municipal needs governed by Russian law;
(11) environment harm compensation claims;
(12) cases that according to the Code of Civil Procedure should be heard as special proceedings in the courts of general jurisdiction, including the establishment of legally significant facts, adoption, declaring an individual dead or missing, etc.
(13) disputes arising from family relations, including disputes arising from the management of children's assets or the assets of individuals lacking full legal capacity, by their respective carers, custodians and guardians, with the exception of cases concerning the division of common property between the spouses;
(14) individual employment disputes;
(15) disputes arising from the relations of inheritance;
(16) personal injury and death compensation claims;
(17) disputes concerning the eviction from living quarters.

Direct legal regulation of non-arbitrability is a great stride towards predictability of court practice development, a pledge for the uniform understanding of the arbitral tribunals' competence.

If objective arbitrability is based on the nature of the case, the subjective one is determined by the status of the parties to the legal relationship. It permits the conclusion of arbitration agreements by some participants of civil relations. Subjective arbitrability is the legal permission for the specified persons to submit disputes with their participation to arbitration, to conclude arbitration agreements for this purpose.

Subjective arbitrability, or arbitrability *ratione personae*, concerns, in particular, the entitlement of states and public entities to submit their disputes to arbitration.[24]

Who can submit disputes to arbitration in Russia? First, it is the subjects of civil relationships arising in the course of foreign trade and other types of economic relations. Second, it is foreign investors in matters related to the implementation of foreign investments in the territory of the Russian Federation, as well as Russian investors in connection with their investments abroad. Their legal capacity to submit disputes to arbitration is beyond doubt. Subjective arbitrability, in this case, has the character of general legal permission but remains a legal mechanism designed to protect public interests.

The conditions for the admissibility of a particular dispute to be resolved by the arbitral tribunal, depending on the composition of its participants, are determined by the law chosen by the parties. However, arbitrability is a criterion for the validity of an arbitration agreement. Therefore, the evaluation of subjective arbitrability takes *lex arbitri* into account.

Particular attention should be paid to the issues of subjective arbitrability in relation to the State or other public legal entities acting as a party in cases related to foreign trade and other types of international economic relations. In international practice, some entities have been found unable to submit their disputes to arbitration because of their special status or their special functions. First, this applies to states, authorities, and local municipal bodies, organisations performing certain public functions. It should be noted that the inability to submit their disputes to arbitration correlates with these functions. In this case, one can recall the rights that the parties cannot freely dispose of. Subjective arbitrability becomes a mechanism based on public policy considerations to limit the possibility of submitting disputes involving certain persons or organisations to the resolution in international commercial arbitration.

The legal capacity of public law entities and public law organisations is determined by their personal law, thus the subjective arbitrability is primarily determined by the relevant national legislation. However, issues of subjective arbitrability are also reflected in international agreements. For instance, the European Convention on International Commercial Arbitration 1961 to which Russia is a party confirms the capacity of public legal entities to participate in arbitration. In accordance with Article 2 of the Convention, [for the purpose of settling disputes arising from international trade], legal persons considered by the law which is applicable to them as 'legal persons of public law' have the right to conclude valid arbitration agreements.

Modern Russian legislation allows one to conclude, on the topic of subjective arbitrability, that the state and other public legal entities are capable of concluding valid and binding arbitration agreements when they are parties to investment disputes or cases related to the implementation of foreign trade and other types of international economic relations.

24. Fouchard P., Gaillard E., Goldman B., *supra* note 12, at 313.

§7.06 ARBITRABILITY OF CORPORATE DISPUTES

Much has been said about the arbitrability of corporate disputes in Russia.[25] The uncertainty of the previous legal provisions of the Commercial Procedure Code of the Russian Federation entailed the ambiguous approaches to their application. During the arbitration reform, the lawmakers clearly defined a list of corporate disputes which may and may not be submitted to arbitration. *In general, corporate disputes may be referred to arbitration but only to arbitration seated in Russia.* Corporate disputes' arbitration must be administered by a permanent arbitral institution which has adopted and duly published the special arbitration rules for corporate disputes. According to the law, corporate disputes are cases concerning the setting up of a legal entity, its management or participation in a legal entity which is a commercial organisation, as well as in a non-commercial partnership, association (union) of commercial organisations, other non-commercial organisation where commercial organisations and individual entrepreneurs participate, self-regulating non-commercial organisation.

The following types of corporate disputes in respect of the legal entity incorporated in Russia may be referred to arbitration:

- disputes relating to the incorporation, reorganisation and liquidation of the legal entity;
- claims by the participants for the recovery of damages caused to the legal entity (derivative action);
- claims by the participants for declaring transactions made by the legal entity invalid and/or for application of consequences of invalidity of such transactions (derivative actions seeking declaratory relief), as well as other claims of the participants in connection with the legal relations between the legal entity and a third party when participants are entitled to file such claims;
- claims related to the appointment or election, termination, suspension of powers and liability of existing and former CEOs, as well as disputes arising out of civil-law relations between the said persons and the legal entity in connection with the exercise, termination or suspension of powers of such persons;
- disputes arising out of agreements between the participants in relation to the management of the legal entity, including disputes arising out of corporate agreements (shareholder agreements);
- disputes related to the issuance of securities, including disputes concerning the challenge of resolutions of the issuer's management bodies, the transactions made in the course of the offering of mass-issue securities, and approval of reports (notifications) on the results of issuance (additional issuance) of mass-issue securities;
- disputes on challenging resolutions of the management bodies of the legal entity;

25. *See*, e.g., Pettibone P., *The Nonarbitrability of Corporate Disputes in Russia*, 2 Arbitration International, 263-274 (2013).

- disputes on the provision of information by the legal entity to the participants;
- other corporate disputes to which the legal entity is a party unless the applicable law provides otherwise.

It should be mentioned that, as before, some types of corporate disputes cannot be submitted to arbitration. These are:

- cases related to the exclusion (expulsion) of founders, members and participants from a legal entity;
- disputes about convening a general meeting of a legal entity's participants;
- cases related to actions of a notary public in the course of certifying transactions with the shares in limited liability companies' registered capital;
- disputes on challenging individual legal acts, decisions and actions (omissions) of state agencies, municipal bodies or legal entities authorised to act as a state agency and officials on matters related to disputes on the acquisition and buyout of outstanding shares by public joint-stock companies, and to acquiring of more than 30% of a public company's shares.

Other corporate disputes which have arisen between a legal entity and its participants may be submitted to arbitration if two conditions are fulfilled. First, the legal entity, all participants of the legal entity and the other person acting as a claimant or a respondent must conclude an agreement to submit the specified disputes to arbitration. Second, the arbitration should be seated in Russia and the proceedings should be administered by a permanent arbitral institution which has adopted the special arbitration rules for corporate disputes.

CHAPTER 8

The Arbitration Procedure

§8.01 PRINCIPLES OF ARBITRATION PROCEDURE

Russian law treats the principles of arbitration procedure as the basic postulates underlying the arbitral legislation.

Arbitration principles form a system that ensures the functioning of this institution. The system must be logically consistent and the principles must correlate with each other. Taken together, the principles must guarantee the stability of the system of arbitration and the consistency of the smaller institutions within it.

It has been pointed out in Russian literature that one should approach the principles with extreme caution, because 'hasty and unjustified expansion of their number could result in depreciation and erosion of this category that is crucial for the society and the law. But the decrease in the principles' reach and number will reduce the guarantees of judicial protection of the rights of organisations and citizens'.[1] This observation is valid and important for the system of general legal principles, as well as the principles of individual areas of law and particular legal institutions.

Adopting a statute, the legislator does not always stipulate the principles for the legal regulation of any particular social sphere. For example, the Provisional Rules for the Resolution of Economic Disputes by an Arbitration Tribunal that regulated arbitration previously did not contain any provisions that would define the principles of arbitration. There are no rules laying down the legal principles in the ICA Act 1993 either.

In the Arbitration Act 2015, the Russian legislator introduced the system of principles for the arbitration of domestic disputes in Russia.

1. Sherstuk V.M., *The New Provisions of the Third Commercial Procedure Code of the Russian Federation*, 4 (Moscow, 2003) [Shyerstuk V.M. Novyye polojyeniya tryetyego Arbitrajnogo procyessualnogo kodyeksa Rossiiskoi Fyedyeracii. M., 2003. S. 4]; Sherstuk V.M., *Development of the Principles of Commercial Procedural Law*, 9 (Moscow, 2004) [Sherstuk V.M. Razvitiye principov arbitrajnogo procyessualnogo prava. M., 2004. S. 9].

Russian legal scholarship sometimes draws little distinction between the principles of civil procedure and the principles of the arbitration procedure. This approach is incorrect. Some principles of arbitration, of course, coincide to an extent with the principles of civil procedure. However, neither the list of principles nor their content could allow one to claim that they are identical. The distinction manifests itself most clearly in the requirement of confidentiality in arbitration. In this sense, the arbitration process and the procedure in state court are direct opposites. The trial in a state court is open and public, whereas arbitration proceedings, as a rule, are non-public and confidential.

There is no unanimous view in the doctrine about the system of principles of arbitration. The legislator also is not consistent in defining the set of arbitration principles. Thus, the Arbitration Act 2002 contained a list of principles that differ from the system of arbitration principles in its modern understanding.

The current Russian statute provides that arbitration rests on the principles of independence and impartiality of arbitrators, the autonomy of the parties (dispositivity), adversarial proceedings, and equal treatment of the parties.

One must note that the system of principles in the Arbitration Act 2015 resembles closely those applicable to the determination of civil rights and obligations, which found their expression in Article 6 of the Convention for the Protection of Human Rights and Fundamental Freedoms of 1950 (ECHR). In this sense, the principles of dispute resolution rely on the trends of harmonisation, leading to the adoption of uniform standards across diverse legal orders.

Both Russian literature and court practice engage in the discussions about the list and extent of the principles of arbitration proceedings. In one judgment, the court identified the following principles of arbitration: non-public process, the informal nature of the proceedings, the simplified procedure for the obtaining and presentation of evidence, the lack of information about the awards, and the impossibility of their review on the merits.[2]

The lack of consensus on a common list of principles leads to the 'minimalist' approach of the legislator who is responsible for 'formalising' the principles by putting them in the statute books.

[A] Independence and Impartiality of Arbitrators

The independence of individuals resolving the dispute is a necessary condition that ensures the proper organisation of the process. Only being independent, such a person can remain impartial and thus ensure a fair and lawful resolution of the dispute. Political scientists and lawyers of many countries have long come to the unanimous conclusion that the principle of judicial independence is the cornerstone of great significance and the basis of any democratic state.

2. The Decree of the Federal Commercial Court for the Moscow Circuit of 7 November 2016, case No. A40-2650 / 2016. *See* also the letter of the Deputy President of the Supreme Court of 29 August 2014 No. 4-VS-3513/14 (published in: 5 Treteysky Sud, 20 (2014)).

Independence and impartiality of judges as the organising principle of the dispute proceedings are crucial for both the public litigation and arbitration and in this sense represent the general principle of the jurisdictional system. Although arbitration, by virtue of the Federal Constitutional Law 'On the Judicial System of Russia', is not part of the judicial system, its objectives generally coincide with the objectives of the state courts – the protection of violated or disputed civil rights through a fair, lawful and effective resolution of civil-law disputes. This results in the common policy framework for these activities carried out by sovereign and impartial decision makers, regardless of whether they are public or private judges (the arbitrators). At the same time, arbitrators are also subject to the requirements set forth in the European Charter on the Statute for Judges of 10 July 1998: judges must show, in discharging their duties, availability, respect for individuals, and vigilance in maintaining the high level of competence which the decision of cases requires on every occasion. This gives rise to the doctrinal conclusion that the concept of 'independence of the arbitrators' is analogous to the concept of 'independence of state judges'.[3]

The independence of arbitrators is enforced through a number of legal mechanisms. In particular, according to Article 56(3)(7) of the Criminal Procedure Code, an arbitrator cannot be questioned as a witness about facts which became known to him during arbitration. There are sufficient grounds to believe that an arbitrator cannot be questioned about the circumstances that have become known to him in the course of the arbitration proceedings, both in criminal proceedings and in administrative, civil, or commercial proceedings.

As neither international law nor the Russian legislation contains a definition of the concept of 'independence and impartiality of an arbitrator', the question arises about the criteria for deciding whether an arbitrator is, in fact, independent and impartial or not. The legislator leaves the interpretation of this concept to the discretion of a decision maker (typically, a court). According to Professor I.S. Zykin, 'this wording covers, among other things, the cases of arbitrator's personal interest (direct or indirect) in the outcome of the case, the familial relationship with a party or its representative, professional dependence on such persons, involvement in their business activities, and so on. The wording, therefore, covers largely the situations where a person is involved with the subject matter of the dispute or has a sufficiently close connection with the party or its representative. However, the circumstances may differ depending on the specific facts of every case'.[4] The author of this comment draws attention to the stretchable nature of the definition at hand.

3. Arbitration in the Russian Federation: the Textbook, 77 (O.Yu. Skvortsov, ed., Moscow: Wolters Kluwer, 2010) (author of the chapter – S.A. Kurochkin) [Tryetyeiskoye razbiratyelstvo v Rossiiskoi Fyedyeracii: uchyebnoye posobiye. / Pod ryed. O.Yu. Skvortsova. – M.: Wolters Kluwer, 2010. S. 77 (avtor glavy S.A. Kurochkin)].
4. *Commentary to the Law of Russian Federation 'On International Commercial Arbitration': Clause-by-Clause, Academic and Practical*, 62 (A.S. Komarov, S.N. Lebedev and V.A. Musin, eds, compiled by G.V. Sevastyanov, Saint Petersburg, 2007) (author of the commentary – I.S. Zykin) [Kommyentarii k Zakonu Rossiiskoi Fyedyeracii «O myejdunarodnom kommyerchyeskom arbitrajye»: postatyeinyi, nauchno-praktichyeskii. / Pod ryed. A.S. Komarova, S.N. Lebedeva, V.A. Musina / Sost. G.V. Sevastyanov. – SPb.: ANO «Ryedakciya jurnala «Treteysky Sud», 2007. S.62 (avtor kommyentariya – I.S. Zykin)].

The international legal community has made considerable efforts in its search for guidance in the determination of independence and impartiality. The first results emerged in the field of international arbitration. In 1987, the International Bar Association (IBA) published the Rules of Ethics for International Arbitrators, which laid down the approaches to these important concepts.

Consequently, the International Bar Association formed a working group of nineteen experts who produced the Guidelines on Conflicts of Interest in International Arbitration.[5] The IBA Council approved the Guidelines by its resolution in 2004. The Working Group considered that the promotion of greater consistency and avoidance of unnecessary challenges, arbitrator withdrawals, and removals could be achieved by listing specific situations and indicating whether they warrant the disclosure of information or disqualification of an arbitrator. This idea led to the adoption of three lists of hypothetical circumstances designated 'Red', 'Orange', and 'Green'. The Working Group developed the common standards and the lists relying on the legislation and judicial practice of various countries, as well as on the personal judgment and experience of the Working Group members and other international commercial arbitration stakeholders. The Working Group attempted to balance the diverging interests of the parties, their representatives, arbitrators and arbitral institutions, all of which have the responsibility for the integrity, reputation, and efficiency of international commercial arbitration.

Following the international example, the Rules on Impartiality and Independence of Arbitrators have been developed in Russia. They were approved by the order of the President of the CCI of 27 August 2010 No. 39.

However, the lack of clear ideas about the criteria of arbitral independence was noticeable within the Russian legal practice. In the end, it was not the representatives of academic theory but the judges of commercial courts who were actively engaged in the search for these criteria. This brought into being the so-called *objective impartiality doctrine*.

This doctrine has its historical roots. In modern Russia, up until the moment of its abolition, the Supreme Commercial Court (SCC RF) was the main 'overseer' of arbitration. This was because arbitration became most widespread in the field of the economic jurisdiction where this court was the main 'ideologist' of the law enforcement practice. The period from the early 1990s until the mid-2000s, despite all the complexities of arbitration's acceptance within the Russian jurisdictional system, was positive because the leadership of the commercial courts adopted a careful attitude to arbitration as a means of dispute resolution. The situation has changed dramatically in 2006 with the arrival of the new leaders of the commercial justice system.

The degree of distrust to arbitration by the official judicial authorities was so high that it led in 2011 to questioning de jure the constitutionality of arbitration, which de facto put into question their very existence. One must pay tribute to the balanced position of the Constitutional Court,[6] which to some extent managed to extinguish the

5. Russian translation of the Guidelines was published in the Treteysky Sud journal - *see* 2 Treteysky Sud, 33-52 (2008).
6. Decree of the Constitutional Court of 26 May 2011 No. 10-P.

heated debates. At the same time, the anti-arbitration approach in the practice of state commercial courts has not disappeared and has even become more radical.

One must admit that the activities of arbitration in Russia indeed gave rise to many difficult questions. However, these difficulties were an indicator not so much of any inherent defects in arbitration, as the very condition of Russian society. Faced with such a complex tangle of intertwined conflicts, the government had to find a way – if not to eliminate, then at least to minimise – the negative consequences of such activities of private jurisdictional entities. At a time when there were no specially designated authorities which would monitor the activities of arbitration, the state commercial courts, and especially the SCC of Russia, de facto assumed this function. Countering near-fraudulent arbitrations in the absence of a coherent legislative framework caused the doctrinal approaches to appear in the practice of the SCC RF that indicated the desire to squeeze arbitration out of the Russian jurisdictional sphere. One of the manifestations of the anti-arbitration approach was the creation of the doctrine of objective independence and impartiality of an arbitration tribunal. The forerunner of this doctrine was a perfectly sensible idea that an arbitration tribunal that hears a dispute should be free from any influence by the disputing parties.

The 'objective impartiality theory' evolved from the positions of the European Court of Human Rights (ECtHR). In particular, with regard to the state judges, ECtHR practice draws a distinction between objective and subjective impartiality. Objective impartiality is the visible, external impartiality that leaves no room for any doubt. Subjective (personal) impartiality is the personal attitude of the judge to the parties in a dispute.[7]

One of the consequences of the objective impartiality theory was the disappearance of a number of corporate arbitral institutions from the Russian jurisdictional sphere. The apotheosis of this line of jurisprudence was the Presidium of the SCC RF cases that declared illegitimate the awards of such arbitration centres as the Arbitration Court at the JSC 'Lukoil', the NGO 'Centre of Arbitration', the Arbitration Court at the OJSC 'Gazprom'[8] and some others.

From a formal legal point of view, the SCC RF attempted to formulate a theory of arbitral independence and impartiality that would provide clear criteria for eliminating any suspicions of partiality on the part of the tribunal. A central element of independence in the context of this doctrine is the so-called objective independence, which means the absence of any formal affiliation of the parties with the founders of the arbitral institution.

7. Rozhkova M.A., Glazkova M.E., Savina M.A., *Topical Problems of the Unification of Civil Procedural and Commercial Procedural Legislation*, 37-38 (M.A. Rozhkova, ed., Moscow, 2015) [*Rozhkova M.A., Glazkova M.E., Savina M.A. Aktualnyye problyemy unifikacii grajdanskogo procyessualnogo i arbitrajnogo procyessualnogo zakonodatyelstva. / Pod obsh.ryed. M.A. Rozhkovoi*. – M., 2015. S. 37-38].
8. The Decree of the Presidium of the Supreme Commercial Court of 24 May 2011 No. 17020/2010; The Decree of the Presidium of the Supreme Commercial Court of 22 May 2012 No. 16541/11; The Decree of the Presidium of the Supreme Commercial Court of 16 July 2013 No. 1567/13; The Decree of the Presidium of the Supreme Commercial Court of 29 October 2013 No. A40-147862/2012.

In the above cases, the SCC RF concluded that the principles of equality and autonomy of the parties had been violated, citing the fact that an organisation affiliated with a party (its parent company) established and funded an arbitration centre which dealt with the dispute. In turn, this led to a violation of the guarantee of impartiality. Thus, the SCC RF findings rely on the assessment of the relationship between a party to the arbitration and a founder of the arbitral institution. In turn, this assessment is based on assigning a particular degree of importance to such a connection. SAC believed that the relationship is so significant that it affects the independence and impartiality of the tribunal hearing the case.

The objective impartiality doctrine evolved over time in the judgments of the Supreme Court, and in its eventual form is embodied in a number of decisions of the Supreme Commercial Court, and thereafter the Russian Supreme Court (SC RF).[9]

The objective impartiality doctrine sparked a fierce controversy among the experts.[10]

---

9. The Decree of the Presidium of the Supreme Commercial Court of 24 May 2011 No. 17020/2010; the Decree of the Presidium of the Supreme Commercial Court of 28 June 2011 No. 1308/2011; the Decree of the Presidium of the Supreme Commercial Court of 22 May 2012 No. 16541/11; the Decree of the Presidium of the Supreme Commercial Court of 18 September 2012 No. 4011/2012; the Decree of the Presidium of the Supreme Commercial Court of 16 July 2013 No. 1567/13; the Decree of the Presidium of the Supreme Commercial Court of 29 October 2013 No. A40-147862/2012; the Decree of the SC RF of 24 February 2015 No. 304-ES14-495; the Decree of the SC RF of 19 March 2015 No. 310-ES14-4786; the Decree of the SC RF of 26 October 2015 No. 305-ES15-4679.
10. Sevastyanov G., *Permanent Arbitrations - Creation of a System of Trust!*, 1 Treteysky Sud 2013 [*Sevastyanov G.V. Postoyanno dyeistvuyushiye tryetyeiskiye sudy – sozdaniye sistyemy dovyeriya! // Tryetyeiskii sud. 2013. No. 1*]; Korchin A.A., *The Fight against 'Pocket' Arbitration and the Issues in the Russian Judicial Practice, the Independence and Impartiality of Arbitrators*, 1 Bulletin of International Commercial Arbitration (2013) [*Korchin A.A. Borba s «karmannymi» tryetyeiskimi sudami i voprosy nyezavisimosti i byespristrastnosti arbitrov v rossiiskoi sudyebnoi praktikye. // Vyestnik myejdunarodnogo kommyerchyeskogo arbitraja. 2013. No. 1*]; Skvortsov O.Yu., *Objective and Independent Arbitration: in Search of a Theoretical Framework*, 2 Treteysky Sud (2013) [*Skvortsov O.Yu. Obyektivnaya nyezavisimost arbitraja: v poiskah tyeoryetichyeskoi osnovy. // Tryetyeiskii sud. 2013. No. 2*]; Khvalei V.V., *On the Independence of Arbitration Institutions in General and the Russian Arbitration Association in Particular*, 5 Treteysky Sud (2013) [*Khvalyei V.V. O nyezavisimosti arbitrajnyh institucii voobshye i Rossiiskoi Arbitrajnoi Associacii v chastnosti. //* Treteysky Sud. *2013. No.* 5]; Skvortsov O.Yu., *The Doctrine of Objective Impartiality and Its Impact on the Practice of Arbitration*, 6 Treteysky Sud (2013) [*Skvortsov O.Yu. Doktrina obyektivnoi byespristrastnosti i yeye vliyaniye na praktiku tryetyeiskogo razbiratyelstva. //* Treteysky Sud. *2013.* No. 6]; Kurbatov A., *Arbitration Proceedings in Russia: Realities and Prospects* (Moscow, Yustitsinform, 2014) [*Kurbatov A. Tryetyeiskoye (arbitrajnoye) razbiratyelstvo v Rossii: ryealii i pyerspyektivy. – M.: Yusticinform, 2014*]; Skvortsov O.Yu., *The Objective Impartiality in the Context of Arbitration Theory*, 14(3) Bulletin of St Petersburg State University (2014) [*Skvortsov O.Yu. Ob obyektivnoi byespristrastnosti v kontyekstye tyeorii tryetyeiskogo razbiratyelstva. // Vyestnik Sankt-Pyetyerburgskogo univyersityeta. Syeriya 14: Pravo. 2014.* No. 3]; Skvortsov O.Yu., *New Trends in the Development of the Judicial Doctrine of Objective Independence in Relation to Arbitration*, 5 (95) Treteysky Sud. 2014 [*Skvortsov O.Yu. Novyye tyendyencii razvitiya sudyebnoi doktriny obyektivnoi nyezavisimosti v otnoshyenii tryetyeiskih sudov. //* Treteysky Sud. *2014. No. 5* (95)]; Fetyukhin M.V., *Commentary on the Decree of the Constitutional Court of the Russian Federation of 18 November 18 2014 No 30-P*, 6 Journal of Civil Procedure (2014) [*Fetyukhin M.V. Kommyentarii k postanovlyeniyu KS RF ot 18 noyabrya 2014 goda No. 30-P. // Vyestnik grajdanskogo procyessa. 2014. No.* 6]; Skvortsov O.Yu., *The Theory of Objective Impartiality: Assessment from the Viewpoint of Constitutional Principles*, 6 (96) Treteysky Sud (2014) [*Skvorcov O.Yu. Tyeoriya obyektivnoi*

Eventually, the Constitutional Court also addressed the issue.[11] The Constitutional Court pointed out that the principle of independence and impartiality of arbitrators is derived from the requirements to the judges of state courts. Therefore, the approaches to the fundamental guarantees of their activities should also be similar. Independence and impartiality requirements in both arbitration and state civil justice aim to ensure the right of citizens and their associations (organisations) to a fair hearing by an independent and impartial tribunal. The Constitutional Court noted that the independence of an arbitrator from the parties means, as a rule, the lack of an employment relationship between them (employee-employer, manager-subordinate), civil-law relations (debtor-creditor) and other legal relations (such as administrative, financial, or family). The specific legislative requirements to arbitrators ensure their impartiality: an arbitrator cannot have any direct or indirect interest in the outcome of the case and must be independent of the parties. This approach is consistent with the legal position of the Constitutional Court, according to which the absence of prejudice and bias on the part of judges is a prerequisite for a fair trial.[12] The Constitutional Court

byespristrastnosti: ocyenka s pozicii konstitucionnyh principov. // Treteysky Sud. *2014. No.* 6 (96)]; Sevastyanov G., *The Arbitration Reform in Russia: a Chronology of Major Events and Their Specific Content. International Commercial Arbitration and the Issues of Private Law* (Moscow, Statute, 2015) [*Sevastyanov G.V. Tryetyeiskaya ryeforma v Rossii: hronologiya osnovnyh sobytii i spyecifika sodyerjaniya. // Myejdunarodnyi kommyerchyeskii arbitraj i voprosy chastnogo prava. – M.: Statut,* 2015]; Skvortsov O.Yu., *Constitutional Court: Again the Objective Impartiality (Commentary to the Ruling of the CC),* 1(97) Treteysky Sud (2015) [*Skvortsov O.Yu. Konstitucionnyi Sud Rossiiskoi Fyedyeracii: vnov ob obyektivnoi byespristrastnosti (kommyentarii k opryedyelyeniyu KS RF). //* Treteysky Sud. *2015. No. 1 (97)*]; Skvortsov O.Yu., *The Doctrine of Objective Impartiality of the Arbitration Tribunal: End of an Era or the Beginning of a New Understanding?,* 2/3 Treteysky Sud (2015) [*Skvortsov O.Yu. Doktrina obyektivnoi byespristrastnosti tryetyeiskih sudov: konyec epohi ili nachalo novogo osmyslyeniya? //* Treteysky Sud. *2015. No. 2/3*]; Karabelnikov B.R., *The Supreme Court to Arbitration, 'Welcome, but Do Not Forget That There Is No Admittance',* 4 Bulletin of Economic Justice (2015) [*Karabelnikov B.R. Vyerhovnyi Sud – sudam tryetyeiskim: «Dobro pojalovat, no nye zabyvaitye, chto vhod vospryeshyen». // Vyestnik ekonomichyeskogo pravosudiya. 2015. No.* 4]; Skvortsov O.Yu., *Constitutional Principles and Objective Impartiality,* 14(2) Bulletin of St Petersburg State University (2015) [*Skvortsov O.Yu. Konstitucionnyye principy i obyektivnaya byespristrastnost. // Vyestnik Sankt-Pyetyerburgskogo univyersityeta. Syeriya 14: Pravo. 2015. No.* 2]; Karabelnikov B.R., *The Supreme Court on the Impartiality of the Arbitrators: There Are Questions and No Answer,* 12 Bulletin of Economic Justice (2015) [*Karabelnikov B.R. Vyerhovnyi Sud o byespristrastnosti arbitrov: voprosy yest, a otvyeta nyet. // Vyestnik ekonomichyeskogo pravosudiya. 2015.* No. 12]; Skvortsov O.Yu., *Main Trends in the Development of Arbitration in Russia (Doctrine, Law Reform, Litigation, the Practice of Arbitration, Education, Self-Regulation),* 4(100) Treteysky Sud (2015) [*Skvortsov O.Yu. Osnovnyye tyendyencii razvitiya tryetyeiskogo razbiratyelstva v Rossii (doktrina, zakonodatyelstvo, ryeforma, sudyebnaya praktika, praktika tryetyeiskih sudov, obrazovaniye, samoryegulirovaniye). // Tryetyeiskii sud. 2015.* No. 4 (100)]; Zaitseva A.G., *The Problem of Regulation of the Impartiality and Independence of Arbitrators in Russia,* 8 Universum: Economics and Law (2016) [*Zaitseva A.G. Problyema ryegulirovaniya byespristrastnosti i nyezavisimosti arbitrov v Rossii. // Universum: ekonomika i yurisprudyenciya. 2016.* No. 8]; Litvinova M., *Evaluation of Subjective and Objective Impartiality of the Judges,* 5 Corporate Lawyer (2016) [*Litvinova M. Ocyenka subyektivnoi i obyektivnoi byespristrastnosti sudyei. // Korporativnyi yurist. 2016.* No. 5]; Popova A.V., *Approaches to the 'Pocket' Arbitration,* 7 Arbitration and Civil Procedure (2016) [*Popova A.V. Podhody sudov k «karmannym» tryetyeiskim sudam. // Arbitrajnyi i grajdanskii procyess. 2016. No. 7*].

11. The Decree of the Constitutional Court of 18 November 2014 No. 30-P.
12. The Decree of the Constitutional Court of 25 March 2008 No. 6-P.

also indicated that in assessing the impartiality of the arbitrator, one must take into account his personal position on a particular case, as well as the objective criterion, namely the existence of links between the arbitrator and one of the parties or its representative. Proceeding on the assumption that a dependent arbitrator may also be biased, this approach allows one to question the arbitrator's independence from such a party or determine whether sufficient guarantees were in place to exclude a possibility of bias against the other side of a dispute. Summing up the reasoning, the Constitutional Court concluded that in order to find out whether a violation of the principle of impartiality had occurred, one has to focus on the impartiality of the tribunal members. However, this does not exclude the need to consider the organisational and legal ties between the arbitrator and the parties. This principle, expressed in a maxim that 'no one should be a judge in his own case', is one of the main components of the right to a fair trial under Article 6(1) of the ECHR.

Thus, in cases that require an assessment of the impartiality of the tribunal members, the courts should take into account the arbitrators' organisational and legal ties with the parties to the dispute, and the impact such links may have on the emergence of any, even the smallest, doubts about the particular arbitrator's impartiality. Where one cannot exclude even the smallest doubt as to the impartiality of specific arbitrators, including due to the organisational and legal ties with one of the parties, the principle of impartiality of the proceedings is under threat. The position of the arbitral tribunal will then depend on the second party, who can either agree with its competence despite such links, or object to putting its dispute before a body that is not objectively independent but has a potential flaw – the presence of a doubt as to the subjective impartiality of the arbitrators comprising this body.

[B] Autonomy of the Parties (The Principle of Dispositivity)

Autonomy of the parties (or the principle of dispositivity in the terminology of Russian law; hereinafter, this chapter will use the former expression) is one of the fundamental principles of both civil procedural law and arbitration. The essence of this principle lies in the empowerment of the disputing parties to dispose of their substantive and procedural rights as they see fit.

Professor A.T. Bonner defines the autonomy of the parties as a regulatory guideline of civil procedure, which determines the source and the driving mechanism of the procedure.[13]

From a theoretical point of view, the party autonomy principle is crucial for understanding the nature of arbitration as an alternative method of dispute resolution, where jurisdictional activity constitutes the core of the dispute settlement mechanism, but the parties and the decision maker can establish the procedural rules.[14]

---

13. Bonner A.T., *The Principle of Legality in the Soviet Civil Procedure*, 18-19 (Moscow, 1989) [Bonner A.T., Princip zakonnosti v sovyetskom grajdanskom procyessye. M., 1989. S. 18-19].
14. Valeev D.H., Zaitsev A.I., Fetyukhin M.V., *Commentary to the Federal Law of 24 July 24 2002 No 102-FZ 'On Arbitration in the Russian Federation' (Clause-by-Clause)* (Moscow, 2015) [Valeev

There is a close connection between the autonomy of the parties and the other principles of arbitration, which is conducive to the accomplishment of the goal of arbitral proceedings - the fair, full, and comprehensive investigation of all the circumstances of the case in the resolution of the dispute. Most experts consider the procedural autonomy of the parties to be an extension of the principle of autonomy in substantive civil law.[15]

Thus, the starting point for understanding the autonomy of the parties is seeing it from the standpoint of civil law, which defines it as freedom of the participants of civil relations to exercise their subjective rights (to acquire, enjoy and dispose of such rights) in their discretion, within the limits established by the law.[16] This concept found its expression in the legislation. Thus, in accordance with Article 9(1) of the Civil Code of the Russian Federation, citizens and legal entities exercise the civil rights belonging to them at their own discretion. The consistent development of this concept leads to the conclusion that the principle of autonomy of the parties is inherent in all contexts where the law needs to be applied, and the whole system of civil jurisdiction of Russia is the sphere of its application.[17]

However, the content of the procedural principle of autonomy of the parties is not the same as the substantive autonomy of the parties, although it does represent an extension (development) of the latter.

It would be equally incorrect to say that the principle of party autonomy is common for civil procedure and arbitration. Thus, A.I. Zaitsev considers that party autonomy should be viewed as a fundamental principle of arbitral procedure, which in turn is a species of civil procedure.[18] Along with other considerations, this approach allows one to treat arbitration as part of the civil procedural law, which also, in our view, does not reflect the legal nature and the relationship of these legal phenomena. One has to agree with A.G. Pleshanov, who believes that 'the characteristic of party autonomy as one of the principles of civil and commercial procedure that the legislator transplanted to the arbitral soil is imprecise. It does not contribute to a comprehensive study of autonomy in the framework of arbitration. If one puts the problem this way, all the research is reduced only to the identification and analysis of the manifestations

---

D.H., Zaitsev A.I., Fetyukhin M.V. Kommyentarii k Fyedyeralnomu zakonu ot 24 iyulya 2002 g. N 102-FZ 'O tryetyeiskih sudah v Rossiiskoi Fyedyeracii' (postatyeinyi). - M., 2015].

15. *See*, e.g., *Commercial Procedure: a University Textbook*, 34 (M.K. Treushnikov, ed., Moscow, 1997) (author of the chapter - M.K. Treushnikov) [Arbitrajnyi procyess: uchyebnik dlya vuzov. / Pod ryed. prof. M.K. Treushnikova. – M., 1997. S. 34 (avtor glavy M.K Treushnikov)].
16. Krasavchikov O.A., *Dispositivity in the Civil-Law Regulation*, 1 The Soviet State and the Law, 42 (1979) [Krasavchikov O.A. Dispozitivnost v grajdansko-pravovom ryegulirovanii. // Sovyetskoye gosudarstvo i pravo. 1979. No. 1. S. 42].
17. Anokhin V.S., *Commercial Procedural Law of Russia*, 55 (Moscow, 1999) [Anokhin V.S. Arbitrajnoye procyessualnoye pravo Rossii. – M., 1999. S. 55]; Pleshanov A.G., *Dispositive Elements in the Field of Civil Jurisdiction. Problems of Theory and Practice*, 110 (Moscow, 2002) [Pleshanov A.G. Dispozitivnoye nachalo v sfyerye grajdanskoi yurisdikcii. Problyemy tyeorii i praktiki. – M., 2002. S. 110].
18. A.I. Zaitsev, Dispositivity - a Fundamental Principle of Arbitration, 1 Treteysky Sud, 34 (2000) [Zaicyev A.I. Dispozitivnost – osnovopolagayushii princip tryetyeiskogo sudoproizvodstva. // Treteysky Sud. 2000. No. 1. S. 34].

of autonomy in arbitral proceedings, at best accompanied by the cataloguing of its particular features.[19]

We must emphasise once more: arbitration is not an element or a component of the civil procedure. The arbitration process is a complex independent legal institution that does not form part of the civil procedural law or commercial procedural law, though it is closely associated with them.

Researchers often considered party autonomy to be the leading principle of arbitration that occupies the most prominent position in the system of other principles.[20] Such an approach reflects the importance of this principle for arbitration. In procedural terms, the principle of autonomy allows the party, in its sole discretion, to exercise its procedural rights, including the right to waive any of them altogether. For example, the respondent is entitled to present to the claimant and the tribunal an answer to the statement of claim outlining its objections against the claim. However, the respondent is free to forego the presentation of its objections. The failure by the respondent to present its objection to the claim is not an admission of the claimant's demands. The autonomy in the respondent's behaviour, in this case, is guaranteed by the absence of direct procedural sanctions resulting from a choice to pursue any particular line of defence.

The principle of party autonomy manifests itself in a variety of legal structures set out in the legislation. For example, the tribunal might be interested in hearing a testimony of an expert witness in order to resolve its doubts relating to a particular area of knowledge. However, the parties are free to agree that they shall not seek expert evidence of this issue. One should bear in mind that all possible adverse procedural consequences of such a decision will fall to the parties because the tribunal will have to make a decision with an uncertainty pertaining to some important issue.

As far as the content is concerned, i.e., from the viewpoint of the number and range of procedural possibilities, party autonomy in civil procedure is narrower than party autonomy in arbitration. The broader autonomy in the arbitration proceedings, in comparison with the content of the 'civil procedural autonomy', is noticeable in various aspects of arbitration. For instance, in arbitration, the existence of the autonomy of the parties is obvious before the proceedings even begin. The parties are choosing not only arbitration as a method of dispute resolution, but also its form (institutional or ad hoc), the seat of arbitration; they select candidates for the tribunal,

19. Pleshanov A.G., *Dispositive Elements in the Field of Civil Jurisdiction. Problems of Theory and Practice*, 112 (Moscow, 2002) [Pleshanov A.G. Dispozitivnoye nachalo v sfyerye grajdanskoi yurisdikcii. Problyemy tyeorii i praktiki. – M., 2002. S. 112].

20. Pleshanov A.G., *Dispositive Elements in the Field of Civil Jurisdiction. Problems of Theory and Practice*, 111 (Moscow, 2002) [Pleshanov A.G. Dispozitivnoye nachalo v sfyerye grajdanskoi yurisdikcii. Problyemy tyeorii i praktiki. – M., 2002. S. 111]; A.I. Zaitsev, Dispositivity - a Fundamental Principle of Arbitration, 1 Treteysky Sud, 34 (2000) [Zaitsev A.I. Dispozitivnost – osnovopolagayushii princip tryetyeiskogo sudoproizvodstva. // Treteysky Sud. 2000. No. 1. S. 34]; Chung Hoang Hai, *Hearing and Resolution of Economic Disputes by Arbitration in the Socialist Republic of Vietnam: Abstract of the Doctor of Law Dissertation*, 17 (Moscow, 2002) [Chung Hoang Hai. Razbiratyelstvo i razryeshyeniye v tryetyeiskom poryadkye hozyaistvyennyh sporov v Socialistichyeskoi Ryespublikye Vyetnam: Avtoryef. diss. ... kand. yurid. nauk. – M., 2002. S. 17]; Tarasov V.N., The Arbitral Process. Textbook, 50 (St Petersburg, 2002) [Tarasov V.N. Tryetyeiskii procyess. Uchyebnoye posobiye. – SPb., 2002. S. 50].

define the rules of arbitration, and so forth. Such possibilities are not available in the civil procedure where the litigants, despite relying on the principle of autonomy, do not have the same range of possibilities in defining their own procedural rights and obligations.

At the same time, autonomy in arbitration differs from autonomy in civil proceedings, not only in terms of the number of options available to the parties in the process. The difference is also qualitative. The parties are free to determine the rules of arbitration, setting such rules of dispute resolution that the current legislation does not envision. In general, the arbitration law does not formally limit the parties in their choice of arbitration rules. This, of course, does not mean that the party-made procedural rules can be contrary to the law or the essence of arbitration. But the legislation does not set a specific framework for the parties' choice of the rules of arbitration. In civil procedure, the legislative framework always limits the autonomy of the parties. Thus, the restrictions on party autonomy in civil proceedings are always formalised, whereas, in arbitration, the limits of autonomy arise not so much from the formal legal framework, as from the essential principles of the arbitration process, which the implementation of one of its principles cannot contradict.

The qualitative difference between arbitration and civil procedure also manifests itself in the comparison between an arbitration agreement and a prorogation agreement. The difference here is that the parties in arbitration are free to conclude such arbitration agreements that contain clauses on jurisdiction; they can select any arbitral institution and any tribunal or constitute an entirely new one, which would come into existence exclusively by virtue of the agreement. The litigants in civil procedure do not enjoy similar freedom when they enter into a prorogation agreement. In addition, the civil procedural law imposes other limitations on prorogation agreements. First, the parties have a limited choice between the state courts that are in existence on the date of the agreement. Second, the procedural law only allows the parties to alter the general territorial jurisdiction (Article 35 of the Commercial Procedure Code, Article 28 of the Code of Civil Procedure) and alternative jurisdiction (Article 36 of the Commercial Procedure Code, Article 29 of the Code of Civil Procedure). It is impossible to change by agreement the competence to resolve the disputes in the enumerated categories (Article 34 of the Commercial Procedure Code and Articles 23-27 of the Code of Civil Procedure) and the exclusive territorial jurisdiction (Article 38 of the Commercial Procedure Code and Article 30 of the Code of Civil Procedure).

The broader autonomy of the parties in arbitration, compared to civil justice, is also noticeable in certain procedural aspects. For state courts, the legislator often establishes mandatory rules that do not provide litigants with any discretion in the process, while the parties themselves resolve similar issues in the arbitration. A pertinent example is the language of the proceedings. The commercial court procedure operates under the mandatory rule that the proceedings in all commercial courts must be in Russian (Article 12 of the Commercial Procedure Code). In general civil courts, the proceedings are conducted in the Russian language – the official language of the Russian Federation, or in the official language of the Republic within the Russian Federation where the relevant court is located (Article 9 of the Code of Civil Procedure).

At the same time, in arbitration, the parties are free to agree to any language of the proceedings at their joint discretion.

It is important that the parties are free to determine the range of evidence to use in arbitral proceedings – to admit only the written or only the oral evidence; to exclude certain types of evidence; to determine the range of admissible evidence. Although the arbitral tribunal can conclude that the evidence is insufficient, and has the right to invite the parties to submit additional evidence, such an invitation by the tribunal is not binding for the claimant and respondent. In civil proceedings, the parties are not entitled to limit the range of evidence that can serve as a basis for a judgment (though, of course, they can refrain from presenting certain evidence to the court, thus taking on the risk of adverse procedural consequences). Courts of general jurisdiction and commercial courts will proceed on the premise that any information about the facts relevant for the proper resolution of the case and obtained in a manner prescribed by the law is admissible as evidence. If the parties in civil or commercial procedure enter into an agreement depriving certain evidence of their status and admissibility, such an agreement will be invalid as contrary to the legislation.

In some of its manifestations, party autonomy in arbitration is similar to the procedural instruments that embody the autonomy in civil and commercial court procedure. For example, in both arbitration and civil proceedings, the claimant (plaintiff) determines who shall be the respondent or respondents (defendants), formulates the claim, reduces or increases the quantum of the claim, decides which facts are material for the claim and presents the relevant evidence before the decision maker.

Thus, the autonomy of the parties is not a common principle for civil (commercial) and arbitration procedure. It would be more precise to say that the autonomy of the parties in arbitration and the autonomy of the parties in civil procedure are the eponymous principles.[21]

[C] Adversarial Character of the Proceedings

The procedural principle that requires the proceedings to be adversarial, just like the autonomy of the parties, has its origins in substantive law. The scholars have pointed out that 'the adversarial character of the proceedings as a guiding principle arises from

21. It is interesting to note in this regard that, during the period when arbitration in the Soviet legal system was not considered as a judicial authority, Professor A.T. Bonner, speaking about the effect of the principle of autonomy for the resolution of disputes in arbitration, came to the same conclusion. He also noted that party autonomy in arbitration has the same name as party autonomy in civil proceeding, but these principles do not coincide and have different content. *See* A.T. Bonner, *The Principle of Dispositivity in Soviet Civil Procedural Law*, 3-4 (Moscow, 1987) [Bonner A.T. Princip dispozitivnosti sovyetskogo grajdanskogo procyessualnogo prava. – M., 1987. S. 3-4].

the opposition of the parties' substantive interests. This competitive element predetermines the adversarial form of civil proceedings'.[22]

This view relating to civil proceedings is equally applicable to arbitration. The driving force of the arbitration process is the conflicting substantive interests of the parties.

However, the implementation of the adversarial principle in arbitration differs somewhat from the way in which it is implemented in the civil and commercial procedure. The reason is that, whereas the adversarial form of civil procedure is predominantly underpinned by legislative provisions, in arbitral proceedings it is the institutional and ad hoc rules, as well as the parties' contracts, that act as a normative source of the adversarial principle.

The adversarial principle finds its expression in arbitration proceedings through various legal mechanisms. One central rule of evidence is that each party must prove the circumstances on which it relies as a basis for its claims and objections. This fundamental requirement shapes the allocation of the burden of proof in the arbitration process. Both parties are involved in the examination of the evidence, can express their views on any piece of evidence, and put forward their own opinion on all matters arising in the course of the proceedings. The same is enshrined in the civil proceedings as well. However, in the civil and commercial process, the law regulates the process of proof within a rigid procedural framework. The parties can only use the types of evidence that procedural law allows. A fact proved otherwise than according to the procedural legal regulations cannot form the basis for a judicial decision of a state court in civil or commercial proceedings. In arbitration, the parties can establish their own rules of evidence, as long as such rules do not directly contradict the law. The parties are free to determine which forms of evidence will be admissible, including such forms that are unknown to civil procedural law. For example, claimant and respondent have the right to agree on a particular manner of presenting evidence, the rules to govern the relevance of evidence, shifting the burden of proof to one of the parties, the requirements to evidence, presumptions and *res judicata*, and so on.

In arbitration, the adversarial principle takes more radical forms than in civil procedure. Despite the competing theories of adversarial proceedings, it is common in the legal doctrine to recognise that 'pure' adversarial proceedings could not, or should not, exist in civil justice.[23]

In the Russian civil and commercial procedure, the legislator has left the state court certain powers to influence the development process and thus to some extent limit the adversarial nature of a trial. For example, the court plays an active role in investigating and determining the material facts that will be the subject of proof in the case. The court has the right to determine which circumstances are relevant to the case,

22. Shishkin S.A., *The Adversarial Element in Civil and Commercial Procedure*, 97 (Moscow, 1997) [Shishkin S.A. Sostyazatyelnost v grajdanskom i arbitrajnom sudoproizvodstvye. – M., 1997. S. 97].
23. Shishkin S.A., *Adversarial Element in Civil and Commercial Proceedings*, 73 (Moscow, 1997) [Shishkin S.A. Sostyazatyelnost v grajdanskom i arbitrajnom sudoproizvodstvye. – M., 1997. S. 73].

which party must prove them, even if none of the parties referred to these circumstances (Article 56(2) of the Code of Civil Procedure). Of course, this kind of authority of the affects competitiveness in the civil process, limiting it to a certain extent. An arbitral tribunal, on the other hand, does not have procedural powers to influence the development of the process without the mutual consent of the participants in the process. Placing the burden of proof on the parties and relieving the court of this duty means that 'the parties who present evidence become the masters of evidentiary material. This results in their ability to narrow down the sources of knowledge and methods of the court's inquiry into the disputed legal relations of the parties. The parties' dominance over the evidentiary material derives from their freedom to dispose of all the procedural means to protect an individual right, which has its roots in the substantive private law.[24]

Thus, the adversarial principle in arbitration exists in much 'purer' forms, free from the influence of the 'investigative' element that in some degree is characteristic to the civil and commercial procedure. An infringement of the adversarial principle by arbitral tribunal can have serious legal consequences. One such infringement that occurs often in practice is the lack of due notice about the appointment of arbitrators or the start of arbitration proceedings, which deprives the party of its opportunity to present its case. This infringement occurs where the arbitral tribunal does not follow the rules of notification established by the agreement of the parties, institutional rules or the law.

Another frequent practical situation that has a potential to infringe the adversarial principle is where the tribunal fails to give due consideration to the fact that a duly notified party 'was otherwise unable to present its case'. Professor V.A. Musin gives one example of such violation of the adversarial principle: 'The refusal of the tribunal to grant one of the parties' request, sent at once after receiving the notice of the hearing date, to adjourn the hearing to a later date because the applicant would within a certain time obtain a document of considerable importance for the case.'[25]

[D] Equal Treatment of the Parties

The principle of equal treatment of the parties in arbitration proceedings follows from Article 19 of the Russian Constitution.

The previous legislation referred to 'equality' or 'equal rights of the parties' in arbitration proceedings. Thus, the Provisional Rules for the Resolution of Economic Disputes by an Arbitration Tribunal provided that the resolution of disputes by an arbitration tribunal must proceed on the principle of equality of the parties. Each side

24. Ferentz-Sorotsky A.A., *Some principles of the Commercial Procedure*, Code-info, 53 (July-August 2004) [Ferentz-Sorotsky A.A. O nyekotoryh principah arbitrajnogo procyessa. // Kodyeks-info. 2004. Iyul-avgust. S. 53].
25. Musin V.A., *On the Relationship between Arbitration and Commercial Courts*, 1(25) Arbitration Disputes, 100 (2004) [Musin V.A. O vzaimootnoshyeniyah arbitrajnyh i tryetyeiskih sudov. // Arbitrajnyye spory. 2004. No. 1 (25). S. 100].

should have an equal opportunity to present its position and protect its rights (Article 9). The same principle was enshrined in the Arbitration Act 2002.

Naturally, this principle had to be enshrined in the new legislation on arbitration. In the Arbitration Act 2015, it received a new name – the principle of equal treatment of the parties.

The principle of equal treatment of the parties is as fundamental as the other principles discussed above. The principle of the equality of citizens in all areas of public and social life is so significant that in a generalised form it is enshrined in the Constitution, i.e., it is a constitutional principle. The equality of citizens is ensured regardless of origin, social status, language, race, gender, nationality, place of residence, religious beliefs, property, and official status. With regard to legal persons, the principle of equality reflects in the fact that they are all equal before the law regardless of the place of incorporation, legal form, activities, ownership, affiliation, and other circumstances.

The legal literature recognises the multidimensional legal content of the principle of equality, at the same time highlighting one of its aspects: 'it is forbidden for the legislative and other rule-making state authorities to establish an unequal legal framework for the different subjects in similar or virtually identical circumstances'.[26] But there are, of course, many other aspects of the principle of equality. Among other things, it would be important to emphasise the prohibition of unequal treatment in the law enforcement practice and in the application of the law.

The principle of equality finds its expression in the protection of civil rights generally, and in arbitration in particular. The equality of participants of civil relations is twofold. It involves, first, the recognition of their equal substantive and procedural rights and, second, the provision of equal opportunities to them for seeking protection in arbitration. Thus, the principle of equality of the parties in arbitration is a necessary guarantee for the establishment of the truth in cases considered by arbitral tribunals and for the rendering of lawful, correct, and just awards.

One aspect of equality is the prohibition for any of the parties to obtain procedural advantages over its opponent. None of the parties should be burdened by additional procedural obligations or put into a more advantageous position by additional procedural rights, just as none of the parties can be exempt from fulfilling its procedural duties. A variety of procedural structures conveys the same idea. For example, each party has an equal right to provide evidence as well as to participate in its assessment. Each side should have equal opportunity to present its position and protect its rights and interests.

In addition, the principle of equal treatment of the parties is reflected in the fact that the consideration and resolution of disputes by an arbitral tribunal takes place in a single procedural order, established either by the law or by an agreement. In the event

26. Hajiyev G.A., Constitutional Principles of Market Economy (the Development of Civil Law in the Decisions of the Constitutional Court), 131 (Moscow, 2002) [Hajiyev G.A. Konstitucionnyye principy rynochnoi ekonomiki: (Razvitiye osnov grajdanskogo prava v ryeshyeniyah Konstitucionnogo Suda Rossiiskoi Fyedyeracii). – M., 2002. S. 131].

that one of the parties in the arbitration agreement waives its procedural rights, the relevant provisions of the arbitration agreement should be considered invalid.

Infringement of the principle of equal treatment of the parties can be a ground for setting aside of an arbitral award or refusal to recognise and enforce it.[27]

[E] The Principle of Confidentiality

Whereas the previous legislation treated confidentiality as a principle of arbitration proceedings, the current regulation declined to consider it as a fundamental principle. However, the Arbitration Act 2015 does contain provisions on confidentiality.

The legal doctrinal literature often refers to confidentiality as one of the key principles of commercial arbitration. In the discussions of the benefits of international commercial arbitration, one frequently encounters a view that the possibility of closing the proceedings for outsiders is one of its central advantages. Indeed the importance of confidentiality to arbitration can hardly be overestimated. Entrepreneurs often refer their disputes to international commercial or domestic arbitration and not to the state courts precisely because they prefer the public not to know about their disagreements with their commercial partners. Resolution of commercial disputes *in camera* is an important advantage of commercial arbitration over state courts.

Meanwhile, the legislation does not contain the rules guaranteeing the principle of confidentiality in arbitral proceedings. There are no such rules in the UNCITRAL Model Law; there is none in the Russian ICA Act 1993, either.

Many institutional arbitration rules contain provisions on the principle of confidentiality of the proceedings.

The concept of confidentiality has several aspects. First, confidentiality means the closed character of the consideration of disputes by international commercial arbitration. Second, confidentiality entails the system of guarantees for the members of the arbitral tribunal dealing with the dispute.

One of the goals that confidentiality helps to achieve is the protection of arbitrators from the possible influence of the public authorities. Such danger may arise, in particular, in criminal and administrative investigations into the circumstances that were considered in a case before the arbitral tribunal. Some jurisdictions prohibit questioning the arbitrators in criminal investigations about the circumstances that became known to them in the course of arbitral proceedings. The Criminal Procedure Code of the Russian Federation contains such a rule. In addition, an arbitrator cannot be questioned about the circumstances that became known to him in the course of resolving a dispute in administrative and civil proceedings as well (Article 21(3) of the Arbitration Act 2015).

The prohibition on the disclosure of information obtained in the course of arbitral proceedings applies not only to the arbitrators, but also to other persons assisting the arbitral proceedings – rapporteurs, executive secretaries of the permanent arbitral institutions, interpreters, and so on. The same prohibition applies also to both parties

27. The Decree of the Presidium of the SCC RF of 20 July 2010 No. 4325/2010.

in arbitration. It seems reasonable to suggest that an infringement of confidentiality principle is actionable and may lead to a recovery of damages.

At the same time, the implementation of the principle of confidentiality of arbitral proceedings has not been free of contradictions.

The Arbitration Act 2015 established the duty of permanent arbitral institutions, when considering a corporate dispute, to post on their Internet websites the information about the claims within three days of their receipt by the institution. This provision narrows down the content of the principle of confidentiality.

Another example of an internal conflict in the implementation of the confidentiality principle has been retained from the previous legislation. The parties do not always comply with arbitral awards voluntarily. Sometimes, the winning party has to go to the state court asking for assistance in its enforcement. Meanwhile, the procedure in state courts, according to the general rule, is public, open, and non-confidential. This significantly reduces the confidentiality the parties enjoyed in arbitration since the wider public becomes aware of the proceedings. Parties interested in shielding their dispute from the attention of third parties will have to justify the need for the *in-camera* proceedings before the state court. Typically, such a justification relies on the considerations of commercial confidentiality that the dispute involves. It appears that the changes to the legislation are necessary in this regard, which would provide that applications for setting aside and enforcement of arbitral awards should be heard in a closed court session.[28]

One must also note that while in international commercial arbitration, both legislation and court practice tend to uphold confidentiality, in investment arbitration there is a trend to reject confidentiality. Investment disputes, as a rule, involve a claim by a private investor against a sovereign state. Due to the public significance of such disputes, the rules emerge aiming to inform the public about their details. In particular, this trend has found its expression in the UNCITRAL Rules on Transparency in Treaty-based Investor-State Arbitration.

§8.02 DETERMINING THE RULES OF THE ARBITRATION PROCEDURE

The Arbitration Act 2015 limited the parties' freedom to determine the rules of arbitration, compared with the position under the previous legislation. The conservative principles that underpinned the arbitration reforms of 2015-2017, among other things, have produced this effect.

The general formula for determining the arbitration rules is as follows: subject to any legislative requirements, the parties are free to agree on the rules of the arbitration

28. *See* Skvortsov O.Yu., *The Principle of Confidentiality in Arbitration and its Relationship with Related Institutions of Public Law*, 4 Bulletin of St. Petersburg State University, Series 14: Law. 2014 [*Skvorcov O.Yu. Princip konfidyencialnosti tryetyeiskogo razbiratyelstva i yego sootnoshyeniye so smyejnymi institutami publichnogo prava. // Vyestnik Sankt-Pyetyerburgskogo univyersityeta. Syeriya 14: Pravo. 2014. No. 4*].

procedure (Article 19(1) of the Arbitration Act 2015). This rule follows the recommendation contained in the UNCITRAL Model Law on International Commercial Arbitration.

In addition, the parties may authorise the arbitral tribunal to determine the applicable law. Moreover, the parties are entitled to authorise the chairperson of the arbitral tribunal to resolve unilaterally the matters relating to the arbitration procedure (Article 32(1) of the Arbitration Act 2015).

The Arbitration Act 2015 introduced a new concept in the Russian legislation on arbitration agreements. Parties may now enter into a so-called direct agreement that will have priority over the institutional rules of arbitration. The parties have the right to make such agreements in enumerated cases, which concern the following:

(1) an arbitrator selection procedure that eliminates the possibility of resorting to the assistance of a competent court (Articles 11(4) and 13(3) of the Arbitration Act);
(2) a procedure for terminating an arbitrator's mandate (Article 14(1) of the Arbitration Act);
(3) a procedure for the tribunal's ruling on its own competence that excludes the possibility of recourse to the competent state court to challenge the tribunal's competence before and during arbitration proceedings (Article 16(3) of the Arbitration Act);
(4) hearing arrangements – an oral hearing or a procedure solely on the basis of documents (Article 27(1) of the Arbitration Act);
(5) the possibility of excluding the parties' right to challenge an award (Article 40 of the Arbitration Act);
(6) the possibility of limiting the selection of arbitrators to those included on the recommended list of the permanent arbitral institutions (Article 47(1) of the Arbitration Act).

§8.03 THE SEAT OF ARBITRATION

The choice of the seat of arbitration is crucial.

The seat of arbitration is regulated differently for institutional or ad hoc arbitration. The resolution of this issue has a number of legal consequences. Therefore, ideally, the parties should discuss the seat before signing their arbitration agreement.

It is a common misconception is that the seat of arbitration is the same as the location of an arbitral institution whose rules will govern the proceedings. The seat of arbitration and the hearing venue of arbitration do not necessarily coincide, either. The same applies to the place where an award is rendered.[29]

29. Musin V.A., *Some Procedural Matters Related to the Enforcement of Arbitral Awards*, 3 Arbitration Disputes (2006) [*Musin V.A. O nyekotoryh procyessualnyh voprosah, svyazannyh s ispolnyeniyem ryeshyenii tryetyeiskih sudov // Arbitrajnyye spory. 2006. No.* 3]; *International*

The Rules of a vast majority of international commercial arbitration institutions stipulate that the seat of arbitration may be in any state chosen by the parties or specified by the arbitral institution or the arbitral tribunal. Article 20(1) of the UNCITRAL Model Law contains a similar recommendation, stipulating that the parties are free to agree on the place of arbitration. In the absence of such agreement, the place of arbitration shall be determined by the arbitral tribunal having regard to the circumstances of the case, including the convenience of the parties.

The foregoing considerations apply equally to the choice of the seat by Russian arbitral tribunals. Article 20 of the Arbitration Act does not contain any mandatory requirements to conduct the arbitration in the same location as the permanent arbitral institution. According to this rule, the parties are free to agree on the place of arbitration or a procedure for determining it. In the absence of such agreement, the arbitral tribunal, taking into account the circumstances of the case and the convenience of the parties, will determine the place of arbitration.

Thus, the seat of arbitration in the proceedings governed by the Rules of a permanent arbitral institution may be different from the location of the institution itself. In this respect, the rules for determining the seat of arbitration are in contrast with the rules governing the proceedings in state courts, where, as a rule, the relevant general court or the commercial court will hear cases at its official location.

In ad hoc arbitration, the agreement of the parties determines the seat of arbitration. In the event that the parties have not determined the place of arbitration, the arbitral tribunal, taking into account all the circumstances, among which the convenience of the parties is paramount, will resolve this issue. Second, the selection of the seat should take into account the convenience of the arbitrators, the availability, and cost of ancillary services that the proceedings might require, the proximity to the object of the dispute, as well as the location of the bulk of the evidence. Other circumstances may also influence the selection of the seat if they help to ensure maximum efficiency and cost-effectiveness in the resolution of a dispute. Such additional circumstances may include the distance from the parties and the availability of a convenient transport scheme; availability of technology and administrative services; availability of qualified arbitrators that would satisfy the requirements of the parties; availability of qualified lawyers who can represent the interests of the parties in arbitration; the costs of the proceedings.

An indication of the seat of arbitration is an indispensable element of an arbitral award. This is because the place of arbitration affects the supervisory jurisdiction of a competent national court. An application to set aside an award must be submitted to the court at the seat of arbitration.

In permanent arbitral institutions, the general principle of determining the seat of arbitration is that the matter is governed by the Rules of that institution. However, this does not exclude the option of the Rules providing simply that the parties' agreement will establish the mechanism for determining the place of arbitration.

Commercial Arbitration: A Textbook. – (St Petersburg - Moscow, 2018, author of the chapter - A.I. Muranov) [Myejdunarodnyi kommyerchyeskii arbitraj: Uchyebnik. – SPb.-M., 2018 (avtor razdyela – A.I. Muranov)].

Some Russian authors suggested that a non-conformity with the rules on the seat of arbitration, like any other procedural violation, should be a sufficient ground for setting aside or refusal to issue a writ of execution to enforce the award.[30] This point of view seems incorrect. First, neither the Arbitration Act 2015 nor the procedural legislation contains such a ground for setting aside or refusal to enforce an arbitral award. Second, a violation of the rules on the place of arbitration can only result in annulment of the award or refusal to issue a writ of execution where such violations lead to one of the enumerated consequences. These consequences may include a failure to provide the losing party in arbitration with a due notice of the time and place of the hearing or the losing party's inability to present its case before the arbitral tribunal.

On occasion, courts have adopted a similar approach to the argument on 'violations' of the rules on the place of arbitration.[31]

§8.04 STAGES OF ARBITRAL PROCEEDINGS

The Arbitration Act 2015 defines the commencement of arbitration as the date when the claim is received by the respondent. The practical value of this rule is that the period during which the arbitral tribunal must resolve the dispute starts to run from this date. The law contains no provision that would oblige the arbitral tribunal to resolve the case within a certain period, but the Rules of permanent arbitral institutions usually contain such requirements.

The commencement of arbitration proceedings can also define other time limitations. For example, the rules of arbitration may provide for time limits within which the respondent must submit an answer to the claim.

This rule is not mandatory: the parties may agree to determine the commencement of arbitration in a different way. For example, the parties may enter into an agreement linking the commencement of arbitration to the receipt of the statement of claim by the permanent arbitral institution.

The procedure for registering the claim in arbitration, as well as the formal requirements to the statement of claim, is regulated in accordance with the traditions of the civil procedural law. However, as is characteristic of arbitration, some procedural aspects are left at the discretion of the parties.

According to Article 25(1) of the Arbitration Act, the claimant shall set out its demands in the statement of claim, which must be communicated in writing to the

30. RF Commercial Procedure Code 2002. The Official Text. The Arbitration Act 2002. Comments to the Law, 183-185 (Novosibirsk, 2002, author of the commentary – M.E. Morozov) [Arbitrajnyi procyessualnyi kodyeks RF 2002. Oficialnyi tyekst. Zakon o tryetyeiskih sudah v Rossiiskoi Fyedyeracii 2002. Kommyentarii k zakonu. – Novosibirsk, 2002. S. 183-185 (avtor kommyentariya – M.E. Morozov)].

31. *See* the Decree of the Presidium of the Supreme Commercial Court of 29 November 2005 No. 8660/05; the Decree of the Federal Commercial Court for the North-Caucasian Circuit of 8 December 2010, case No. A32-27122/2010; the Decree of the Federal Commercial Court for the Urals Circuit of 9 August 2012, case No. A07-4753/2011.

respondent, unless the parties agreed otherwise. The parties can agree on alternative forms and methods of submitting a claim, for example, in electronic form.

The requirements to the content of the statement of claim are also non-mandatory. The parties are entitled to determine the content of the statement of claim. If they have not done so, the statement of claim must meet the legal requirements, namely, include:

(1) date of the statement of claim;
(2) name (surname, first name and, if available, patronymic) and registered address (place of residence) of the parties in arbitration;
(3) explanation of why the arbitral tribunal has jurisdiction;
(4) claimant's request for relief;
(5) circumstances on which the claimant relies;
(6) evidence supporting the claim;
(7) monetary amount (equivalent) of the claim;
(8) list of documents and other materials attached to the statement of claim.

As for the answer to the claim, its submission is the right of a party. The respondent is free to refrain from providing an answer, although, according to the adversarial principle, such a decision carries with it the risks that might arise from a failure to prove the circumstances of the case and justify the respondent's legal position.

The answer shall be submitted within the time specified in the Rules of the permanent arbitral institution, and if such a time limit is not set – at any time before the first session of the arbitral tribunal.

The law does not impose any formal requirements for the answer to the claim. In practice, these requirements are contained in the Rules of the permanent arbitral institutions.

The law provides that in the course of proceedings a party may amend or supplement its claim or defence and submit additional evidence unless the parties agree otherwise. In this case, the arbitral tribunal has the right to refuse to accept the amended statement of claim, the objection against the claim or additional evidence on the grounds of a delay in their submission.

The regulation of the hearing procedure before the arbitral tribunal is also fairly scant.

The main provisions of the Arbitration Act 2015 relating to the hearing are based on the UNCITRAL Model Law on International Commercial Arbitration (Article 24).

In contrast with the civil procedure, the parties in arbitration are free to decide whether to hold an oral hearing or to limit the proceedings to the consideration of documents and other materials. If the parties did not settle the matter in their agreement, the arbitral tribunal can decide independently whether to conduct hearings for the presentation of evidence or for oral argument, or whether the proceedings shall be based only on documents. However, if the arbitral tribunal decides to confine itself to a study of documents, it is obliged to hold oral hearings if either of the parties should request them.

Hearings as a form of arbitration procedure include an oral hearing in a strict sense of the word and a hearing held for other purposes. The aim of an oral hearing *sensu stricto* is to present evidence or hear the oral argument of the parties. In turn, the oral argument is the presentations by the parties and their representatives. Other purposes of a hearing include the inspection of goods, other property or documents.

In general, an oral hearing in arbitration is similar in its structure to a hearing in state court.

The Arbitration Act's provisions on the termination of the proceedings are based on the UNCITRAL Model Law.

According to Article 35(1) of the Arbitration Act, arbitration proceedings are terminated by a final award or by an order of the arbitral tribunal (an order for the termination of arbitration). Thus, an award or an order of the tribunal is the final stage of the arbitration process.

The arbitral tribunal renders an award when it resolves the dispute between the parties on the merits, and it makes an order on matters which, although not affecting the merits of the dispute, lead to the necessity of ending the arbitration in accordance with Article 36(2) of the Arbitration Act. In addition to an award and a relevant order, arbitral proceedings can also be terminated if it is impossible to designate (select) an arbitrator, and a direct agreement of the parties rules out the possibility of recourse to a competent court that could take the necessary measures (Article 11(4) of the Arbitration Act).

The arbitral tribunal shall issue an order terminating the arbitration if:

(1) *The claimant withdraws his claim, unless the respondent objects to the termination of arbitration and the arbitral tribunal recognises a legitimate interest on his part in obtaining a final settlement of the dispute.* This rule is novel for Russian legislation. The legislative objective behind such wording is to prevent an abuse of right by the claimant, who may come to realise in the course of the arbitration proceedings the high probability of losing the case and try to terminate the proceedings by withdrawing the claim. Meanwhile, the respondent, in the presence of an adverse claim, may have an interest in eliminating the legal uncertainty. As a result, the respondent has the right to object to the termination of the proceedings.

(2) *The parties agree on the termination of the proceedings.* This ground for the termination of proceedings is logical in the context of the parties' freedom of will in choosing to arbitrate and the principle of autonomy on which arbitration is based. The parties' reasons for making this decision do not matter, and the arbitral tribunal is bound to respect the will of the parties.

(3) *The arbitral tribunal finds that the continuation of the proceedings has become unnecessary or impossible, including when there is a decision of the court of general jurisdiction, commercial court or an arbitral award that entered into legal force, rendered in a dispute between the same parties concerning the same subject and involving the same grounds of the claim.* This item makes the list of grounds for the termination of arbitration

non-exhaustive.[32] This is evidenced by the use of the terms 'unnecessary' and 'impossible'. Those terms, being stretchable, provide the arbitral tribunal with the right to assess the factual circumstances that lead to 'uselessness' or 'impossibility' of continuing the proceedings. The law cannot foresee all such cases. One example of a situation where it may be impossible or unnecessary to continue the arbitration is where the organisation that was a party to the arbitration is liquidated. In cases involving individuals, where a party (a citizen-entrepreneur or an ordinary private individual) has died, was declared dead or missing, it may also become impossible or unnecessary to continue the proceedings. Another case of impossibility to continue the arbitration proceedings may be the permanent arbitral institution's loss of legitimacy, for example, due to the fact that its list of arbitrators does not meet the legislative requirements.

A special case of the impossibility to continue the arbitration is a decision of the court of general jurisdiction, commercial court or an arbitral award that entered into legal force, rendered in a dispute between the same parties concerning the same subject and involving the same grounds of the claim (*res judicata* principle).

According to Article 36(3) of the Arbitration Act, after the making of an order on the termination of the proceedings, its copy signed by the arbitrators must be handed over (sent) to each party of arbitration. An arbitrator's dissenting opinion, if any, shall be attached to the order. When the tribunal includes more than on arbitrator, signatures of the majority of the members of the tribunal are sufficient, but the reasons for the absence of other signatures must be provided.

§8.05 EVIDENCE AND PROOF IN ARBITRATION

Unlike civil procedural law, arbitral legislation devotes little attention to evidence. There is neither a statutory definition of evidence nor a list of the types of evidence and the description of rules applicable to each type. Thus, scholars and practitioners are left to rely on the theory and terminology of procedural law.

From a doctrinal point of view, *the evidence* is the information about facts as well as the means by which this information may be obtained (means of evidence).[33]

---

32. The previous Arbitration Act contained an exhaustive list of grounds for termination of the arbitration proceedings. However, the commentators indicated a discrepancy between the legislative regulation and the reality. *See* Valeev D.H., Zaitsev A.I., Fetyukhin M.V., Commentary to the Federal Law of 24 July 2002 No. 102-FZ 'On Arbitration in the Russian Federation' (Clause-by-Clause) (Moscow, 2015) (Cited according to the publication in the Legal Information System 'Consultant Plus') [*Valeev D.H., Zaitsev A.I., Fetyuhin M.V. Kommyentarii k Fyedyeralnomu zakonu ot 24 iyulya 2002 g. No. 102-FZ «O tryetyeiskih sudah v Rossiiskoi Fyedyeracii» (postatyeinyi). M., 2015 (cit. po IPS «Konsultant Plyus»)*].
33. *See: Clause-by-Clause Commentary to the Commercial Procedure Code of the Russian Federation* (P.V. Krasheninnikov, ed., Moscow, 2013, the publication in the Legal Information System 'Consultant Plus'') [Postatyeinyi kommyentarii k Arbitrajnomu procyessualnomu kodyeksu Rossiiskoi Fyedyeracii / Pod ryed. P.V. Krasheninnikova. M., 2013 (SPS «KonsultantPlyus»)].

Procedural legislation defines evidence as information about facts obtained in a manner prescribed by law on the basis of which the court determines the presence or absence of circumstances supporting the claims and objections of persons participating in the case, as well as other circumstances that are material for the correct resolution of the case (Article 55 Code of Civil Procedure, Article 64 of the Commercial Procedure Code).

The Arbitration Act 2015 reiterates the traditional rule of the law of evidence that each party must prove the circumstances on which they rely to support their claims and objections (Article 26).

As mentioned, the Arbitration Act does not provide a list of admissible types of evidence. Various articles of the Act devoted to other issues mention several types of evidence in passing. Thus, Article 22(1) refers to written and physical evidence (para 4) and witnesses (para 5), and Article 27 names an expert opinion as a possible means of evidence.

In most cases, arbitral tribunals rely primarily on written evidence. According to Article 75 of the Commercial Procedure Code, contracts, acts, reference notes, business correspondence and other documents containing information on the circumstances material to the case and made in the form of digital or graphical records or in any other form that allows ascertaining the authenticity of a document, are written evidence. Arbitration Act operates with the term 'documents' (Articles 27, 28), using it as a synonym of 'written evidence'.

Unlike state courts, an arbitral tribunal is not bound by statutory rules on admissibility, relevance, and significance of any evidence. According to Article 19(2) of the Arbitration Act, in the absence of the parties' agreement on the procedure, the arbitral tribunal may conduct the arbitration in such manner as it considers appropriate, including in relation to the admissibility, relevance, and weight of any evidence.

The arbitral legislation also reiterates the traditional rule of civil procedure on the allocation of the burden of proof: the obligation to provide evidence lies with the party who must prove the relevant circumstances.

A feature of the taking of evidence in arbitration is that the arbitral tribunal cannot carry out any evidence gathering on its own initiative. However, the tribunal is entitled (but not obliged) to invite the parties to submit additional evidence.

§8.06 COURT ASSISTANCE IN THE TAKING OF EVIDENCE

Article 30 of the Arbitration Act 2015 deals with the court assistance to arbitration in the taking of evidence, establishing the right of the arbitral tribunal and the parties to approach the competent court with a *request for assistance in obtaining evidence*. The court will perform the request in accordance with the procedural legislation. Article 74.1(1) of the Commercial Procedure Code provides that the commercial court of the first instance at the relevant region of the Russian Federation where the evidence in question is located shall be competent to deal with the request for assistance. The arbitral tribunal can send the request directly or pass it on to a party in arbitration for presenting in the commercial court.

One must note that the range of evidence that can be thus obtained is limited. The arbitral tribunal has the right to request assistance in the taking of written evidence, physical evidence and other materials and documents. Therefore, the arbitral tribunal is not entitled to request the assistance of the competent court in obtaining other types of evidence, such as witness statements or expert opinions.

The competent court may refuse the request in the following cases:

(1) the request aims to obtain evidence which cannot be obtained in this way according to the law;
(2) performance of the request may infringe the rights and legitimate interests of third parties not involved in the arbitral proceedings;
(3) the request relates to a dispute that arbitral tribunals are incompetent to resolve (a non-arbitrable dispute);
(4) the request enables access to state secrets;
(5) the request enables access to official, commercial, banking or other secret information protected by law, in respect of persons not involved in the arbitration.

§8.07 COSTS AND FEES IN ARBITRATION

The parties involved in arbitration proceedings incur various expenses. Legal regulation of costs in arbitration differs for permanent arbitral institutions and ad hoc tribunals.

According to paragraphs 9 and 10 of Article 45(4) of the Arbitration Act 2015, Rules of a permanent arbitral institution must prescribe a fixed amount for any kind of arbitration fees and lay down the rules for their determination, as well as the rules on the distribution of arbitration costs between the parties.

The costs associated with the resolution of a dispute in arbitration include (unless the parties agree otherwise):

(1) arbitrator fees;
(2) expenses incurred by the arbitrators in connection with participation in the proceedings, including the costs of travel to the place of arbitration;
(3) amounts payable to experts and interpreters;
(4) expenses incurred by the arbitrators in connection with the inspection and examination of written and physical evidence at their location;
(5) expenses incurred by witnesses;
(6) costs of party representation;
(7) costs of organisational, financial and other support of arbitration;
(8) other costs determined by the arbitral tribunal.

The parties have to pay the arbitration fee in arbitral proceedings, just as they need to pay a state duty in domestic courts. This fee includes, as a rule, the arbitrators' fees, as well as the cost of organisational, financial, and other support of arbitration. The Rules of arbitral institutions often distinguish, within the overall amount of the arbitration fee, the following components: (1) an honorarium part, i.e., the arbitrators' fees and (2) an administrative fee, which remains with the institution and compensates it for the costs of assistance in the conduct of the arbitration. The Rules of some arbitral institutions provide that the honorarium part also includes remuneration for persons who support the arbitration proceedings (a rapporteur or a tribunal secretary). The administrative fee may include a registration fee that covers the costs of the arbitral institution before the arbitral proceedings begin or at their early stages. The registration fee allows the party to commence arbitral proceedings without the need to pay the arbitration fee immediately in full.

If ad hoc arbitration (in the absence of agreement between the parties that a permanent arbitral institution would perform some individual functions of assistance to the proceedings) the parties pay all expenses directly. In the proceedings administered by an arbitral institution, its Rules can determine which expenses shall be paid directly by the parties, and which shall be channelled through the arbitral institution.

Usually, the additional expenses of the arbitrators and those of the arbitral institution are paid through the institution. The amounts payable to experts and interpreters, as well as the costs incurred by witnesses, can be paid either by the parties directly or through the arbitral institution.

The Rules of permanent arbitral institutions stipulate the amounts and procedures for the payment of arbitration fees. The law requires that Rules define the amounts of honorarium fees and the rules for their determination.

In ad hoc arbitration, the agreement of the parties determines the fees of the arbitrators, and in the absence of an agreement, the tribunal makes the appropriate ruling on this matter. It is conventional to take into account such factors as the amount in dispute, complexity of the case, the duration of the proceedings and other similar circumstances.

The value of a claim usually determines the amount of arbitration fees, which can be expressed as a fixed amount or as a percentage of the disputed sums. Where the claims are non-monetary, the value of the property in dispute can define the amount of arbitration fees.

Distribution of costs between the parties in the proceedings is governed by their agreement, often reached by reference to the Rules of an arbitral institution. In the absence of such an agreement, the costs are borne by the losing party. If the claim is granted in part, the costs are distributed among the parties in proportion.

In contrast to the procedural codes that govern proceedings in state courts, arbitral legislations does not rely on the criterion of reasonableness in the reimbursement of party expenses. This, however, does not mean that the arbitral tribunal cannot use this criterion. If the tribunal concludes that the requested costs are unreasonably high, it can order the losing party to reimburse them within reasonable limits. The award should contain a justification for this approach. However, commentators often welcome the approach that if the losing party does not object to the requested amount of the legal representation costs, then the tribunal should not question its reasonableness, and such costs should be reimbursed in full.[34]

34. Rozhkova M.A., *The Problems of Reimbursement of the Costs of Representation and Other Legal Damages,* 596, in: *Damages and the Practice of Their Compensation* (M.A. Rozhkova, ed., Moscow, Statute, 2006) [*Rozhkova M.A. Problyemy vozmyeshyeniya rashodov na oplatu uslug pryedstavityelyei i inyh sudyebnyh ubytkov. // Ubytki i praktika ih vozmyeshyeniya. / Otv.ryed. M.A. Rozhkova.* – M.: Statut, 2006. S. 596]; M.Yu. Savransky, *Reimbursement of Legal Expenses: Some Topical Issues and the Practice of the ICAC,* 380, in: International Commercial Arbitration: Current Problems and Solutions: A Collection of Articles on the 75th Anniversary of the International Commercial Arbitration Court at the Chamber of Commerce of the Russian Federation (A.S. Komarov, ed., Moscow, Statute, 2007) [*Savransky M.Yu. Vozmyeshyeniye rashodov na yuridichyeskih pryedstavityelyei: nyekotoryye aktualnyye voprosy i praktika MKAS pri TPP RF. // Myejdunarodnyi kommyerchyeskii arbitraj: sovryemyennyye problyemy i ryeshyeniya: Sbornik statyei k 75-lyetiyu Myejdunarodnogo kommyerchyeskogo arbitrajnogo suda pri Torgovo-promyshlyennoi palatye Rossiiskoi Fyedyeracii. / Pod ryed. A.S. Komarova.* – M.: Statut, 2007. S. 380].

CHAPTER 9
Conservatory and Interim Measures in Arbitration

§9.01 PROVISIONAL MEASURES IN ARBITRATION

As a component of the civil justice system, arbitration is an important way of protecting the rights and legitimate interests of civil turnover participants. The effectiveness of arbitration directly depends on the enforceability of arbitral awards. Unscrupulous parties often take actions aimed at the alienation of property and the creation of obstacles to the execution of the final award, the destruction of evidence and the object of the dispute. The practice of dispute resolution in arbitration required the establishment of a mechanism to deal with such problems – the institution of interim measures.

Before the Russian arbitration reform, the practice of application of the interim measures for claims considered by the arbitral tribunals did not exhibit much uniformity. Scholars have also expressed a variety of positions on this issue.[1] The result was an ambivalent interpretation by the courts of the rules on the application of interim measures in arbitration.

In international practice, interim measures are understood as any temporary measures – regardless of whether they are adopted in the form of an award or in any other form, – where at any time prior to the final decision, the arbitral tribunal orders a party to maintain or restore the *status quo* pending resolution of the dispute, take

1. *See*, e.g., Valeev D., Zaytsev A., Fetyukhin M., *Commentary to the Federal law of 24 July 2002 No. 102-FZ 'On Arbitration in the Russian Federation'*, 86-100 (Moscow, 2015) [Valeev D.H., Zaytsev A.I., Fetyukhin M.V. Kommyentarii k Fyedyeralnomu zakonu «O tryetyeiskih sudah v Rossiiskoi Fyedyeracii». M., 2015. S. 86-100]; Skvortsov O., *Commentary to the Federal law 'On Arbitration in the Russian Federation'*, 190 (Moscow, 2003) [Skvortsov O.Yu. Kommyentarii k Fyedyeralnomu zakonu «O tryetyeiskih sudah v Rossiiskoi Fyedyeracii». M., 2003. S. 190]; *Commentary to the Federal law 'On Arbitration in the Russian Federation'* / Ed. by A. Makovsky, E. Sukhanov, 110-111 (Moscow, 2003) [O tryetyeiskih sudah v Rossiiskoi Fyedyeracii: kommyentarii k fyedyeralnomu zakonu / pod ryed. A. L. Makovskogo, E. A. Sukhanova. M., 2003. S. 110-111], etc.

steps to prevent current or imminent harm or prejudice to the arbitral process itself, or refrain from taking action that could cause such damage, provide the means to preserve the assets from which a subsequent award may be enforced, retain evidence that may be relevant and material to the settlement of the dispute.

Interim measures in arbitration are remedies aimed at maintaining the *status quo* in the parties' relations, preventing the possible infringement of legitimate interests of the parties in the course of the proceedings, preserving the subject matter of the dispute as well as the possibility of future enforcement of the arbitral award.

What are the conditions for the application of interim measures? R. Zykov notes that legal practice, regardless of the legal system and method of dispute resolution, is based on three basic criteria that underlie any decision to take interim measures. The first is that interim measures become necessary because of the urgency of the situation, which can often be found in the reasoning of the decisions on interim measures. ... Second, interim measures should be proportionate to the contingency they are intended to prevent. The third criterion is that interim measures are temporary. [2] Thus, interim measures are special protective remedies and time-bound restrictions on the actions of the parties proportionate to the consequences they are intended to prevent.

The main condition for the application of interim measures in arbitration is economic. The arbitrators or judges shall take account of whether harm may be caused that is not adequately remedied by the award of damages, or such harm substantially outweighs the costs incurred by the party against whom the measure is taken if the measure is ordered. The second condition is that there is a reasonable possibility that the requesting party will succeed on the merits of the claim. It is clear that any conclusion on this possibility does not affect the discretion of the arbitral tribunal in making any subsequent determination.

The party against whom interim measures are ordered may comply with the restrictions voluntarily or as a result of coercion. In the world practice, several approaches have developed to the application of interim measures in arbitration. In some countries, only the arbitral tribunal is empowered in this area, in others – only state courts. The third group of states provides a wide range of opportunities to the parties and provides both arbitral tribunals and state courts with the power to adopt interim measures in respect of the claim in arbitration.

Russia has adopted the principle of 'concurrent jurisdiction' – the rule that courts and arbitrators have concurrent powers to order provisional measures. Currently, in Russia, both courts and arbitrators can order interim measures in claims considered by arbitral tribunals. It is generally accepted that there are three consequences of this principle: [3]

2. Zykov R., *International Arbitration in Sweden: Law and Practice*, 150 (Moscow, 2014) [Zykov R.O. Myejdunarodnyi arbitraj v Shvyecii: pravo i praktika. M., 2014. S. 150].
3. Fouchard P., Gaillard E., Goldman B., *On International Commercial Arbitration*, 711 (The Hague, 1999).

(1) the arbitrators themselves have jurisdiction to order provisional or protective measures;
(2) the parties are entitled to apply to the courts, despite the existence of an arbitration agreement, to obtain provisional or protective measures;
(3) such request for interim measures addressed to a judicial authority shall not be deemed incompatible with the arbitration agreement.

All these consequences have been adopted in Russian legislation, practice and doctrine. Both Russian arbitration statutes allow a party to apply to a competent state court for measures to secure a claim both before and during arbitration. Such applications and the court's adoption of interim measures are not deemed incompatible with the arbitration agreement. In addition, upon a request of any party, the arbitral tribunal may order interim measures it considers necessary. Provisions reflecting the content of the principle of 'concurrent jurisdiction' are enshrined in international conventions (e.g., Article VI of the European Convention on International Commercial Arbitration of 1961) to which Russia is a participant, as well as in many arbitration rules.

The principle of 'concurrent jurisdiction' may be limited[4] by parties' arbitration agreement, as well as by the legislative provisions on the exclusive competence of state courts. Thus, the court shall refuse to order interim measures upon a request of a party if the dispute cannot be the subject of arbitral proceedings (non-arbitrable cases), for instance, is of a public nature or affects the exclusive jurisdiction of state courts.[5] The parties may decrease the power of the arbitral tribunal to order interim measures (excluding only some of them) by expressly indicating this in their agreement, and in international commercial arbitration may even waive the right of recourse to the court with an application for interim measures.

Before the reform, there were some studies in Russia on the experience of countries where the competence of arbitral tribunals and state courts in ordering interim measures was delimited to a greater extent. For instance, in the United States, a party may apply to the court on the issue in question only before the formation of a 'competent' arbitral tribunal and the emergence of its competence to make the appropriate decisions.[6] After an arbitrator is appointed and is authorised and able to act, a party to arbitration proceedings may petition the court for a provisional remedy only if the matter is urgent and the arbitrator is not able to act timely or the arbitrator cannot provide an adequate remedy (section 8 of the United States Uniform Arbitration Act 2000). In Russia today, both arbitration statutes allow the following options:

(1) interim measures may be ordered by the arbitral tribunal itself;

4. *Ibid.* 718-720.
5. Resolution of Plenum of Supreme Commercial Court of the Russian Federation of 12 October 2006 No. 55 'On Application of Interim Measures by Commercial Courts' (paragraph 34).
6. Nosyreva E.I., *Alternative Dispute Resolution in the United States,* 112 (Moscow, 2005) [Nosyreva E.I., Altyernativnoye razryeshyeniye sporov v SSHA. M., 2005. S. 112].

(2) prior to the formation of the arbitral tribunal, a permanent arbitral institution may order an interim measure of protection;
(3) a party may request the court to order protective measures before arbitration (provisional measures);
(4) a party may request the court to order interim measures during the arbitration.

§9.02 POWER OF ARBITRAL TRIBUNAL TO ORDER INTERIM MEASURES

Unless otherwise agreed by the parties, the arbitral tribunal may, at the request of any party, order interim measures it deems necessary (Article 17 of the Federal law 'On Arbitration in the Russian Federation', Article 17 of the Law 'On International Commercial Arbitration'). The arbitral tribunal may require any party to provide adequate security in connection with the said measures. In international practice, a party requesting an interim measure may also be held liable for any costs and damages caused by the measure to any other party if the arbitral tribunal subsequently determines that the measure should not have been ordered in the circumstances then existing. The arbitral tribunal may award such costs and damages at any time during the proceedings.

The arbitral tribunal may modify, suspend, or revoke an interim measure of protection ordered by it at the request of either party or, in exceptional circumstances and upon prior notice to the parties, on its own initiative. In addition, the arbitrators may require any party to disclose without delay a material change in the circumstances under which the interim measure was requested or granted.

In Russia, interim measures are generally taken in the form of a reasoned order or an award. Regardless of the form, parties must comply with the procedural acts of the arbitral tribunal. The adoption by the arbitral tribunal of an order for interim measures of protection in the form of an award, rather than a determination, does not indicate the possibility of issuing a writ of execution for the enforcement of the relevant act of arbitral tribunal.[7]

The resolution of the issue of interim measures by the arbitration itself is based on the voluntary subordination of the parties to the jurisdiction of the arbitral tribunal, so in the Russian literature, one can find very critical assessments of this method of protecting legitimate interests. Of course, in such an assessment, the importance of arbitrators in the adoption of interim measures is seriously underestimated, and the worldwide practice of arbitration is good evidence of this. In most cases, the parties

7. Item 7 of the Review of Practice in Cases on Setting Aside of Arbitral Awards and Issuing Writs of Execution for Enforcement of Arbitral Awards / approved by the Presidium of the Federal Commercial Court of the Ural Circuit on 7 July 2010.

comply voluntarily with the tribunal-ordered interim measures of protection, whatever form they take.[8]

Arbitration is a private element of the social system, but it also has some public features. Any act of the arbitral tribunal ordering interim measures is subject to implementation by the parties and ix binding on them. As a rule, interim measures apply to persons who have signed the arbitration agreement. Arbitrators may only impose acts of a coercive nature on the parties[9] and not any other third persons, and only in disputes in which the tribunal has exclusive jurisdiction on the merits.[10]

The voluntary enforcement of interim measures ordered by the arbitral tribunal is often stimulated by a number of factors. Among them are reputational risks, the credibility of the arbitration institution administering the dispute, procedural responsibility and much more. The *sui generis* nature of arbitration provides an opportunity to put the question about the possibility of using different methods of compelling the parties to execute orders on interim measures, both private and procedural.

§9.03 INTERIM MEASURES ORDERED BY ARBITRAL INSTITUTION

The agreement of the parties may also provide (including by reference to the arbitration rules) that before the formation of the arbitral tribunal, a permanent arbitration institution may order a party to take such interim measures as it deems necessary (Article 17 of the Federal law 'On Arbitration in the Russian Federation', Article 17 of the Law of the Russian Federation 'On International Commercial Arbitration').

In some cases, the law empowers the chairperson of permanent arbitration institutions to adopt interim measures. Thus, in cases to be resolved by the International Commercial Arbitration Court, its Chairman may, upon the request of one of the parties, order interim measures (paragraph 10 of the ICAC Rules of Arbitration). In cases to be resolved by the Maritime Arbitration Commission, the Chairman may, upon the request of a party, determine the amount and form of security for the claim and, in particular, order the seizure of the vessel or cargo of the other party in the Russian port (paragraph 4 of the Rules of Maritime Arbitration Commission).

It is known that many arbitration rules (ICC Arbitration, Arbitration Institute of the Stockholm Chamber Commerce, etc.) envisage some protective measures before the arbitral proceedings are initiated or referred to the arbitral tribunal. The party seeking urgent interim or provisional measures, adoption of which cannot wait until the formation of the arbitral tribunal may file a petition for adoption of such measures and request a ruling by an emergency arbitrator. It should be noted that the party applying for the appointment of an emergency arbitrator, when submitting the application, must pay the costs of the emergency procedure, including the fee of the

8. Bruntseva E., *International Commercial Arbitration*, 196 (St. Petersburg, 2001) [Bruntseva E.V., Myejdunarodnyi kommyerchyeskii arbitraj. SPb., 2001. S. 196].
9. Redfern A., Hunter M., *Law and Practice of International Commercial Arbitration, 232* (London, 1986).
10. Reisman M., Craig L., Park W., Paulsson J., *International Commercial Arbitration. Cases, Materials and Notes on the Resolution of International Business Disputes*, 754 (Wesbury, New York, 1997).

arbitrator and the fee for filing the application. In the future, the costs of this extraordinary procedure may be apportioned by the arbitral tribunal between the parties in the final award.

An emergency arbitrator is normally appointed by the head of the institutional arbitration as soon as possible (usually within one or two days after the arbitration institution receives the party's request). An emergency arbitrator shall not be appointed if it is clear that there is no institutional arbitration competence. In addition, an emergency arbitrator may not be appointed after the case has been referred to the arbitral tribunal. As a rule, an emergency arbitrator should not act as an arbitrator in further proceedings in a dispute that gave rise to an application.

After the appointment of the emergency arbitrator, the permanent arbitral institution shall notify the parties and refer the case to him. The emergency arbitrator shall draw up the procedural schedule and conduct the proceedings on its basis in such manner as he considers appropriate, taking into account the nature and urgency of the application. Meetings with the emergency arbitrator may be held in person or by videoconference, telephone, or similar means. In all cases, the emergency arbitrator should act fairly and impartially and ensure that each party has a real opportunity to present its case.

The decision of the emergency arbitrator shall be made in the form of an order. Such order shall be issued in writing, specifying the reasons on which it is based, usually no later than 15 days from the date of referral of the case to the emergency arbitrator. The parties shall comply with any order made by the emergency arbitrator. The order shall cease to be binding on the parties after the arbitral tribunal has rendered a final award (unless the arbitral tribunal expressly decides otherwise) or the arbitral proceedings have been terminated before the final award has been made. At the reasoned request of the party before the submission of the case to the arbitral tribunal, the emergency arbitrator may modify, terminate, or cancel the order. It should be noted that the order of the emergency arbitrator does not bind the arbitral tribunal, and therefore the arbitrators may change, terminate, or cancel the order adopted by the emergency arbitrator. The arbitral tribunal is not bound by the motives and decision of the emergency arbitrator.

The provisions on the emergency arbitrator do not limit the right of any party to seek urgent relief or interim measures of protection before the competent court at any time, neither before the request for such measures is made not thereafter. An application for such measures to a competent court does not constitute a waiver of the arbitration agreement.

§9.04 COURT-ORDERED INTERIM MEASURES

In Russia, interim measures may be ordered by a court at the request of a party at the location of the arbitral tribunal, or at the domicile of the debtor, or at the location of the debtor's property. Interim measures of protection may be ordered if failure to take such measures can make it more difficult or impossible to enforce the arbitral award, including where the enforcement of the arbitral award is expected outside the Russian Federation, as well as in order to prevent significant damage to the applicant.

The method under consideration is based on fundamentally different positions in comparison with the resolution of the issue of interim measures by the arbitral tribunal itself. The person concerned shall seek the assistance of the public authorities of the state in which the dispute is being heard. The state court shall take interim measures on the application of a party under the general rules, taking into account the peculiarities of the arbitration form of dispute resolution based on the agreement of the parties. In considering such applications, the court shall verify the validity of the arbitration agreement.

An advantage of the party request to the state court is the possibility of enforcement of the order on interim measures, *inter alia* against third parties. Request to the state court allows protecting the property interests of the claimant before the arbitral tribunal is formed. However, the request to take protective measures may be ineffective for international commercial arbitrations when such measures are required in several States.

The request shall be submitted by the party at the location of the arbitral tribunal, or at the location or residence of the debtor, or at the location of the debtor's property. The application shall be accompanied by evidence of filing a claim to arbitration (sending an ad hoc request for arbitration to the other party); evidence of payment of the state fee; a certified copy of the arbitration agreement.

Consideration of the application by the competent court and its order on interim measures or refusing to provide it shall be carried out in the manner prescribed by Chapter 8 of the Commercial Procedure Code and Chapter 13 of the Code of Civil Procedure of the Russian Federation. The law does not preclude the parallel application of interim measures by state courts and arbitral tribunals, but the practice has developed a rule requiring the arbitral tribunal considering a dispute to be informed of the adoption of the relevant acts by the competent state courts.

The court that ordered an interim measure to assist the arbitral proceedings may later set it aside on an application by one of the parties. The arbitral award dismissing the claims on the merits is a ground for cancellation by a competent court of the interim measures adopted earlier.

§9.05 PRELIMINARY CONSERVATORY MEASURES

Arbitration is a process that develops over time. This temporal factor may benefit unscrupulous parties who sometimes attempt to render legally enforceable arbitral awards practically useless. The institute of emergency arbitrators allows the parties to apply for interim measures before the arbitral proceedings are commenced or the case is referred to the arbitral tribunal. However, this is often not enough. Russian legislation provides the parties with a right to petition the state court for interim measures to secure the claim. State courts and the majority of Russian scholars, based on the provisions of Article 99 of the Commercial Procedure Code of the Russian Federation, consistently hold the that the competent court may also take preliminary interim measures to protect the property interests of the applicant even before the arbitral proceedings are initiated.[11]

A competent court may adopt preliminary interim measures of protection before a request for arbitration is communicated to the other party and the arbitral institution, in order to safeguard the applicant's property interests. Preliminary interim measures of protection are to be taken under the general rules provided by the Commercial Procedure Code, taking into account the peculiarities of the arbitral form of dispute resolution, to preserve the possibility of enforcement of the future award if there are grounds for their application under Article 90 of the Commercial Procedure Code.[12] Current Russian legislation only allows the parties to apply for preliminary interim measures protecting the applicant's property interests in one category of cases, namely those related to the entrepreneurial and other economic activities, but not in other categories of disputes.

The application for preliminary interim measures is submitted to the court at the location of the applicant, or at the location of funds or other property in respect of which the applicant applies for measures to ensure property interests, or at the place of infringement of the applicant's rights. Such an application may be submitted to the court by filling out a form posted on its official website, in which case it shall be signed by an enhanced qualified electronic signature.

A mandatory condition is a submission to the court of a document confirming the provision of a counter-security in the amount equal to that specified in the application. In its absence, the court leaves the request for the protection of property interests without consideration until the applicant submits a document confirming the counter-security.

If the application is granted, the court makes a relevant ruling and establishes the time limit not exceeding 15 days for the filing of the statement of claim in connection with which the court took measures for ensuring property interests of the applicant. The claimant shall inform the court which ordered provisional measures about the filing of a claim in arbitration. If the applicant has not filed a claim within the period established in the court's order on the protection of property interests, the measure shall be cancelled by the same court. After the claim is filed, preliminary interim measures of protection continue to act as the regular interim measures, so no further application is required.

The court, taking into account the specific circumstances of the case, may refuse to take preliminary measures upon the application of a party if it considers the provisional measures previously taken by a permanent arbitral institution or an emergency arbitrator to be sufficient and the applicant has not provided evidence that they are not complied with voluntarily. In addition, the court shall refuse to take

11. Skvortsov O.Yu., *Arbitration of Commercial Disputes in Russia: Problems, Trends, Prospectives*, 480 (Moscow, 2003) [Skvortsov O.Yu. Tryetyeiskoye razbiratyelstvo pryedprinimatyelskih sporov v Rossii. M., 2003. S. 480].

12. *Review of the Practice of Commercial Courts in Applying Interim Measures of Protection*. Information letter of Presidium of the Supreme Commercial Court of the Russian Federation of 7 July 2004 No. 78 (paragraph 23).

preliminary measures on the application of a party to the arbitration if the dispute cannot be the subject of arbitration. [13]

§9.06 TYPES OF CONSERVATORY AND INTERIM MEASURES

What types of interim measures can be taken in arbitration? In international practice, interim measures fall into two main categories: measures taken to avoid harm, loss, or damage and measures designed to facilitate the subsequent enforcement of an award. Such a division was proposed by the UNCITRAL Working Group on Arbitration in 2002.[14] In the former case, interim measures are taken to avoid or minimise loss or damage (by, for example, maintaining a certain *status quo* until the dispute is resolved) and to avoid harm (for example, by maintaining confidentiality). In the latter case, interim measures are intended to facilitate the subsequent enforcement of the award.

In the doctrine, interim measures are divided into three main groups. The first group includes measures those that have to do with the taking, preservation, and production of evidence concerning the dispute. The second group consists of measures those that have to do with preserving the subject matter of the dispute and avoiding prejudice to the rights of the parties during the pendency of the proceedings. The third group consists of measures that are designed to permit the effective execution of the award to be rendered on the merits.[15]

The purpose of the first set of measures is to ensure the formation of the evidential base in case there is a threat of the possible loss of some evidence in the future. These measures include inspection of the goods or the subject matter of the dispute by the arbitral tribunal or a third independent person before the qualities (properties) of the goods are lost, or the subject of the dispute leaves the possession of the parties. As a rule, such interim measures are taken by the arbitral tribunal itself.

The second group of interim measures is aimed at preserving the *status quo* between the parties, preventing possible changes in the position of the claimant and the respondent in the proceedings, and preserving the object of the dispute. Such measures include use (operation) of equipment; completion of construction in cases where it is necessary to prevent irreparable damage; actions aimed at protecting trade secrets or information protected by law, preventing its unauthorised dissemination. Measures of this kind involve the voluntary active participation of the parties in their implementation and are taken by the arbitral tribunal.

Finally, the third group of interim measures is aimed at enforcement of the future award. This category of measures often requires placing restrictions on the respondent and may affect the third parties in possession of the relevant property or money. For this reason, this type of interim measure in Russia is most often applied by state courts. The tribunal, in this case, may, with the active assistance of the parties, take measures

13. *Ibid.* at paragraphs 24, 25.
14. *Report of the Working Group on Arbitration on the Work of its Thirty-Sixth Session* (New York, 4-8 March 2002), https://documents-dds-ny.un.org/doc/UNDOC/GEN/V02/533/86/PDF/V0253386.pdf (accessed 25 February 2019).
15. *Reisman M., Craig L., Park W., Paulsson J., supra* note 10, at 754.

to preserve the goods, transfer them to a third party for storage or sale, if the goods may lose their quality while the proceedings are being conducted; require the parties to provide a bank guarantee, place funds in the amount necessary for the possible enforcement of the award on a deposit with a third independent party; depositing funds with a bank (third party) on agreed conditions. Among the powers to grant interim measures mentioned above, there are those that arbitral tribunals and state courts have a 'concurrent jurisdiction' to adopt and those in the exclusive competence of the state courts.[16]

It should be noted that the arbitral tribunals do not have the power to enforce interim measures that the parties are unable to perform independently. If it becomes necessary, the parties to the arbitration may apply directly to the state court for interim measures.[17]

When applying for interim measures to the state court, the party may ask for any measures provided for by procedural law (Article 91 of the Commercial Procedure Code, Article 140 of the Code of Civil Procedure of the Russian Federation), including the seizure of funds or other property belonging to the respondent and held by him or other persons; the prohibition for the respondent and other persons to perform certain actions relating to the subject matter of the dispute; the imposition on the respondent of the obligation to perform certain actions in order to prevent damage or deterioration of the disputed property; on transfer of disputable property to the custody of the claimant or another person.

§9.07 CONSEQUENCES OF PARTIES' FAILURE TO COMPLY WITH INTERIM MEASURES

The orders and other procedural acts of the arbitral tribunal on interim measures of protection are subject to implementation by the parties. International practice shows that this does not always happen. Two types of adverse consequences of non-compliance with arbitral awards on interim measures are the most common in arbitration practice. First, these are unfavourable inferences of the arbitral tribunal. Second, the award of costs and (or) damages. The arbitral tribunal may impose on the respective party a costs sanction and (or) award damages resulting from its failure to comply with the interim measure.[18]

16. *See* Redfern A., Hunter M., *supra* note 9, at 232.
17. Decree of the Federal Commercial Court for the North-Western Circuit of 20 October 2011, case No. A56-13008/2011; Decree of the Federal Commercial Court for the Volga Region of 20 May 2003, case No. A12-30011/03-13.
18. Yerpyleva N., Lopatina D., *Interim Measures in International Commercial Arbitration*, 4 International Commercial Arbitration, 68-69 (2008) [Yerpyleva. N.Yu., Lopatina D.A., Obyespyechityelnyye myery v myejdunarodnom kommyerchyeskom arbitrajye, Myejdunarodnyi kommyerchyeskii arbitraj. 2008. No. 4. S. 6].

CHAPTER 10

Award

§10.01 DEFINITION OF AWARD

An arbitral award is the ultimate result of the proceedings, and parties normally expect their arbitration to end in a final and binding award.[1] It is therefore unsurprising that Article 2 of the Arbitration Act 2015 defines arbitration as a process whereby the tribunal resolves a dispute and renders an award. This definition places a special emphasis on two aspects of the arbitral mechanism: the process and the award.

It is important to distinguish between arbitral awards and other acts and decisions that do not qualify as awards. There are two logical stages in this process. First, a decision maker must review whether the dispute had been submitted and resolved by arbitration and not another method of dispute resolution. Second, it is necessary to ascertain whether the decision is an award and not any other type of decision by the tribunal.[2]

Arbitral awards – but, generally, not other decisions and orders of the tribunal – are capable of enforcement with the assistance of competent national courts. The possibility of enforcing an arbitral award in other jurisdictions under the New York Convention 1958 is the key reason for the popularity of arbitration in international commerce. Enforceability is also crucial in the domestic context because the final and binding character of arbitral awards constitutes domestic arbitration's main difference from, and an advantage over, other methods of alternative dispute resolution. The parties can usually challenge an arbitral award before the relevant national courts; other kinds of the tribunal's orders and decisions, with a few notable exceptions, are not subject to separate challenge proceedings.

Just like the previous Russian legislation, the Arbitration Act 2015 does not contain a definition of an arbitral award, although several individual provisions of this

1. Margaret L. Moses, *International Commercial Arbitration*, 201 (3rd ed., CUP, 2017).
2. *ICCA's Guide to the Interpretation of the 1958 New York Convention. A Handbook for Judges*, 16 (The Hague 2011).

statute do shed some light on its nature.[3] Article 34 of the 2015 Act sets out the detailed requirements to the form and content of an arbitral award. In particular, according to Article 34(2)(8), the operative part of the award contains the tribunal's conclusions on upholding or refusing each of the parties' requests for relief. Article 35 of the Arbitration Act 2015 stipulates that on the matters that do not concern the merits of the dispute, the tribunal shall render an order (and not an award).

At the doctrinal level, I.M. Chupakhin has suggested the following comprehensive definition of an arbitral award, listing its nine essential characteristics:

(1) The arbitral award is, first and foremost, a result of the application of the law, and in order to distinguish it from the acts of other bodies and authorities performing jurisdictional functions – notably, the courts – one must keep in mind the private legal nature of an arbitral tribunal.
(2) An award must follow a procedure agreed by the parties, and this procedure must comply with the mandatory rules of law.
(3) Only the arbitrators selected or appointed in the manner agreed by the parties can render an award.
(4) Since arbitration is not a universal or a default method of protecting the individual rights, an arbitral award can only concern the civil legal relationships, provided that there is a valid and enforceable arbitration agreement between the parties.
(5) An arbitral award resolves the dispute on the merits in full or in part.
(6) The arbitral award is final, which implies its immediate entry into legal force and the impossibility of review on the merits (with some exceptions as provided for in the law of some legal systems).
(7) An arbitral award can be set aside by a competent court within a dedicated type of proceedings on a limited number of grounds.
(8) Since an award is the result of the actions of private persons, as a rule, the parties comply with it voluntarily; otherwise, the state may exercise its enforcement powers in the form of an exequatur.
(9) An arbitral award can act as a legally significant fact of both substantive and procedural law.[4]

3. In fairness to the Russian statute, there is no internationally accepted definition of the term 'award' either – *see* Nigel Blackaby, Constantine Partasides QC, Alan Redfern, and Martin Hunter, *Redfern and Hunter on International Arbitration*, §9.05 (6th ed., OUP, 2015).
4. Chupakhin I.M., *Arbitral Award: Theoretical and Practical Issues*, 28 (Moscow, 2015) [Chupakhin I.M. Ryeshyeniye tryetyeiskogo suda: tyeoryetichyeskiye i prikladnyye problyemy. M., 2015. S. 28].

§10.02 CATEGORIES OF AWARD

[A] Partial, Interim and Separate Awards

The authoritative ICCA's Guide to the Interpretation of the 1958 New York Convention, arguably, defines an arbitral award more broadly than the Russian statutory law and doctrine. In order to understand why this is the case, it is useful to start from a review of the international position.

According to the Guide, an award is a decision putting an end to the arbitration in whole or in part, or a ruling on a preliminary issue the resolution of which is necessary to reach a final decision. Consequently, the Guide lists the following arbitral decisions that qualify as awards:

- final awards putting an end to the arbitration;
- partial awards that give a final decision on part of the claims and leave the remaining claims for a subsequent phase of the arbitration proceedings;
- preliminary or interim awards that decide a preliminary issue necessary to dispose of the parties' claims, such as a decision on whether a claim is time-barred;
- awards on costs;
- consent awards recording the parties' settlement of the dispute.[5]

This classification is a useful starting point for discussing the different categories of arbitral awards. In international practice, an even wider variety of adjectives is used to describe various kinds of arbitral awards, such as 'interlocutory' and 'preliminary' awards. Adding to the confusion, what is referred to as a partial award in some civil-law countries is called an interim award in certain common law countries. The courts in different jurisdictions took various positions as to whether each particular type of award could be enforced under the New York Convention.[6]

In an attempt to simplify the terminology and reduce the grounds for refusal of recognition and enforcement, some arbitration rules have introduced a wider notion of a 'separate' award. For instance, the UNCITRAL Arbitration Rules state in Article 34: 'The arbitral tribunal may make separate awards on different issues at different times.'[7] Likewise, the Rules of the ICAC at the RF CCI provide in paragraph 38 that the arbitral tribunal may make separate awards on individual issues or a part of the claims.[8]

5. *ICCA's Guide to the Interpretation of the 1958 New York Convention. A Handbook for Judges*, *supra* note 2, at 17.
6. Albert Jan van den Berg, *New York Convention of 1958: Refusals of Enforcement*, 12(2) ICC International Court of Arbitration Bulletin, 25 (2007).
7. UNCITRAL Arbitration Rules (with new Article 1, paragraph 4, as adopted in 2013) http://www.uncitral.org/pdf/english/texts/arbitration/arb-rules-2013/UNCITRAL-Arbitration-Rules-2013-e.pdf (accessed 15 January 2019).
8. *The Rules of Arbitration on International Commercial Disputes*. Appendix No. 2 to Order No. 6 of the Chamber of Commerce and Industry of the Russian Federation of 11 January 2017, paragraph 38 http://mkas.tpprf.ru/upload/iblock/fd9/fd91e3315ec67621225835bc71d3de5e.docx (accessed 14 January 2019)

This approach may be of assistance as far as the terminology is concerned, but a national court – which certainly includes a Russian court – would still have to classify such a 'separate' award further to determine its enforceability. 'Separate' awards, therefore, are not a category of an award in its own right in Russia, but rather an umbrella term, which may cover partial and interim awards, as well as the awards on costs.[9]

Russian commentators agree that the tribunal's right to render a separate award implies that such an award must concern the merits of the dispute rather than any procedural aspects of the case.[10] Likewise, Article 35 of the Arbitration Act 2015 stipulates that on the matters that do not concern the merits of the dispute, the tribunal shall render an order (and not an award). Russian legal tradition thus offers a narrower understanding of a term 'separate award', in comparison with its international counterparts. While in other countries the tribunal's decisions on procedural matters may take the form of an award, in Russia such decisions are normally termed 'orders' and denied the status of an arbitral award.[11] For example, there cannot be a separate award on the jurisdiction of the tribunal to hear the case, because statutory law explicitly labels this decision 'an order'.[12] The consequences of a court classifying an award as 'merely procedural' are potentially very serious, because it may result in a refusal to enforce such an award.

It is beyond doubt that Russian law fully recognises final awards (also called 'definitive' awards) that resolve all the issues put before the arbitral tribunal, and such final awards are binding and enforceable in this country. Equally, the statutes on both domestic and international arbitration regulate consent awards in line with the international practice (Article 30 of the ICA Act 1993, Article 33 of the Arbitration Act 2015).

The position of partial and interim awards in an arbitration seated in Russia, however, may be slightly less certain. In principle, there is nothing in Russian statutory law to prevent the tribunal from issuing separate, partial and interim awards, as long as they finally resolve some part of a dispute on the merits and are not merely interlocutory or procedural in character. Moreover, some Russian statutes explicitly mention such a possibility. For example, Article 138 of the Code of Inland Water Transport of the Russian Federation provides that a court of law, a commercial court or an arbitration tribunal may rule by passing an interim decision that an advance sum of money should be paid to the salvor of a vessel, being regarded as equitable and reasonable and provided on such conditions. Article 352 of the Merchant Shipping Code of the Russian Federation contains a similar provision.

9. Chupakhin I.M., *supra* note 4, at 75.
10. The Rules of the International Commercial Arbitration Court at the Chamber of Commerce and Industry of the Russian Federation: Academic and Practical Commentary, §40(2) (Komarov A.S., ed., Moscow, 2012) [Ryeglamyent Myejdunarodnogo kommyerchyeskogo arbitrajnogo suda pri Torgovo-promyshlyennoi palatye Rossiiskoi Fyedyeracii: nauchno-praktichyeskii kommyentarii /pod obsh. ryed. A.S. Komarova. M., 2012. §40(2)].
11. Chupakhin I.M., *supra* note 4, at 76.
12. Article 16 of the ICA Act 1993 and Article 16 of the Arbitration Act 2015 use the term '*postanovlenie*', which could also translate to English as a 'decree' but certainly not an 'award' – *see* below at §10(9)(a).

Russian doctrinal authorities are also quite positive on the potential of interim and partial arbitral awards in the Russian arbitration law, pointing out that such awards could be particularly useful in resolving individual aspects of a dispute. For example, an interim award could declare a transaction void and thus clear the way for a subsequent restitution claim; or it might confirm a fundamental breach of contract thus opening the possibility to seek damages for the non-breaching party.[13]

ICAC at the RF CCI tribunals do use their right to issue separate awards from time to time, and Russian courts do enforce them.[14] However, they do not render such awards very often. To date, there have only been several reported cases where an ICAC tribunal would issue a separate award. It is conceivable that the requirement that such an award must be 'final' and not merely interlocutory or procedural might prompt the tribunals to approach them with caution and, where possible, resolve all the relevant issues in one single final award. The determination of what exactly constitutes a 'final' award, although straightforward in theory, may sometimes present difficulties in practice.

Russian courts argued in one case that only a 'final' (i.e., the 'last' or 'definitive') decision of a tribunal on the merits of a dispute could qualify as a final and enforceable arbitral award. In its Decree No. 6547/10 of 5 October 2010,[15] the Presidium of the Supreme Commercial Court considered the application to enforce a Separate Award of an arbitral tribunal acting under the Arbitration Rules of the Arbitration Institute of the Stockholm Chamber of Commerce. The award required the respondent to reimburse €33,000 to the claimant. This sum represented the respondent's part of the advance payment covering the costs of arbitration. The tribunal specifically noted that such a confirmation of the duty to make advance payment for costs did not preclude the tribunal from allocating the costs as between the parties in the final award on the merits. The Presidium of the Supreme Commercial Court noted that the Separate Award in question was of a provisional character and therefore did not constitute a final award enforceable under the New York Convention. According to the Presidium, in this case, the Separate Award has not yet become binding on the parties (Article V(1)(e) of the New York Convention 1958), and the matter of costs should properly be addressed in the final arbitral award on the merits of the dispute. The court added that interim awards, including orders of the tribunal resolving other procedural matters (allocating costs of arbitration, determining the tribunal's jurisdiction to deal with the dispute, adopting interim measures) are unenforceable in the territory of the Russian

13. Skvortsov O.Yu., *Arbitration of Commercial Disputes in Russia: Problems, Tendencies, Prospects*, 520 (Moscow, Wolters Kluwer, 2005) [Skvortsov O.Yu. Tryetyeiskoye razbiratyelstvo pryedprinimatyelskih sporov v Rossii: problyemy, tyendyencii, pyerspyektivy. M.: Wolters Kluwer, 2005. S. 520].
14. *See*, e.g., the Decree of the Federal Commercial Court for the Moscow Circuit of 7 August 2017 No. F05-10967/2017, case No. A40-32661/2017. It is worth pointing out that in this case, the winning party in arbitration requested the enforcement of two awards simultaneously: a Final Award and a Separate Award.
15. Decree of the Presidium of the Supreme Commercial Court No. 6547/10 of 5 October 2010, case No. A56-63115/2009.

Federation.[16] The judgment did not explore in detail the requirements of Swedish law (*lex arbitri)* to the categories arbitral awards, nor did it consider any prominent case law from other counties on this matter.

In another case, though adopted earlier and by a lower court, the petition to enforce an interim award by a sole LCIA arbitrator was successful. In this 2005 case, the tribunal ordered specific performance (delivery of crude oil) and payment of expenses in an award specifically entitled an 'interim' award. Without any further discussion of this fact, the court granted the enforcement.[17]

An additional complication might emerge from the new wording of the requirements to an award in the Arbitration Act 2015. According to its Article 34(2)(8), the operative part of an award must contain the tribunal's conclusions on upholding or refusing *each* of the parties' requests for relief (emphasis added). Article 31 of the ICA Act 1993 that governs international commercial arbitration is less categorical in this regard, saying only that an award must contain the conclusions on granting or refusing the requests for relief. It remains to be seen whether this new wording would be interpreted as an argument against partial and interim awards as such, or, hopefully, as a requirement that applies only to final (dispositive) awards putting an end to the proceedings but does not preclude the tribunal from issuing other types of awards. As a practical matter, since the requirements of Article 34 are default and not mandatory, i.e., the parties are free to modify these requirements by their agreement, this question will not arise where the arbitration agreement, or the institutional or ad hoc rules incorporated by reference into such agreement, specifically empower the tribunal to issue partial, interim or separate awards.

[B] Award on Agreed Terms

If the parties settle the dispute during arbitral proceedings, the arbitral tribunal shall terminate the proceedings and, if requested by the parties, record the settlement in the form of an arbitral award on agreed terms. An award on agreed terms shall be made in accordance with the general requirements to the form and contents of an arbitral award and shall state that it is an award. Such an award has the same status and effect as any other award on the merits of the case.

The above provision originating in the UNCITRAL Model Law on International Commercial Arbitration had been reproduced in both the 2015 Arbitration Act (Article 33) for domestic arbitration and the ICA Act 1993 (Article 30) for international

16. On the impossibility of enforcing the tribunals' orders dealing with interim measures, the earlier position of the Supreme Commercial Court remains unchanged until this day, and courts often reference it. *See* Information Letter No. 78 of the Presidium of the Supreme Commercial Court of 7 July 2004 'Review of Commercial Court Practice Concerning Preliminary Interim Measures of Protection' (paragraph 26) [punkt 26 Informacionnogo pisma Pryezidiuma Vysshyego Arbitrajnogo Suda Rossiiskoi 70yedyeracii ot 07.07.2004 N 78 'Obzor praktiki primyenyeniya arbitrajnymi sudami pryedvarityelnyh obyespyechityelnyh myer']. The 2006 amendments to the UNCITRAL Model Law concerning the interim measures have not been adopted in Russia.
17. Ruling of the Commercial Court of Moscow Oblast of 20 January 2005, case No. A41-K1-25659/04.

commercial arbitration. One difference between the two statutes is that whereas the ICA Act 1993, following the Model Law, provides that the tribunal shall adopt an award on agreed terms *unless* it has an objection thereto, the Arbitration Act 2015 contains no such condition. Its predecessor, the Arbitration Act 2002 that governed domestic arbitration until the 2015 reform, also did provide the tribunal with a power to control the parties' discretion.[18]

Unfortunately, there is no published drafting history explaining this omission in Article 33 of the Arbitration Act 2015. Therefore, it is difficult to ascertain whether the omission was intentional, and if so, what it means in terms of the procedure for recording the parties' settlement in Russian domestic arbitrations.

So far, commentators of the new Act did not pay much attention to the distinction between the old and new wording. For example, one authoritative commentary to the 2015 Act[19] draws a parallel with the litigation in state commercial courts and courts of general jurisdiction, where it has long been a tradition to provide the court with a degree of control over the parties' discretion in settling a dispute. According to Article 141 of the Commercial Procedure Code and Article 39 of the Code of Civil Procedure, the parties' settlement agreement does not enter into force unless and until approved by the court. The court shall refuse its approval if the terms of the agreement are illegal (contravene the law) or violate the rights and legitimate interests of other persons who did not take part in the proceedings.

If recording the parties' settlement of a dispute in domestic arbitration is indeed subject to the same controls and limitations as settlement agreements in national litigation, as the authors of the above Commentary suggest,[20] this requires an explanation that has to lie in the domain of statutory interpretation. One possible explanation for this legislative omission might lie in the tribunal's general power to conduct the arbitration in such manner as it considers appropriate (Article 19 of the 2015 Act), in conjunction with its discretion as to the content of the arbitral award (Articles 31 and 34 of the 2015 Act). In addition, it is common ground in Russian doctrine that the tribunal's role in dispute resolution goes beyond that of a parties' mere agent, and includes public elements akin to those of the judiciary.[21]

The above interpretation, derogating from the literal meaning of the statutory language, may not be watertight. However, as a matter of legislative policy, it is, in our view, a preferable one. One of the declared rationales for the 2015 arbitration reform was the need to prevent any misuse of arbitration by unscrupulous parties.[22] It is,

18. Article 32(3) of the Arbitation Act 2002.
19. *Commentary to the Federal Law 'On Arbitration (Arbitral Proceedings) in the Russian Federation' (Clause-by-clause, Academic and Practical Commentary)*, Commentary to Article 33, §2 (O.Yu Skvortsov, M.Yu. Savransky, eds), (Moscow, Statut 2016) [Kommyentarii k Fyedyeralnomu zakonu 'Ob arbitrajye (tryetyeiskom razbiratyelstvye) v Rossiiskoi Fyedyeracii' (postatyeinyi, nauchno-praktichyeskii) / pod ryed. O.Yu. Skvortsova, M.Yu. Savranskogo. M.: Statut, 2016. Kommyentarii k statye 33, §2].
20. *Ibid.*
21. *Commercial Litigation: a Textbook*, 643 (V.V. Yarkov, ed., 7th ed., Moscow, 2017, author of the chapter I.G. Renz) [*Arbitrajnyi procyess: Uchyebnik / otv. ryed. V.V. Yarkova. 7-ye izd. M., 2017. C. 643. Avtor glavy – I.G. Renz*].
22. See above, Chapter 1.

unfortunately, not entirely uncommon in Russia that the parties engage in 'staged trials' where no actual dispute exists between them, but rather with a purpose of obtaining an enforceable court ruling approving their settlement agreement, which they can later use against third parties.[23] Just as Russian national courts occasionally decline to grant their approval for in-court settlement agreements, arbitral tribunals in domestic arbitration ought to possess a similar control mechanism at their disposal. Nevertheless, with the current wording of Article 33, a tribunal that resists the request of both parties and refuses to record their settlement in the form of an award on agreed terms may have to answer some difficult questions.

Another aspect of the same problem arose in the context of international commercial arbitration, where an ICAC tribunal felt that it was unable to approve the parties' settlement agreement in its entirety. Having pointed out that the proposed agreement goes beyond the limits of the original statement of claim and covers other relations between the parties the tribunal proceeded to record part of that agreement as an award on agreed terms. An application to enforce this award was later unsuccessful. The court held that if the arbitrators have an objection to the proposed terms that the parties agreed between themselves, they must either continue the proceedings and render an ordinary arbitral award, or suggest that the parties modify their agreement so that it would become acceptable to the tribunal in its entirety. An award that records only part of the agreement is neither an award on agreed terms nor a regular arbitral award, which makes it unsuitable for enforcement.[24]

Where the parties reach a settlement at the post-award stage, in the process of enforcement, a question arises as to the form in which they can record such settlement. The three possible alternatives are treating such an agreement as a purely private contract valid only as between the parties and carrying no enforcement status, recording it in the competent national court whereupon the settlement agreement would become enforceable as a judgment, or allowing the arbitral tribunal to record it. In 2012, the Supreme Commercial Court held that for the purposes of recording the parties' settlement, the arbitral tribunal that rendered the award could reconvene and approve this settlement agreement, thus giving it the same status as that of a 'regular' arbitral award.[25] This amounted to a new exception to the general rule that, upon rendering an award, the tribunal loses its authority and becomes *functus officio*.

§10.03 THE MAKING OF ARBITRAL AWARD

After the close of the proceedings, the tribunal renders an award. If there is more than one arbitrator on the tribunal, the award is adopted, according to the general rule, by a majority of arbitrators. According to Article 34 of the Arbitration Act 2015, all

23. Nestoliy V., *Openness – a Guarantee of Justice*, 45 EJ-Jurist 6, 9 (2012) [Nestoliy V. Glasnost - garantiya spravyedlivosti // EJ-Yurist. 2012. N 45. S. 9].
24. The Decree of the Federal Commercial Court for the North-Western Circuit of 7 October 2015 No. F07-7179/2015, case No. A56-14627/2015.
25. Decree of the Presidium of the Supreme Commercial Court of 7 June 2012 No. 16434/11, case No. A58-1799/2011.

members of the tribunal must sign the award, including the dissenting arbitrators. A dissenting opinion is then attached to the award.

It is customary in Russian arbitration, as it is the norm in the national litigation, to announce the operative part of the award upholding or refusing each of the parties' requests for relief at the end of the final arbitral hearing.[26] After that, the tribunal proceeds to make a reasoned award and send it to the parties. Unlike the procedural codes imposing strict deadlines on the national courts, arbitral legislation does not limit the arbitrators in the length of time they can take drafting the final award. However, with the general trend towards combating delay, institutional rules may provide for such a deadline.

Some arbitral institutions adopt the procedure of a preliminary internal scrutiny of an award, aiming to ensure the quality and enforceability of the award. Before signing the award, the tribunal sends its draft to the institution that may direct the attention of the arbitral tribunal to any formal discrepancies, as well as to any matters going into the merits of the dispute, without encroaching on the independence of the arbitrators. Members of the tribunal do not sign the award until its institutional approval.

In international practice, such a procedure is famously adopted in ICC Rules,[27] as well as in Singapore International Arbitration Centre (SIAC) Rules.[28] It is relatively uncommon in Russia, but the ICAC Rules provide for its abbreviated version. According to §40 of the ICAC Rules, before the award is signed, the arbitral tribunal shall, within a reasonable time in advance, deliver the draft award to the Secretariat. The Secretariat may, without infringing on the independence of the arbitrators to make the award, direct the attention of the arbitral tribunal to discrepancies found, if any, between the draft award and the formal requirements provided by these Rules or other ICAC regulations and rules. If such discrepancies are not rectified, the Secretariat may inform the Presidium of this.[29]

§10.04 CONTENTS OF AN AWARD

Article 34 of the Arbitration Act 2015 formulates the requirements to the contents of an arbitral award. These are default requirements, i.e., the parties in their agreement are free to modify them as they see fit. Under the general rules, an award must contain the following:

---

26. Kurochkin S.A., *Domestic and International Commercial Arbitration*, 156 (Moscow, Statut, 2017) [Kurochkin S.A. Tryetyeiskoye razbiratyelstvo i myejdunarodnyi kommyerchyeskii arbitraj. M.: Statut, 2017. S. 156].
27. Article 34 of the ICC Rues of Arbitration (current as of 1 March 2017), https://iccwbo.org/dispute-resolution-services/arbitration/rules-of-arbitration/#article_34 (accessed 7 February 2019).
28. Rule 32 of the SIAC Rules 2016, http://www.siac.org.sg/our-rules/rules/siac-rules-2016#siac_rule32 (accessed 7 February 2019).
29. *The Rules of Arbitration on International Commercial Disputes*, *supra* note 8, at paragraph 40.

(1) *The date of an arbitral award.* The award is deemed to be adopted on the date indicated in the document itself. Sometimes, institutional rules may modify this rule. For example, the ICAC Rules provide that the date of the award shall be the date of the last signature affixed thereto by an arbitrator of the arbitral tribunal.[30]

(2) *The seat of arbitration.* The parties may designate the seat in their agreement or design a procedure for its determination. Otherwise, the tribunal has the right to determine the seat. The Russian doctrine draws a clear distinction between the juridical seat of arbitration and a venue of the hearings.[31] Therefore, the tribunal is free to hold a hearing in any location; this will not, as a rule, influence the juridical seat of arbitration.

(3) *The composition of the arbitral tribunal and the procedure that led to its selection or appointment.*

(4) *Name and address of the parties in arbitration.* The information about the parties in the award relies on that supplied by the parties themselves. According to Article 3 of the Arbitration Act 2015, unless the parties agreed otherwise, documents and other materials shall be sent to the last known address of an organisation or the home address of an individual. Such documents and materials are deemed delivered in the day of delivery or an attempt to deliver them, even if the party in question no longer lives or conducts business at this address. In the context of litigation, the equivalent wording of the procedural codes in relation to organisations, including companies, has been interpreted primarily with the registered address of a company in mind, which for Russian organisations is freely available to the public as a part of the Unified State Register of Legal Entities. With foreign organisations, one option that the Supreme Court recommended to the lower courts was to consult the official Internet websites of registering authorities in the respective foreign countries containing information about the registered address of a party.[32]

(5) *The substantiation of the tribunal's jurisdiction.* In the award, the tribunal should address the matter of jurisdiction and explain its reasons for arriving at the conclusion that it had jurisdiction to hear the dispute. According to Article 16 of the Arbitration Act 2015, a party may raise a plea that the arbitral tribunal does not have jurisdiction until its first submission on the merits of the dispute. If the tribunal does not rule on this plea as a preliminary matter, it must include its reasoning in the award on the merits.

(6) *Claimant's submissions and respondent's objections, as well as any motions raised by the parties.* An award should describe the requests that the parties made and the grounds on which they relied, together with any objections

30. *Ibid.* at paragraph 37.
31. Kurochkin S.A., *supra* note 26, at 154.
32. Decree of the Plenum of the SC RF of 27 June 2017 N 23 'On the Consideration in Commercial Courts of Economic Disputes Arising from Relations with a Foreign Element'.

of the opposing party, according to the statement of claim and the answer to the statement of claim. The tribunal should arrive at a conclusion on each claim and objection and reflect this in the award.

(7) *Circumstances of the case, evidence and legal rules.* The arbitrators should record in the award the factual circumstances they considered proven; the evidence on which their conclusions relied; and the applicable legal rules on the basis of which the tribunal arrived at its conclusions. It is very common in Russia that the tribunal will resolve the case on the basis of Russian law. In cases where the parties selected foreign law to govern their relations, the tribunal will apply the parties' chosen rules of law. Failing any designation by the parties, the arbitral tribunal shall apply the law determined by the conflict of law rules that it considers applicable.

(8) *The operative part of the arbitral award* containing the tribunal's conclusions on upholding or refusing each of the parties' requests for relief.

(9) *Distribution of the costs of arbitration between the parties.* The provisions dealing with costs are also included in the operative part of the award. The tribunal will ascertain the overall amount of costs incurred in the process of arbitration and designate the party liable for the payment of such costs, in proportion to the tribunal's decision as to which party, and to what extent, prevailed on the merits, taking into account any agreement of the parties as to costs. The detailed rules on costs of arbitration and their distribution between the parties are contained in Article 22 of the 2015 Act.

(10) *An award may also contain the time limits and the procedure for the parties' compliance with its operative part*, e.g., where the sums awarded are to be paid in instalments.

The ICA Act 1993 governing international commercial arbitration contains fewer requirements to the contents of an award. According to Article 31 of this Act, the arbitral award shall state reasons on which it is based, the conclusions on upholding or refusing the claims, the quantification of arbitration fees and other costs, and their distribution between the parties. The award should also state its date and the place of arbitration.

The institutional rules may prescribe more detailed requirements for arbitral awards. For example, ICAC Rules require arbitral awards to contain:

- case number;
- date of the award;
- place of arbitration;
- the composition of the arbitral tribunal and its formation procedure;
- names (last name, first name and patronymic, if any), place of location (place of residence) of the parties to arbitral proceedings;
- a brief description of the conduct of arbitral proceedings;
- claims and statements of defence of the parties;
- substantiation of the jurisdiction of the arbitral tribunal;

- circumstances of the case established by the arbitral tribunal, evidence on which the conclusions of the arbitral tribunal on these circumstances are based, and legal norms applied by the arbitral tribunal when making an award;
- reasons for the award, with reference to the applicable legal norms;
- conclusions of the arbitral tribunal on the granting or dismissal of the claim;
- amounts of arbitration costs of the case and apportionment thereof between the parties; and
- signatures of the arbitrators.[33]

An arbitral award must contain the reasons on which it is based. If an arbitral award rendered in Russia does not contain the reasons on which it is based, it may be a ground for its challenge or refusing its enforcement. Neither the Arbitration Act 2015 nor the ICA Act 1993 authorise tribunal to resolve disputes *ex aequo et bono* or as *amiable compositeurs.* Likewise, enforcement of an unreasoned foreign arbitral award may be refused in Russia if the court establishes that the national arbitral law of the seat required the award to contain reasons.

§10.05 LEGAL EFFECTS OF AN AWARD

As far as the parties in arbitration are concerned, an arbitral award is final and binding for them, meaning that both parties are under an obligation to comply with its operative part, and neither of the parties is at freedom to challenge the findings of an arbitral tribunal on its merits.

The extent to which arbitral awards should have *res judicata* effect for subsequent legal and arbitral proceedings is more controversial. The issue has been in the spotlight of international debate over the last decades. An important step forward in this area had been made in the International Law Association Report on *Res Judicata* and Arbitration. Among other things, the Report suggested that national law does not necessarily have to govern the *res judicata* effect of an arbitral award, and it can instead be determined under the transnational rules applicable to international commercial arbitration.[34] In practical terms, this means that foreign courts and tribunals might hold that awards made in Russia possess *res judicata* effect regardless of the position of the national law on the issue. Russian national courts, however, have not been known to employ similar reasoning to date.

The effect of a *res judicata* decision is that it disposes finally and conclusively of a dispute in question so that the same subject matter cannot be relitigated between the same parties.[35] National laws differ as to the precise rules that apply to this effect of *res judicata,* in particular on what exactly constitutes the 'same subject matter'. Another aspect of *res judicata* belongs to the realm of evidence and concerns the question of

33. The Rules of Arbitration of International Commercial Disputes, *supra* note 8, at paragraph 37. Kurochkin, *supra* note 26, at 167.
34. *ILA Final Report on Res Judicata and Arbitration*, 25 Arbitration International 67 (2009).
35. Peter Barnett, *Res Judicata, Estoppel and Foreign Judgment,* paragraph 1.11 (OUP, 2011).

whether the parties are entitled to rely on – or are they at freedom to challenge in subsequent proceedings – the factual determinations made in an earlier judgment.[36] Russian doctrine treats these two effects or *res judicata* as two aspects of the legal force of judgments and arbitral awards;[37] for simplicity, these will be termed 'preclusive effect' and 'evidential effects' of an award in this chapter.

Article 150 of the Commercial Procedure Code and Article 220 of the Code of Civil Procedure define the preclusive effect of arbitral awards in national litigation. They stipulate that a competent court shall terminate legal proceedings if it finds that there exists an arbitral award rendered in a dispute between the same parties, about the same subject matter, and on the same grounds, except where a court has earlier refused the enforcement of such an award or set it aside.

Thus, as a general rule, arbitral awards preclude the litigation of further identical claims in national courts. It is logical that an award that has been set aside by a competent court loses its effect because after the entry into force of the respective judgment the award becomes a legal nullity – with a possible though highly unusual exception of enforcement of an annulled award in other countries.[38]

The argument is similar where the court refuses to enforce an arbitral award. This rule is best understood in conjunction with Article 240 of the Commercial Procedure Code that defines the consequences of a refusal to enforce an arbitral award. According to paragraphs 3 and 4 of this article, a refusal to enforce an arbitral award does not prevent the parties from re-initiating arbitral proceedings if the possibility of such reference has not been lost, or from starting legal proceedings in the commercial court according to the general rules.

Different rules apply to cases where the court refused the enforcement of an award in full or in part on one of the following grounds:

(1) invalidity of the arbitration agreement;
(2) the award dealing with a dispute not contemplated by or not falling within the terms of the submission to arbitration, or containing decisions on matters beyond the scope of the submission to arbitration;
(3) non-arbitrability of the subject matter of the dispute;
(4) an inconsistency of award with the public policy of the Russian Federation.

In such cases, the parties are free to begin legal proceedings in the commercial court according to the general rules but are unable to return to arbitration under the same arbitration agreement.

36. *Carl-Zeiss Stiftung v Rayner & Keeler Ltd (No 2)* [1966] 2 All ER 536 at 564 (HL), per Lord Guest.
37. *International Commercial Arbitration: a Textbook*, 764 (O.Yu. Skvortsov, M.Yu. Savransky, G.V. Sevastyanov, academic eds, 2nd ed., Moscow, 2018, author of the paragraph A.V. Asoskov) [Myejdunarodnyi kommyerchyeskii arbitraj: uchyebnik / Nauch. ryed.: O.Yu. Skvortsov, M.Yu. Savransky, G.V. Sevastyanov. M., 2018. S. 764. Avtor paragrafa A.V. Asoskov].
38. This is unusual but not unheard of for the awards in Russian-seated arbitration. A recent example is *Yukos v Rosneft*, Amsterdam Court of Appeal, 28 April 2009, case No. 200.005.269/01 where the Dutch court granted enforcement of an award earlier set aside in Moscow.

This regulation explains why an arbitral award the enforcement of which has been denied by a competent court loses its preclusive effect in Russian national litigation. In the foundation of the claim preclusion effect lies the presumption that the previous judgment or arbitral award is final as between the parties, which is not the case where enforcement of an award has been denied.

A condition required for an arbitral award's preclusive effect is the test of 'triple identity',[39] which in Russian procedural law means the identical claim, the identical legal grounds of this claim, and the same parties. By definition, therefore, arbitral awards have no preclusive effect for the third parties who did not sign an arbitration agreement and did not take part in arbitral proceedings. As the Supreme Commercial Court explained, this conclusion follows from the content of the right of access to justice guaranteed by Article 6 of the ECHR and Article 46 of the Russian Constitution, which provides each party with a right to be heard in an adversarial court hearing. In the absence of an opportunity to present its objections and its position on the subject matter of a dispute, a person cannot be bound by the conclusions in the arbitral award.[40]

Turning to the evidential effect of *res judicata*, Russian legislation does not contain any provisions that would relieve the interested parties of their burden of proof in relation to the facts established in an arbitral award (Article 69 of the Commercial Procedure Code, Article 61 of the Code of Civil Procedure). State courts are bound neither by the facts that that arbitral tribunal established nor by their conclusions.[41] Other arbitral tribunals (even if identical in their composition), likewise, are not bound by previous awards.[42] The lack of the evidential *res judicata* effects in arbitral awards has been confirmed by the Supreme Commercial Court[43] and consistently applied in subsequent judgments.[44]

One could argue, however, that the awards that have been enforced by a competent court do, to a certain extent, possess evidentiary *res judicata* effect. In this case, the circumstances relating to the dispute that that competent court reiterated in its judgment will have *res judicata* effect according to the general rules of procedural law, thus indirectly giving a similar effect to portions of the underlying award.[45] In this case, according to the national rules of civil procedure, the 'triple identity' test is not required. It would be enough that both parties are the same in the previous and the subsequent proceedings, regardless of their subject matter and legal grounds.[46]

39. See Gary Born, *International Commercial Arbitration*, 2886 (Hague, 2009).
40. Decree of the Presidium of the Supreme Commercial Court of Russian Federation of 11 February 2014 N 15554/13, case No. A40-116181/12-11-1051.
41. Kurochkin, *supra* note 26, at 189.
42. *Ibid.*
43. Decree of the Presidium of the Supreme Commercial Court of Russian Federation of 18 March 2014 N 16918/13, case No. A40-164314/12.
44. *See*, e.g., the Decree of the Federal Commercial Court for the Moscow Circuit of 25 April 2014, case No. A40-52599/13-129-284; the Decree of the Federal Commercial Court for the North-Western Circuit of 18 September 2014, case No. A66-4423/2013.
45. Yarkov V.V., *Legal Facts in Civilistic Process*, 175 (Moscow, 2012) [Yarkov V.V. Yuridichyeskiye fakty v civilistichyeskom procyessye. M., 2012. S. 175].
46. See Article 69 of the Commercial Procedure Code, Article 61 of the Code of Civil Procedure.

It has been suggested that arbitral tribunal should voluntarily adopt the approach whereby the previous arbitral awards have evidential *res judicata* effect in subsequent arbitrations between the same parties.[47] This has been the prevailing approach in the published practice of ICAC at the RF CCI.[48] Thus, the evidential *res judicata* effects may also arise in Russian arbitration in its 'soft' form, as part of an attempt to achieve legal consistency on the part of arbitrators, rather than as a strict legal rule.

§10.06 CORRECTION AND INTERPRETATION OF AN AWARD. ADDITIONAL AWARD

According to Article 37 of the Arbitration Act 2015, within thirty days of receipt of the arbitral award, unless the parties agreed another time period, a party, with notice to the other party, may request the arbitral tribunal to correct in the award any errors in computation, any clerical or typographical errors or any errors of similar nature. The arbitral tribunal may correct any error of this type on its own initiative within thirty days of the date of the award.

If so agreed by the parties, a party, with notice to the other party, may request the arbitral tribunal to give an interpretation of a specific point or part of the award. If the arbitral tribunal considers the request to be justified, it shall make the correction or give the interpretation within thirty days of receipt of the request. The interpretation shall form part of the award.

This provision represents a verbatim adoption of the UNCITRAL Model Law wording and is also identical to its counterpart in the ICA Act 1993 regulating international commercial arbitration.

The procedure of correction and interpretation of the award cannot be deployed to change the mistaken pronouncements of the tribunal regarding the facts, and its conclusions on the merits of the claim. It has been rightly pointed out that such requests pose a dilemma for the tribunal that needs to distinguish very carefully between the need to ensure clarity through this statutory mechanism and the attempts to review the tribunal's conclusions or lead new arguments in support of the parties' positions.[49]

According to the prevailing international practice, the term 'errors in computation, any clerical or typographical errors' must be understood literally. There is no need for an error to be significant and affect the conclusions of the tribunal or lead to any doubts as to the correctness of the award. Any errors of such nature must be corrected, however minor and insignificant they might seem.[50]

---

47. *International Commercial Arbitration: a Textbook, supra* note 37, at 765.
48. See *Awards 9, 41, 45, 61, 75, 87* in: *Practice of the ICAC at the RF CCI 2004-2016: for the 85th Anniversary of the ICAC* (A.N. Zhiltsov, A.I. Muranov, eds, Moscow, 2017) [*Ryeshyeniya 9, 41, 45, 61, 75, 87 // Praktika MKAS pri TPP R70: 2004-2016: K 85-lyetiyu MKAS (pod ryed.* A.N. Zhiltsova, A.I. Muranova, *M.: 2017*).
49. Margaret Moses, *The Principles and Practice of International Commercial Arbitration*, 201 (2nd ed. NY, 2012).
50. See G. Nerdrum, *Correction of Errors in Arbitral Awards*, 260, in: *International Commercial Arbitration: Contemporary Problems and Solutions: A Collection of Articles in Honour of the*

There are two most common technical approaches to the correction of an award. First, the tribunal may prepare a new, updated, and corrected edition of the same arbitral award, acknowledging the fact of the amendment and other details relating to its correction. Second, the tribunal can prepare a separate additional award pointing out the errors and offering their correction. Russian commentators expressed a preference for the second option, particularly in the view of the possibility of the chairperson of the arbitral tribunal correcting and signing such an award alone, due to its technical nature.[51]

Unless otherwise agreed by the parties, a party, with notice to the other party, may request, within thirty days of receipt of the award, the arbitral tribunal to make an additional award as to claims presented in the arbitral proceedings but omitted from the award. If the arbitral tribunal considers the request to be justified, it shall make the additional award within sixty days.

The arbitral tribunal may extend, if necessary, the period of time within which it shall make a correction, interpretation or an additional award.

The same Article 37 of the Arbitration Act 2015 contains another provision often found in other countries' statutory provisions concerning the setting aside of arbitral awards. According to paragraph 6 of this Article, if the court considering an application to set aside or enforce an award suspends the proceedings for a period of time in order to give the arbitral tribunal an opportunity to resume the arbitral proceedings and eliminate the grounds for setting aside or refusing to enforce the award, the tribunal may resume the arbitral proceedings on the request of a party submitted during such suspension of the proceedings. Paragraph 7 of the same Article 37 of the Arbitration Act 2015 envisions that the result of such resumption of the proceedings may be an additional award.

Considering the location of the above rules within the 2015 Act, one may conclude that, in deciding whether it is appropriate to suspend the legal proceedings for this purpose, the competent court will be guided by the same considerations as described above in relation to the correction and interpretation of an award. Namely, the potential action that the tribunal might undertake should not entail a dramatic change of the tribunal's conclusions, nor should it be used for correcting any factual mistakes in the tribunal's reasoning. Instead, this procedure will be most appropriate for ensuring that the arbitral award is clear, unambiguous, and free of any errors in computation, any clerical, or typographical errors. Likewise, this procedure will be appropriate to deal with claims presented in the arbitral proceedings but omitted for any reason from the award.

International Commercial Arbitration Court at the Chamber of Commerce and Industry of the Russian Federation 80th Anniversary (Kostin A.A., ed.) [Nerdrum G., Ispravlyeniye oshibok v arbitrajnyh ryeshyeniyah // Myejdunarodnyi kommyerchyeskii arbitraj: sovryemyennyye problyemy i ryeshyeniya: Sbornik statyei k 80-lyetiyu Myejdunarodnogo kommyerchyeskogo arbitrajnogo suda pri Torgovo-promyshlyennoi palatye Rossiiskoi Fyedyeracii / Pod ryed. A.A. Kostina. M., 2012. S. 260].

51. Zykov Roman, *International Arbitration in Sweden: Law and Practice*, 176 (Moscow, 2014) [Zykov R.O. Myejdunarodnyi arbitraj v Shvyecii: pravo i praktika. M., 2014. S. 176].

However, the procedural codes hint at a potentially broader range of actions that the tribunal may be required to perform if a court has suspended the legal proceedings to give it an opportunity to eliminate the grounds for setting aside or refusing to enforce the award. For example, according to Article 232 of the Commercial Procedure Code, the court may suspend the proceedings for this purpose if the application to set aside an award is made on the grounds of the lack of proper notice of the appointment of an arbitrator or of the arbitral proceedings; or inability otherwise to present the applicant's case; or on the grounds that the award deals with a dispute not contemplated by or not falling within the terms of the submission to arbitration, or contains decisions on matters beyond the scope of the submission to arbitration; or that the composition of the arbitral tribunal or the arbitral procedure was not in accordance with the agreement of the parties or the federal law. As a practical matter, such drawbacks of the award may go beyond being merely technical ones, and the resumption of arbitral proceedings may result in the adoption of a new award, as well as correction or amendment of the original award.[52]

Correction, interpretation, and amendment of an award may lead to additional expenses. However, the tribunal, as a rule, cannot claim any additional fees for these actions.[53]

§10.07 OTHER DECISIONS AND ORDERS IN ARBITRATION

The decisions of an arbitral tribunal, according to the Russian legislation on both international and domestic arbitration, come in two main forms: awards and orders. In addition to those, legislation and the Rules of permanent arbitral institutions also mention other forms of documents, such as 'requests' and notifications'. A separate category of arbitral decisions does not originate from the tribunal but instead comes from various officials and committees within the structure of a permanent arbitral institution.[54] We shall discuss these three categories below.

[A] Orders of the Arbitral Tribunal

An order is the act of an arbitral tribunal dealing with matters that do not concern the merits of the dispute and the essence of the parties' claims. Instead, orders resolve various procedural, technical, or financial issues that arise during the proceedings.

To begin with, the matter of terminology deserves some attention. According to Article 35 of the Arbitration Act 2015, on the matters that do not concern the merits of the dispute, the tribunal shall render an order ('*postanovlenie*'). This Russian word

52. *International Commercial Arbitration: a Textbook*, 760 (O.Yu. Skvortsov, M.Yu. Savransky, G.V. Sevastyanov, academic eds, 2nd ed., Moscow, 2018, author of the chapter I.P. Greshnikov) [Myejdunarodnyi kommyerchyeskii arbitraj: uchyebnik / Nauch. ryed.: O.Yu. Skvortsov, M.Yu. Savransky, G.V. Sevastyanov. M., 2018. S. 760. Avtor glavy I.P. Greshnikov].
53. Kurochkin, *supra* note 26, at 190.
54. *International Commercial Arbitration: a Textbook*, *supra* note 52, at 729.

'*postanovlenie*' is often translated into English as 'decree'.[55] The ICA Act 1993 also uses this term.

A further terminological confusion stemmed previously from the Arbitration Act 2002 that, unlike the ICA Act 1993, used the term '*opredelenie*' (ruling) to denote the same type of decisions by the tribunal. Article 37 of the 2002 Act provided that on the matters that do not concern the merits of the dispute, the tribunal shall render a ruling ('*opredelenie*'). Since the entry into force of the Arbitration Act 2015 that replaced the 2002 Act, the discrepancy has now disappeared.

The UNCITRAL Model law (on which the Russian ICA Act 1993 relies) terms such decisions as 'orders', e.g., in Article 32. Since the word 'order' in the Model Law was translated as '*postanovlenie*' in the ICA Act 1993,[56] this book also uses the term 'order' to mean the broad range of acts that concern arbitral proceedings but do not resolve the dispute on the merits.

The legislation explicitly mentions the following orders of the arbitral tribunal:

- an order on the tribunal's jurisdiction to resolve the case (Article 16 of the ICA Act 1993 and Article 16 of the Arbitration Act 2015);
- orders and other acts of the tribunal concerning interim measures (Article 17 of the ICA Act 1993 and Article 17 of the Arbitration Act 2015);
- an order for the termination of the arbitral proceedings (Article 32 of the ICA Act 1993 and Article 36 of the Arbitration Act 2015);
- orders concerning costs of arbitration (Article 22 of the Arbitration Act 2015);
- an order referring the parties to mediation (Article 49 of the Arbitration Act 2015).

Due to the broadly permissive wording of Article 35 of the 2015 Act, the Rules of arbitral institutions and tribunals themselves may adopt other categories of orders, so the list above is not exhaustive.[57]

As a practical matter, orders of an arbitral tribunal in Russia often mirror those in the armoury of the national civil procedure, in particular, the commercial procedure. Thus, by analogy with the Commercial Procedure Code that regulates litigation in Russian commercial courts, arbitral tribunals commonly utilise:

- *An order on the acceptance of the statement of claim*. In Russian commercial procedure, plaintiff's first communication with the court is in the form of a statement of claim. If this document satisfies the formal requirements, the

55. *See*, e.g., MAC Award No. 8/2002 of 10 February 2003 and MAC Award No. 51/1992 of 5 July 1995 in: *From the Practice of the Maritime Arbitration Commission at the Chamber of Commerce and Industry of the Russian Federation 1987-2005*, 197-213 and 318-344 (Sergey Lebedev, Andrey Loboda and Dmitry Filimonov, eds, Moscow, 2009). Quoted according to: Roman Khodykin, *Arbitration Law of Russia: Practice and Procedure*, 133 (Juris, 2013) [Iz praktiki Morskoi arbitrajnoi komissii pri Torgovo-promyshlyennoi palatye Rossiiskoi Fyedyeracii za 1987-2005 gg./Pod ryed. S.N. Lyebyedyeva, A.I. Lobody, D.B. Filimonova. Moskva, Statut, 2009, S. 197-213, 318-344. Tsit. po: Roman Khodykin, *Arbitration Law of Russia: Practice and Procedure*, 133 (Juris, 2013)].
56. Roman Khodykin, *Arbitration Law of Russia: Practice and Procedure*, 133 (Juris, 2013).
57. *International Commercial Arbitration: A Textbook*, *supra* note 52, at 733.

court makes an order on the acceptance of the statement of claim, which initiates the proceedings in the case (Articles 125-127 of the Commercial Procedure Code). In arbitration, statement of claim may not be the first document that claimant exchanges with the respondent, tribunal, or the arbitral institution. However, unless the parties agreed otherwise, the arbitral proceedings in respect of a particular dispute commence on the date on which the respondent receives a statement of claim (Article 21 of the ICA Act 1993). If the claimant fails to communicate his statement of claim, the arbitral tribunal shall terminate the proceedings (Article 25 of the ICA Act 1993). Unlike the Model Law, those articles of the ICA Act 1993 do not differentiate between a 'request for arbitration' and a 'statement of claim'. Just as it is the practice in the national civil and commercial procedure, often only a statement of claim is required; preliminary requests for arbitration are less common in Russia. This, of course, is subject to any provisions to the contrary in the applicable arbitration rules. The Arbitration Act 2015 also fails to mention a request for arbitration and provides instead a detailed set of formal requirements to a statement of claim in Article 25.

- *An order on the preparation of the case for arbitral proceedings*. Such an order would usually summon the parties or their representatives for a preliminary hearing and offer them to disclose the evidence to prove their claims and objections. Such an order could broadly be in line with a similar type of orders in the commercial civil procedure (Articles 133-135 of the Commercial Procedure Code).
- *An order setting a hearing date* (by analogy with Article 137 of the Commercial Procedure Code) where the tribunal summons the parties to a hearing.
- *Orders on joinder or separation of claims* (by analogy with Article 130 of the Commercial Procedure Code), where an agreement of the parties or the applicable rules allow this. The Russian statutory arbitration law does not explicitly mention joinder and separation of claims but they are possible as a matter of practice.[58]
- *An order on the suspension of the proceedings* (by analogy with Articles 143-147 of the Commercial Procedure Code). Suspension of the proceedings means their temporary stay for an indeterminate period, until the circumstances that caused the suspension cease to exist. A frequently used ground for the suspension is the impossibility of resolving the case at hand until another case in the Constitutional Court of the Russian Federation, a court of general jurisdiction or a commercial court, comes to its conclusion. Article 45 of the Arbitration Act 2015 requires permanent arbitral institutions to include the relevant provisions on the suspension of the proceedings in their Rules, otherwise leaving them to regulate the matter as they see fit.

58. *See*, e.g., the Decree of the Federal Commercial Court for the Moscow Circuit of 13 September 2016 No. F05-13069/2016, case No. A40-41858/16; the Decree of the Federal Commercial Court for the Urals Circuit of 08 December 2016 N F09-10934/16, case No. A60-32732/2016.

The practice of issuing *procedural orders* of a complex character, addressing multiple matters and dealing with a plethora of issues at once, is fairly common in the international practice, e.g., in the LCIA, ICC and SCC. This practice is also becoming more widespread in Russia, in particular in ICAC at the RF CCI.[59] Typically, such procedural orders contain some or all of the following provisions:

- a timetable for the proceedings, including the time(s) and place(s) of oral hearings;
- a suggestion for each party to produce the original documents on which it relies, as well as the documents confirming the right of representatives to act on behalf of the respective parties (powers of attorney, minutes of company boards, and so on) at the oral hearing;
- a reminder for each party to disclose all the evidence on which they intend to rely in good time before the hearing, and a suggestion to produce the list of such evidence by a particular date;
- a suggestion for the parties to produce certain documents or classes of documents that the tribunal deems particularly relevant, e.g. the documents proving the applicable interest rates in the relevant country where the claimant seeks to recover interest or the translation of documents in foreign languages;
- a request for the parties to produce their written comments on various aspects of the case;
- a suggestion for the respondent to produce a statement of defence or the statement of a counterclaim, if applicable;
- a suggestion for both parties to put forward any motions or requests of procedural nature;
- a suggestion for both parties to consider the opportunities for settling the dispute, in particular with the assistance of a mediator;
- a reminder of the parties' entitlement to produce their comments on the other side's motions, statements and documents from the other parties, as well as the procedural order of the tribunal, by a certain date.[60]

The crucial feature of the tribunal's orders that distinguishes them from arbitral awards is that they are not capable of enforcement nationally or under the New York Convention 1958, and the parties cannot challenge them on their own, independently of the resulting award. The parties can only bring their objections before the court in the proceedings on setting aside or enforcing the award. Both of these rules are, however, subject to some statutory exceptions.

The parties can challenge two categories of the tribunal's orders in front of a competent court independently of the final award:

- an order refusing a challenge of an arbitrator (Article 13 of the Arbitration Act 2015 and Article 16 of the ICA Act 1993);

59. *International Commercial Arbitration: A Textbook, supra* note 52, at 734.
60. *Ibid.*

- an order where the arbitral tribunal rules as a preliminary question that it has jurisdiction to consider the case (Article 16 of the Arbitration Act 2015 and Article 16 of the ICA Act 1993).

Other categories of procedural orders may be called into question only after the final award has been made, for example as evidence of bias or lack of due process. Just like in other jurisdictions, it is advisable to put one's objections against an order to the tribunal first to increase or, indeed, preserve the chances of such an argument succeeding in the court at a later stage.[61] Article 4 of the Arbitration Act 2015 stipulates that a party shall be deemed to waive its right to object if it continues to participate in arbitral proceedings without raising a timely objection.

[B] Requests, Notifications and Subpoenas

In some cases, instead of referring to the documents originating from the tribunal as 'orders' (*'postanovlenie')*, the drafters of Russian arbitration statutes used other terms, such as 'requests', 'notifications' and 'subpoenas'. Typically, this means that the acts in question serve a more technical purpose (however important it may be) and do not as such determine the rights and obligations of the parties.

An important example of this kind of acts is the *request for assistance in obtaining the evidence.* According to Article 27 of the ICA Act 1993 and Article 30 of the Arbitration Act 2015, an arbitral tribunal in an arbitration administered by a permanent arbitral institution, or a party with the tribunal's permission, may request the competent court to provide assistance in the obtaining of evidence. Procedural legislation (Article 74.1 of the Commercial Procedure Code and Article 63.1 of the Code of Civil Procedure) regulates the actions of a competent court that considers such requests. The court performs the request within thirty days unless it considers that there is a ground for refusal to perform it. Such grounds include the possibility of infringing the rights of third parties that do not participate in arbitration; non-arbitrability of the dispute; the information in question beings classified as a state secret, or a commercial, banking or other protected secret. A refusal to perform the request is not subject to appeal.

These provisions concerning court assistance to arbitration are relatively novel and have been introduced in the course of the arbitration reform 2015. Albeit limited (denying ad hoc arbitration this possibility, making the court refusal non-appealable, etc.), they represent an important step in the development of arbitration in Russia.[62]

Notifications and subpoenas are, essentially, technical acts usually regulated by the Rules of permanent arbitral institutions. They allow the tribunal to keep the parties and other interested persons informed about the course of the ongoing proceedings, the constitution of the tribunal, upcoming hearings, and so on.[63] The term 'subpoena' (*'povestka'*) can be deceptive as it does not imply any power of the arbitral tribunal to

61. Nigel Blackaby, Constantine Partasides QC, Alan Redfern, and Martin Hunter, *supra* note 3, at §9.08.
62. *International Commercial Arbitration: A Textbook, supra* note 52, at 731.
63. *Ibid.* at 732.

enforce the attendance of any persons, be it witnesses or the parties themselves as it does in the national civil procedure. Instead, this seems to be yet another example of the use of similar terminology across the distinct contexts of civil procedure and arbitration.

The acts within this category are not subject to a challenge in court independently of the arbitral award. However, they are far from being inconsequential. Their absence or defects, for example, often form the basis of a successful challenge of the final award, for example, due to the lack of notification or the 'lack of due process'.

[C] Acts by the Officials and Committees of Permanent Arbitral Institutions

Officials and bodies of permanent arbitral institutions perform many important functions ensuring that the arbitral proceedings commence and follow their course in an efficient manner. In most cases, the Rules of arbitral institutions define and enumerate their powers and the range of acts they adopt. Just like those that originate with the tribunal, the acts of said officials and bodies may take the form of orders. Other common terms are protocols, rulings, decisions, and so on.

Chairpersons or presidents of permanent arbitral institutions, their presidiums, and the appointment committees typically exercise some discretionary powers that have a procedural significance in arbitration.

Some institutional rules empower the presidium of an arbitral institution to deal with the matters arising during the constitution of a tribunal, challenges of arbitrators and replacements within the tribunal after its appointment. In other institutions, those matters may be within the competence of a chairperson or an appointment committee.[64]

The Rules of the ICAC at the RF CCI empower the Presidium to deal with a broader range of matters. For instance, the Presidium can adopt decisions on the consolidation of arbitral proceedings.[65] It can also make an order on the termination of arbitral proceedings where the issue of the possibility of arbitrating a dispute at the ICAC arises before the formation of an arbitral tribunal and it is manifestly impossible for the dispute to be considered in full or in part by the ICAC.[66]

In the Arbitration Centre at the Russian Institute of Modern Arbitration, the Board discharges the functions of an appointments committee.[67]The Board is a permanent collective body of the Centre performing the functions of appointment and challenge of arbitrators and termination of their mandate as well as other functions,[68] such as the adjustment of the arbitral fees on an application of a party.[69]

---

64. *Ibid.* at 732.
65. *The Rules of Arbitration on International Commercial Disputes, supra* note 8, at paragraph 12.
66. *Ibid.* at paragraph 25.
67. Article 1 of the *Arbitration Rules of the RIMA at the Autonomous Non-Profit Organisation 'Institute of Modern Arbitration'* of 20 December 2016, as amended on 20.09.2017, https://centerarbitr.ru/en/arbitration-rules/ (accessed 14 January 2019).
68. *Ibid.* Article 2.
69. *Ibid.* Article 9.

The acts within this category are also not subject to a direct challenge in court independently of the arbitral award, but their absence or defects may form the basis for a successful challenge of the final award.

§10.08 TERMINATING ARBITRAL PROCEEDINGS WITHOUT ISSUING AN AWARD

One type of orders deserves particular attention because it represents an exception to the general rule that arbitration ends in a final and binding award. Ordinarily, a final award terminates the proceedings and the mandate of the arbitral tribunal. In addition, the proceedings can also terminate without the tribunal issuing an award.

It is normally the task of a tribunal to issue an order on the termination of arbitral proceedings, although there may be some exceptions. We mentioned one such exception above: the Presidium of the ICAC at the RF CCI can make an order on the termination of arbitral proceedings if the issue arises before the formation of an arbitral tribunal and it is manifestly impossible for the dispute to be considered in full or in part by the ICAC.[70]

The tribunal may issue an order on the termination of the proceedings on its own initiative or at the motion of either party in the arbitration. The legislation contains four grounds for the termination of arbitral proceedings, which are identical for domestic and international arbitration in the Russian Federation, and broadly coincide with those in the UNCITRAL Model Law:

(1) Where the mechanism of arbitral appointment agreed by the parties fails to produce a result, and the parties' agreement excludes the possibility of appointment by a competent court (Articles 11 and 36 of the Arbitration Act 2015, Articles 11 and 32 of the ICA Act 1993). Such an exclusion is only possible in institutional but not in ad hoc arbitration. In the case of a total failure of the appointment procedure, there is no need for an order terminating the proceedings, and the claimant can start a case in a competent court according to the general rules of the procedural law.
(2) Where the claimant withdraws his claim unless the respondent objects thereto and the arbitral tribunal recognises a legitimate interest on his part in obtaining a final settlement of the dispute.[71]
(3) The parties agree on the termination of the proceedings.[72]
(4) The arbitral tribunal finds that the continuation of the proceedings has for any reason become unnecessary or impossible.[73]

The ICAC Rules provide some examples of cases where the latter ground for the termination of proceedings might apply. A common reason, for instance, is the

70. *The Rules of Arbitration on International Commercial Disputes, supra* note 8, paragraph 12.
71. Article 36 of the Arbitration Act 2015, Article 32 of the ICA Act 1993.
72. *Ibid.*
73. *Ibid.*

passivity of the claimant that makes it impossible for the proceedings to move forward for more than six months.[74]

The continuation of the proceedings also becomes unnecessary or impossible if the tribunal finds that there is a decision of a competent court or an arbitral award between the same parties, concerning the same subject matter where the claimant relied on the same grounds as in the case at hand.[75]

Each party must receive a copy of an order on the termination of the arbitral proceedings with the signatures of the arbitrators according to the statutory requirements and any requirements of the applicable rules of arbitration.

The mandate of the arbitral tribunal terminates with the termination of the proceedings, subject to the rules concerning the interpretation and correction of an award, additional awards, and the resumption of proceedings on a request of a competent court hearing the case on a challenge of an award or its recognition and enforcement (Article 37 of the Arbitration Act 2015). Where the proceedings are terminated by an order of the tribunal – as opposed to a final arbitral award – the exceptional circumstances listed above are unlikely to arise, thus the tribunal's mandate terminates permanently.

The statutory law of Russia does not give the parties a right to challenge an order on the termination of the proceedings, and a competent court would refuse to hear such a claim.[76] Such orders can only indirectly become a focus of a court's attention if one of the parties were to allege at a later stage that the court must stay the proceedings in favour of arbitration.

There had been cases in the practice of Russian courts showing that claimants might be able to recover from an arbitral institution the fees they paid to initiate the case if the tribunal terminated the proceedings for lack of an arbitral agreement between the parties.[77] This line of cases seems somewhat anomalous and perhaps merits further discussion to determine whether the grounds for such a judicial approach were sound. However, it does also serve as a useful reminder that the view of arbitration as a provision of services may remain prominent among the Russian judiciary, despite the pronouncements to the contrary.[78]

---

74. The Rules of the International Commercial Arbitration Court at the Chamber of Commerce and Industry of the Russian Federation: Academic and Practical Commentary, *supra* note 10, at §45(4).
75. Kurochkin, *supra* note 26, at 124.
76. *See*, e.g., the Ruling of the Supreme Court of the Russian Federation No. 5-G01-28 of 23 March 2001.
77. The Ruling of the Supreme Commercial Court of the Russian Federation No. VAS-6065/11 of 11 May 2011, case No. A40-33705/10-68-311.
78. *See*, e.g., the Decree of the Commercial Court of the Moscow Region of 17 March 2015 in case No. A40-117713/2014 (refusing to treat the resolution of disputes in arbitration as a service that would require the institution to charge the value added tax).

CHAPTER 11
Challenging the Award

§11.01 GENERAL CONDITIONS OF CHALLENGING AN ARBITRAL AWARD

The previous Arbitration Act regulated the procedure for challenging arbitral awards, the grounds for setting aside and the consequences of setting aside of an award. The Arbitration Act 2015 contains no detailed regulation for these issues, instead referring to the procedural law that governs litigation before state courts. This is a welcome approach, both from the point of view of the legal policy and as a matter of statutory drafting. First, it helps to reduce the overall volume of statutory text. Second, it is logical because the relationship concerning the challenge of arbitral awards takes place before the state courts and is regulated by the civil (commercial) procedural law. Third, this approach helps to exclude the possibility of contradictions between different statutes.

Referring to the right of a party to initiate a procedure of declaring the award legally void, Russian legislator uses the term 'challenge'. With regard to the procedures for review of national courts' judgments, the legislation operates with the term 'appeal'. Apparently, this variation in terminology aims to emphasise the difference between the review procedures for arbitral awards and national court judgments. The difference lies in the fact that the challenge of arbitral awards is limited mainly to procedural grounds, whereas litigants can appeal a state court decision on its merits, both due to the incorrect application of the law and due to any inaccuracies of judicial fact-finding.

An application for setting aside is the exclusive recourse against the award. This idea relies on the international legal practice [1] and means that the review of arbitral awards is only possible by a decision of a ***competent state court*** in accordance with the

1. *See The Explanatory Note by the UNCITRAL Secretariat on the 1985 Model Law on International Commercial Arbitration as Amended in 2006*, 35 - 36 (Vienna, United Nations, 2008).

specific procedural rules. No other state authority can deprive the arbitral tribunal's acts of their legal force.

Considering the application to set aside an award, state courts may not review the award on the merits, nor can they re-evaluate the factual circumstances that have been established by the arbitral tribunal in the proceedings (Article 232(6) of the Commercial Procedure Code, paragraph 12 of the SCC RF Information Letter No. 96 of 22 December 2005).

If an arbitration agreement stipulates that the arbitral award shall be final, the competent court should terminate the proceedings against such an award (paragraph 9 of the SCC RF Information Letter No. 96 of 22 December 2005).

§11.02 APPLICATION TO SET ASIDE AN ARBITRAL AWARD

Three categories of persons have the right to challenge arbitral awards:

(1) those who participated in the arbitration proceedings;
(2) persons whose rights and obligations are affected by the award;
(3) the public prosecutor's office, in cases where the arbitral award affects the rights of the Russian Federation, a region of the Russian Federation, or a local authority and the above entity did not participate in the arbitration proceedings (Article 230(3) of the Commercial Procedure Code), as well as in cases where the award affects the rights and lawful interests of citizens who because of health, age, disability or for other valid reasons cannot independently challenge the award (Article 418(1) of the Code of Civil Procedure).

If the award relates to the rights and obligations of a person who did not participate in the arbitration proceedings, the state court should set aside the arbitral award only in the part that affects this person (paragraph 11 of the SCC RF Information Letter No. 96 of 22 December 2005).

If a person who was not a party to the arbitration proceedings, but whose rights and obligations have been affected by the arbitral award, initiates the challenge proceedings, the competent court should ensure that all parties to the arbitration proceedings take part in such challenge proceedings.

The deadline for challenging the arbitration award is three months from the date the person concerned received the award. This time limit is preclusive and the court cannot extend it even if the applicant had a valid reason for missing the deadline. This three-month limit also applies to those persons who were not parties to arbitration proceedings, but in this case, the term is calculated from the date when the applicant first learned or should have learned about the decision.

Unlike under the previous legislation, currently, the Commercial Procedure Code and the Code of Civil Procedure regulate the process of dealing with the applications to set aside an arbitral award.

The interested parties must apply to set aside an arbitral award according to the rules on subject-matter and territorial jurisdiction, either with the first instance commercial court or with the district court of general jurisdiction at the territory where the award was made. This is a default rule, because the parties may agree that applications for setting aside shall be registered at the location or place of residence of one of the parties. Unfortunately, this rule does not correlate with another rule that governs jurisdiction for the enforcement of arbitral awards. The latter rule provides that applications for issuing a writ of execution shall be considered at the location or place of residence of the debtor and, if it is not known – at the territory where the debtor's property is located (Article 236(3) of the Commercial Procedure Code). Such a legislative solution has a potential of leading to contradictory judgments, where a court might issue a writ of execution for an award that had been set aside.

A sole judge shall consider an application to set aside an arbitral award within one month. It is gratifying that the legislator abandoned the previous rule establishing a three-month limit for consideration of applications to set aside an award. The quicker resolution of setting aside applications makes arbitration more attractive among the other methods of dispute resolution.

The procedural legislation provides the judge considering the application to set aside an arbitral award with the right to request the materials of the relevant arbitral proceedings. The court cannot order the delivery of such materials on its own initiative, but only if so requested by the parties. The wording of the relevant rule (Article 232(2) of the Commercial Procedure Code) remains as unclear as it was under the old law. In our view, this wording will give rise to disputes about whether it is enough that one party makes a request, or the court has the right to order the delivery of materials only where so requested by both sides.

The competent court may suspend the setting aside proceedings temporarily, so that the arbitral tribunal could resume arbitration and eliminate the grounds for setting aside or refusal to enforce an arbitral award (Article 37(6) and (7) of the Arbitration Act 2015, Article 232 of the Commercial Procedure Code). This rule also comes from the UNCITRAL Model Law on International Commercial Arbitration. At the same time, experts subjected this rule to valid criticism,[2] because it allows the tribunal to revise the award as a result of subsequently identified deficiencies, such as lack of jurisdiction under the terms of the arbitration agreement, the non-conformity of the arbitral tribunal or the arbitration procedure to the agreement of the parties or the federal law. Meanwhile, such drawbacks entail illegality of the award of arbitration and can only be eliminated by setting aside of the award. In addition, the wording of this rule, unlike that of its counterpart in the Model Law, is unfortunate because its literal reading allows one to conclude that a national court may, *irrespective of any request by a party*, stay the proceedings and refer the case back to the arbitral tribunal for reconsideration.

2. Rozhkova M., Glazkova M., Afanasiev D., *Innovations in the Legal Regulation of Arbitration in the Russian Federation*, 3 The Economy and the Law, 34-35 (2016) [*Rozhkova M., Glazkova M., Afanasiev D. Novacii v pravovom ryegulirovanii tryetyeiskogo razbiratyelstva v Rossiiskoi Federacii. // Hozyaistvo i pravo*. 2016. No. 3. S. 34-35].

The procedural codes delineate the powers of a competent court in setting aside proceedings. Thus, according to Article 232(6) of the Commercial Procedure Code, a commercial court cannot re-evaluate the circumstances established by the arbitral tribunal or review the award on the merits. This provision is very important as it puts the relationship between state courts and arbitration into the conventional legal framework developed in the long-standing international practice of commercial arbitration. The general thrust of this relationship is that the competent national court can only assess the formal (as a rule, procedural) aspects of arbitration while considering an application to enforce an arbitral award. The courts focus their attention primarily on the rules that guarantee a certain minimum standard of respect for the rights of participants in the process: the right to participate in the hearing, the right to be heard, the right to conduct the proceedings in one's own language, and other procedural rights. Only under this condition, the arbitral proceedings can be truly independent of the state judiciary and, accordingly, guarantee the stability of arbitral awards.

The Russian judicial practice consistently holds that failure to follow the procedure for challenging an arbitral award entails negative procedural consequences for the applicant. For example, the Federal Commercial Court for the Volga Circuit stated, reviewing the case on appeal, that Article 231 of the Commercial Procedure Code requires an application to set aside an arbitral award to be accompanied by the original arbitration agreement or its duly certified copy. The applicant did not attach such a document. Therefore, although the applicant attached a motion for a court order that would require a third party to produce the arbitration agreement, the first instance court acted correctly when it returned the application without considering it on the merits.[3]

§11.03 THE GROUNDS FOR SETTING ASIDE OF ARBITRAL AWARDS

There are two categories of grounds for setting aside of an award: those which a party must invoke before the competent court and provide relevant evidence (Article 233(3) of the Commercial Procedure Code), and those that the court can apply on his own initiative (ex officio) (Article 233(4) of the Commercial Procedure Code).

The list of grounds for setting aside of an award corresponds to that in the universally recognised international instruments: the New York Convention (Article V), The European Convention on International Commercial Arbitration (Article IX), The UNCITRAL Model Law on International Commercial Arbitration (Article 34).

The first group of grounds includes those that lead to the annulment of an award only if the applicant refers to them and, moreover, provides evidence to support the allegations. An award can be set aside only where the applicant furnishes proof that:

(1) one of the parties to the arbitration agreement on the basis of which the tribunal resolved the dispute did not have full legal capacity;

3. The Decree of the Federal Arbitration Court for the Volga Circuit of 5 April 2005, case No. A65-8376/2005.

(2) the arbitration agreement is invalid under the law to which the parties have subjected it, or, in the absence of such an indication, under the Russian legislation;
(3) the award deals with a dispute not contemplated by or not falling within the terms of the arbitration agreement, or contains decisions on matters beyond the scope of the arbitration agreement;
(4) the composition of the arbitral tribunal or the arbitral procedure was not in accordance with the agreement of the parties or the mandatory provisions of the legislation on arbitration;
(5) the party against whom the decision was made was not given proper notice of the selection or appointment of the arbitral tribunal or the time and place of the arbitration hearing or was otherwise unable to present his case to the arbitral tribunal.

In all these cases, competent court is bound by the arguments and evidence supplied by the applicant and may not go beyond them. The legislator relies here on the ancient Roman principle *tantum devolutum quantum appellatum* (there is as much of the decision as there is of the complaint) used in the design of the institutions of appeal and review of judicial acts. The competent court is limited both to the grounds for setting aside referenced in the application and to the arguments of the interested party.

The second group consists of two individual grounds for setting aside of an award:

(1) the dispute resolved by the arbitral tribunal cannot be subject to arbitration in accordance with the federal law;
(2) the award of the arbitral tribunal is contrary to the public policy of the Russian Federation.

The court is under an obligation to check the award against these criteria, whether or not a setting aside application contained a reference to such grounds for annulment. Review of the award on these grounds is both a right and the obligation of the competent court, that is, a duty ex officio. It is obvious that the second group of grounds for annulment of an award was introduced into legislation in order to implement the competent court's public function of controlling the activities of arbitral tribunals. The need to provide national courts with such a function is due to the fact that the arbitral tribunal has certain powers over the disputing parties, and the judiciary on behalf of the state must possess a legal mechanism for ascertaining, in the most significant cases concerning public interests, that the arbitral tribunal did not encroach upon these important public interests.

The list of grounds for setting aside of an arbitral award in the procedural codes is exhaustive and must not be constructed expansively (Article 233(1) of the Commercial Procedure Code).

An arbitral award can be set aside if one of the parties to an arbitration agreement did not have the full legal capacity (Article 233(3)(1) of the Commercial Procedure Code). The law does not specify which kind of capacity the drafters of the law had in mind – civil (substantive) or procedural legal capacity. It seems that in this case, a broad interpretation will be appropriate, encompassing both types of legal capacity. The law defines the civil legal capacity as the ability of citizens to acquire and exercise by their actions the civil rights, to create civil duties for themselves and to perform them (Article 21(1) of the Civil Code). With respect to legal persons, the content of legal capacity varies depending on whether it is a commercial or a non-profit organisation. Commercial organisations (except unitary enterprises) may have civil rights and civil obligations necessary to carry out any activity not prohibited by law (Article 49(1) of the Civil Code). Other legal persons may have civil rights and obligations corresponding to their purposes set in their constituent documents, such as a Charter or Articles of Association (Article 49(1) of the Civil Code).

The procedural legal capacity is the person's ability to carry out procedural rights and fulfil procedural obligations, which includes instructing a procedural representative to conduct a case on one's behalf (Article 37(1) of the Code of Civil Procedure). Citizens who have reached 18 years of age and all organisations enjoy the full procedural capacity.

An arbitral award can be set aside if the arbitration agreement is invalid under the law to which the parties have subjected it, or, in the absence of such an indication, under the Russian law (Article 233(3)(2) of the Commercial Procedure Code). For example, an arbitration agreement will be invalid if it does not comply with the requirement of the written form. An arbitration agreement from which it is impossible to ascertain the permanent arbitral institution that should deal with the dispute should also be considered invalid.

An arbitral award may be set aside if it deals with a dispute not contemplated by or not falling within the terms of the arbitration agreement, or contains decisions on matters beyond the scope of the arbitration agreement (Article 233(3)(3) of the Commercial Procedure Code). For example, if the parties have agreed to submit to arbitration the disputes concerning the invalidity of the contract and the tribunal resolved a dispute about its repudiation, the award will be made in a dispute not contemplated by the agreement, and it can be annulled on this basis by the competent state court. At the same time, if the part of the award within the scope of the arbitration agreement can be separated from the part outside that scope, only that part of the award that is outside the scope of the arbitration agreement shall be set aside.

An award may be set aside if the composition of the arbitral tribunal or the arbitral procedure was not in accordance with the agreement of the parties or the federal law (Article 233(3)(4) of the Commercial Procedure Code). For example, Article 10 of the Arbitration Act 2015 requires that the number of arbitrators must be odd unless otherwise provided by federal law. Currently, there is no such provision in the federal legislation. Thus, this rule is mandatory. If the parties select a tribunal consisting of four arbitrators, the composition of the arbitral tribunal will be non-compliant with the above rule.

An arbitral award may be set aside if the party against whom the decision was made was not given proper notice of the selection or appointment of the arbitral tribunal or the time and place of the arbitration hearing, or was otherwise unable to present his case to the arbitral tribunal. The procedure for sending notices is determined in accordance with Article 3 of the Arbitration Act 2015.

An arbitral award can be set aside if the dispute resolved by the arbitral tribunal cannot be subject to arbitration in accordance with the federal law (a non-arbitrable dispute). For example, this includes the disputes arising from privatisation and from relations regulated by the legislation on the contract system in the procurement of goods, works, and services for state and municipal needs (Article 33 of the Commercial Procedure Code).

An arbitral award may be set aside if it is contrary to the public policy of the Russian Federation. The previous statute used the term 'fundamental principles of Russian law', which gave rise to discussions about the content of this notion, as well as its relation to the term 'public policy' in the ICA Act 1993.[4] Legal scholars argued that these terms were, in fact, synonymous.[5] The legislator has now confirmed the correctness of this argument.

The notion of 'public policy' is a stretchable category, which the legislator leaves for the court to interpret. Depending on the current political and legal situation, this notion fills with the meaning that corresponds to modern ideas about the foundations of state and legal system. The doctrine emphasises that public policy is the principles of law which are fundamental. For this reason, setting aside of an arbitral award can only result when the most significant legal provisions have been violated. It is obvious that this category requires interpretation in every particular case. As a result, discussions in judicial practice about the application of this category in specific disputes are never ending.

Reviewing the previous judgments in individual cases as a court of the supervisory instance, the Presidium of the Supreme Commercial Court considered the following to be fundamental principles of Russian law (public policy):

- the principle of legal certainty;[6]
- the principle that judgments which entered into legal force must be complied with;[7]
- the principle of objective impartiality of the court;[8]
- the principle of equality among the creditors in bankruptcy, which militates against the satisfaction of one creditor's claim to the detriment of the others;[9]

4. *See* Skvortsov O.Yu, *On the Approaches to the Notion of 'Fundamental Principles of Russian Law'*, 1 Treteysky Sud, 68-76 (2004) [Skvortsov O.Yu. O podhodah k ponyatiyu «osnovopolagayushiye principy rossiiskogo prava». // Treteysky Sud. 2004. No. 1. S. 68-76].
5. Musin V.A., *On the Relationship between Commercial Courts and Arbitration*, 1(25) Arbitration Disputes, 101 (2004) [Musin V.A. O vzaimootnoshyeniyah arbitrajnyh i tryetyeiskih sudov. // Arbitrajnyye spory. 2004. No. 1 (25). S. 101]; Karabelnikov B.R., *International Commercial Arbitration*, 363 (Moscow, 2012) [Karabelnikov B.R. Myejdunarodnyi kommyerchyeskii arbitraj. - M., 2012. S. 363].
6. Decree of the Presidium of the SCC RF of 5 February 2013 No. 11606/2012.
7. Decree of the Presidium of the SCC RF of 5 February 2013 No. 11606/2012.
8. Decree of the Presidium of the SCC RF of 22 May 2012 No. 16541/2011; Decree of the Presidium of the SCC RF of 13 November 2012 No. 8141/2012.
9. Decree of the Presidium of the SCC RF of 12 February 2013 No. 12751/2012.

– the principle of proportionality of the civil liability.[10]

In addition, the court considered there to be a violation of the fundamental principles of Russian law (it was not specified which principles exactly) in a situation where a member of a company used a procedural settlement agreement confirmed by an arbitral award to dilute the assets of a company and transfer the company's property to himself, thus bypassing the legislative safeguards for major transactions and transactions with a conflict of interest in a company.[11]

Annulment of an award does not entail the loss of a possibility to assert the party's right in law. Setting aside of the award does not preclude the parties from re-initiating arbitral proceedings if such a possibility remains. If this is no longer possible, a party may refer the dispute to a commercial court or a court of general jurisdiction in accordance with the relevant procedural rules.

10. Decree of the Presidium of the SCC RF of 23 April 2013 No. 16497/2012.
11. Decree of the Presidium of the SCC RF of 14 June 2011 No. 1884/2011.

CHAPTER 12
Enforcement of Arbitral Awards

§12.01 THE GENERAL CHARACTERISTIC OF THE ENFORCEMENT OF ARBITRAL AWARDS

Arbitration is a private jurisdictional mechanism, but the state provides it with certain support. Among other things, this support takes the form of facilitating the enforcement of arbitral awards if the losing party refuses to comply with an award voluntarily.

The *exequatur*, or the enforcement of the award, is the stage that lies beyond the arbitral proceedings. Enforcement takes place within the framework of litigation, i.e., before the state courts.

As a rule, the losing party must comply with the award immediately. However, this is merely a default position, and an arbitral tribunal is free to set a different timescale.

If the debtor refuses to comply with the arbitral award or does not proceed to its performance in a timely manner, the creditor is entitled to request enforcement of the award. In Russia, such requests take the legal form of an application to the competent state court for a writ of execution.

The interested party initiates this process by an application in writing. The procedure for dealing with requests for writs of execution is different in its form to the regular court procedure in civil actions.

There is a considerable similarity between the procedure for the enforcement of an arbitral award and the related kind of proceedings that deal with applications to set aside an arbitral award. The Constitutional Court considered this matter in the Ruling of 15 May 2001 No. 204-O. The case in question concerned international commercial arbitration, but these conclusions apply equally to domestic arbitration. According to the Ruling, 'not only an application to set aside but also an application for recognition and enforcement of an award as the forms of access to justice may result in an annulment of the award. The list of grounds for setting aside of an award and for refusing its recognition and enforcement, essentially, is the same – in both cases, the court dealing with a relevant request, having established one of the relevant grounds, must set aside or refuse the enforcement of the arbitral award'.

§12.02 THE PROCEDURE FOR ISSUING A WRIT TO ENFORCE AN AWARD

Article 237 of the Commercial Procedure Code lays down the requirements to an application for a writ of execution and lists the documents that must accompany the application.

An application for a writ of execution to enforce an arbitral award is resolved by a one-judge panel within a period not exceeding one month from the date of its receipt by the commercial court, including the time necessary for preparation of the case for trial. When preparing the case for trial, at the motion of the parties involved in the proceedings, a judge may request an arbitral institution to produce the materials of the arbitral proceedings that led to the award in question. The judge shall make this request according to the procedural rules that regulate the taking of evidence by the court.

The original award of the arbitral tribunal or its duly certified copy must accompany the application. One form of 'due certification' that the Civil Procedural Court explicitly mentions is the certification by a chairperson of the arbitral tribunal (Article 237(3)(1) of the Commercial Procedure Code). A certification of the arbitrators' signatures on the award by a public notary should also satisfy the requirement of due certification.

For ad hoc arbitration, it is a mandatory requirement that a public notary shall certify a copy of the arbitral award.

The original agreement to arbitrate or its duly certified copy must also accompany the application for the issuance of a writ of execution. Even if the validity of the main contract that contains the arbitration clause is confirmed by a court judgment in another case with a *res judicata* effect for the parties, it does not mean that the applicant will be exempt from the duty to produce the original agreement to arbitrate (or its duly certified copy) with the application for the enforcement of the arbitral award.[1]

A document certifying the payment of state fees in the amount prescribed by federal law must accompany the application for a writ of execution.

A writ of execution issued by a commercial court or a court of general jurisdiction is a necessary condition for the enforcement of the award. Writs of execution (but not arbitral awards) are listed among the types of executive documents that the court bailiffs' service will accept for execution under Article 12 of the Enforcement Proceedings Act. The writ is a strictly formal document and must contain a number of details prescribed by Article 13 of the Enforcement Proceedings Act.

The commercial court notifies the parties of the time and place of the hearing, but their absence does not preclude the court from considering the case and rendering a decision.

1. *See* the Decree of the Presidium of the SCC RF of 15 June 2010 No. 693/10.

During the proceedings, the commercial court determines the presence or absence of grounds for refusal to issue a writ of execution. It does so by means of considering the evidence that the parties presented to substantiate their claims and objections. The court does not have a right to re-evaluate the factual circumstances established by the arbitral tribunal or reconsider the arbitral award on the merits.

In practice, there are cases when parallel applications are pending in the same court to issue a writ of execution to enforce an arbitral award and to set the same award aside. In such circumstances, the court must consolidate these actions into one single set of proceedings.

§12.03 THE GROUNDS FOR REFUSING THE ENFORCEMENT OF ARBITRAL AWARDS

In contrast to the previous statute, the Arbitration Act 2015 does not regulate the grounds for refusing the enforcement of arbitral awards, making instead a blanket reference to the procedural law. The relevant grounds can now be found in the Code of Civil Procedure and the Commercial Procedure Code, which govern the litigation in the state courts.

A competent state court must deal with applications for the enforcement of arbitral awards. It has been rightly pointed out in the Russian literature that the material facts the court must ascertain while dealing with an enforcement application or a challenge to an award include only the facts of procedural nature because the court is not entitled to review the award on the merits.[2]

The grounds for refusing to issue a writ of execution for the enforcement of an arbitral award are identical to the grounds for setting an award aside.

The only basis for refusing to enforce an arbitral award that is absent from the list of grounds for setting an award aside is contained in Article 239(2)(5) of the Commercial Procedure Code (and its identical counterpart in Article 426(2)(5) of the Code of Civil Procedure). According to this provision, an application to issue the writ can be refused if an award has not yet become binding on the parties or was cancelled, or if its execution has been suspended by the commercial court or any other court in the Russian Federation or a court of another State where that award was made or the State whose law applied.

The person in whose favour the arbitral tribunal rendered an award may initiate the enforcement proceedings (Article 237 of the Commercial Procedure Code). As it follows from the above provision, no other person is entitled to apply for a writ of execution to enforce an arbitral award. An arbitral tribunal also cannot act as an entity initiating the enforcement of its awards, which is only natural. Having adopted a legally significant decision in the case, the tribunal should not be entitled to dispose of the rights of the parties any further.

2. Yarkov V.V., *Legal Facts in Civilistic Process*, 18 (Moscow, 2012) [Yarkov V.V. Yuridichyeskiye fakty v civilistichyeskom procyessye. M., 2012. S. 18].

The list of grounds for refusing the enforcement of an arbitral award is exhaustive.

The first group of grounds for refusing the enforcement of an award includes the grounds that the resisting party must assert and, moreover, substantiate with evidence. Thus, the enforcement may be refused only where the resisting party proves that:

(1) one of the parties to the arbitration agreement on the basis of which the tribunal resolved the dispute did not have full legal capacity;
(2) the arbitration agreement is invalid under the law to which the parties have subjected it, or, in the absence of such an indication, under the Russian legislation;
(3) the party against whom the decision was made was not given proper notice of the selection or appointment of the arbitral tribunal or the time and place of the arbitration hearing or was otherwise unable to present his case to the arbitral tribunal;
(4) the award deals with a dispute not contemplated by or not falling within the terms of the arbitration agreement, or contains decisions on matters beyond the scope of the arbitration agreement;
(5) the composition of the arbitral tribunal or the arbitral procedure was not in accordance with the agreement of the parties or the mandatory provisions of the legislation on arbitration.

In all these cases, the competent national court is bound by the arguments and evidence contained in the statement of the person concerned and may not go beyond them.

The second group of grounds that may lead to refusal in the enforcement of an arbitral award includes the following:

(1) the dispute resolved by the arbitral tribunal cannot be subject to arbitration in accordance with the federal law;
(2) the award of the arbitral tribunal is contrary to the public policy of the Russian Federation.

The court is under an obligation to check the award against these criteria, whether or not the resisting party referred to them. Review of the award on these grounds is both a right and an obligation of the competent court, that is, a duty ex officio.

§12.04 ENFORCEMENT OF ARBITRAL AWARDS THAT REQUIRE MAKING AN ENTRY IN A PUBLIC REGISTER

In 2015, a new rule appeared in the Russian legislation, which provides that those arbitral awards the performance of which requires making an entry in a public register cannot on their own be a sufficient basis for the making of such an entry. Their enforcement is only possible after an applicant obtains a writ of execution from a competent state court.

This provision emerged as the result of a lengthy doctrinal debate and analysis of the inconsistent jurisprudence concerning the arbitral awards that purported to transfer rights in immovable property.

Commercial courts and courts of general jurisdiction dealing with the enforcement of arbitral awards that resolved disputes about the real property were unable to work out a clear legal position on the jurisdiction that arbitration tribunals could legitimately exercise in this category of disputes. In the end, the Presidium of the Supreme Commercial Court requested the Constitutional Court of the Russian Federation to declare unconstitutional the legislative provisions that could be interpreted to make arbitral awards a sufficient basis for the registration of rights to the immovable property. In the Decree of 26 May 2011 No. 10-P, the Constitutional Court declined to do so.

At the heart of this problem lies the complexity of the legal structure required for a transfer of rights in real property, elements of which include not only the transaction (an act of private law), but also the state registration of rights arising as a result of that transaction (an act of public law). The registering authority does not merely make the entry on request but is under an obligation to assess the legality of such a transaction. On this basis, the national courts considered that the registration authorities cannot be bound by awards of a private decision maker, and should have the right to refuse state registration based on such awards if they conclude that the award is illegal. In practice, the registering authorities started to perform a function equivalent to appellate review of arbitration awards.[3]

After the Constitutional Court has recognised the right of arbitral tribunals to hear disputes involving rights in immovable property, the practice of state courts moved in a different direction. Now, they adopted the approach whereby in order to apply to the registering authority for the recognition of rights in real estate, the interested person should first obtain a writ of execution for the award of the arbitral tribunal from the competent court.

This practice became the basis for the new statutory regulation of the enforcement of arbitral awards that require making an entry in a public register.

Article 43 of the Arbitration Act 2015 contains the following general rule:

> No arbitral award, including an award that does not require compulsory enforcement, can be a basis for making an entry in a state register (including the Uniform State Register of Legal Entities, the Uniform State Register of Individual Entrepreneurs, the Uniform State Register of Rights in Real Property and Transactions With It), a register of security holders or another registry in the Russian Federation, making entries in which entails the establishment, alteration or termination of civil rights and obligations, in the absence of a writ of execution issued on the basis of

3. Skvortsov O.Yu., *New Appeal: Yet Another Initiative of the Rosreestr to Amend the Decision of the Constitutional Court of the Russian Federation*, 3 Treteysky Sud, 8-11 (2012) [Skvortsov O.Yu. Novaya apyellyaciya: ochyeryednyye iniciativy Rosryeyestra po korryekcii postanovlyeniya Konstitucionnogo Suda Rossiiskoi Fyedyeracii. Treteysky Sud. No.3 (2012). S. 8-11].

a judicial act of the competent court (including in respect of an award that does not require compulsory enforcement).

The statutory text provides an indicative list of registers that can be altered on the basis of an arbitral award only if it is confirmed by a writ of execution from a competent state court. Other examples include the registries of the property belonging to the regional governments of the Russian Federation and local authorities, the registry of notification about pledges of movable property maintained by the Federal Chamber of Notaries, and other registers where an entry can affect the civil rights of individuals and legal persons.

A person interested in making an entry in such a register pursuant to an arbitral award must apply to the competent state court for a writ of execution.

§12.05 RECOGNITION AND ENFORCEMENT OF FOREIGN ARBITRAL AWARDS

The recognition and enforcement of foreign arbitral awards in Russia are regulated by Chapter 31 of the Commercial Procedure Code 'Proceedings in Cases on Recognition and Enforcement of Foreign Judgments and Foreign Arbitral Awards' and Chapter 45 of the Code of Civil Procedure 'Recognition and Enforcement of Foreign Judgments and Foreign Arbitral Awards'. Russia is also a party to the New York Convention 1958; USSR as its predecessor joined this Convention in 1960.

Russian law draws a distinction between the foreign arbitral awards in commercial disputes and all other awards. The awards of international commercial arbitration and other arbitration tribunals rendered abroad in disputes and other matters arising from entrepreneurial and other economic activity (the commercial disputes) are recognised and enforced by commercial courts. The courts of general jurisdiction deal with the recognition and enforcement of other types of awards. Recognition and enforcement of foreign arbitral awards in Russia are possible where an international treaty of the Russian Federation and the federal law thus provide. Since the procedures are largely identical, this section will proceed to outline the features of recognition and enforcement of arbitral awards in commercial disputes, which will be applicable mutatis mutandis to the enforcement of arbitral awards in non-commercial disputes.

A party seeking recognition and enforcement of a foreign arbitral award must lodge an application before the first instance commercial court at the location or the place of residence of the debtor. If the registered address or place of residence of the debtor is unknown, then the commercial court at the location of debtor's property will have jurisdiction. The application can be submitted on paper or by filling the relevant form on the commercial court's official Internet website. The application must satisfy several formal requirements. It should list a number of mandatory details: the name of the commercial court to which the application is submitted; the name of the foreign court or arbitral institution and its location; the creditor's name and location or place of residence; the debtor's name and location or place of residence; the information about the decision of a foreign court or of a foreign arbitral award, the recognition and enforcement of which the creditor seeks; and so on. The application must be accompanied by a number of documents: a copy of the decision of a foreign court or a foreign arbitral award, recognition and enforcement of which creditor seeks; a document confirming the entry of a foreign judgment into force (i.e., becoming binding on the parties) if the text of the decision itself does not make this clear; a document confirming that the debtor was notified of the proceedings timely and in proper form; and some other documents. The materials accompanying the enforcement application can also be submitted to the commercial court in the electronic format.

An application for the recognition and enforcement of a foreign court decision or a foreign arbitral award is resolved by a one-judge panel. The time for considering the application is limited to one month.

The commercial court notifies the parties of the time and place of the hearing, but their absence does not preclude the court from going ahead to consider the case and render a decision.

In the proceedings, the commercial court may not review the foreign judgment or arbitral award on the merits. There can be situations where the proceedings to set aside or suspend the execution of the award are ongoing in a foreign court. In this case, the Russian court dealing with an application for recognition and enforcement of such an award may, at the request of one of the parties, adjourn the proceedings on this enforcement application.

Grounds for refusing recognition and enforcement of a foreign judgment or a foreign arbitral award are provided in the relevant international treaties and Russian national legislation.

The grounds for refusal to enforce a foreign judgment are:

(1) under the law of the state where it was rendered, the decision has not yet entered into force;
(2) the party against whom the decision is invoked was not given a timely and proper notice of the time and place of the hearing or was otherwise unable to present his case;
(3) the consideration of the case, in accordance with an international treaty of the Russian Federation or federal law, falls within the exclusive competence of a court in the Russian Federation;
(4) there is a decision of a court in the Russian Federation rendered in a dispute between the same parties, on the same subject, and on the same grounds that has entered into legal force;
(5) the proceedings in a dispute between the same parties, on the same subject, and on the same grounds are ongoing before a court in the Russian Federation, if such proceedings commenced prior to the institution of the proceedings in a foreign court, or a court in the Russian Federation was the first to accept the application initiating the dispute between the same parties, on the same subject, and on the same grounds;
(6) the limitation period for bringing a foreign judgment for enforcement has expired, and the commercial court has not extended this period;

(7) the enforcement of the foreign judgment would be contrary to the public policy of the Russian Federation.

The grounds for refusal to recognise and enforce an arbitral award are stipulated in Article V of the New York Convention 1958 and Article 36 of the ICA Act 1993.

Recognition and enforcement of an award can be refused only where the party against whom the award is invoked furnishes proof that:

(1) one of the parties to the arbitration agreement did not have full legal capacity;
(2) the arbitration agreement is invalid under the law to which the parties have subjected it, or, in the absence of such an indication, under the law of the country where the award was made;
(3) the party against whom the award is invoked was not given proper notice of the selection or appointment of the arbitral tribunal or the time and place of the arbitration hearing or was otherwise unable to present his case;
(4) the award deals with a dispute not contemplated by or not falling within the terms of the arbitration agreement, or contains decisions on matters beyond the scope of the arbitration agreement. If the decisions on matters submitted to arbitration can be separated from those not so submitted, that part of the award which contains decisions on matters submitted to arbitration may be recognised and enforced;
(5) the composition of the arbitral tribunal or the arbitral procedure was not in accordance with the agreement of the parties or not in accordance with the law of the country where the arbitration took place.

Furthermore, recognition and enforcement of an arbitral award may also be refused if the competent court, regardless of any submission of a party, finds that:

(1) the subject matter of the dispute is not capable of settlement by arbitration in accordance with the federal law;
(2) the recognition or enforcement of the award would be contrary to the public policy of the Russian Federation.

Upon review of the application for recognition and enforcement of a foreign arbitral award, competent state court adopts a judicial act, which is termed a ruling.

Those foreign arbitral awards that do not require compulsory enforcement shall be recognised in the Russian Federation if an international treaty of the Russian Federation or the federal law provides for their recognition. Such awards are recognised without any further proceedings unless an interested person submits their objections in this regard. If an interested person does submit such objections to the competent court, they are considered in the same manner as the debtor's objections against the enforcement of an award.

Enforcement of a foreign arbitral award proceeds on the basis of a writ of execution issued by the competent court that made the ruling on the enforcement application. A foreign arbitral award may be presented for enforcement within a period not exceeding three years from the date of its entry into force. In case the applicant misses this deadline for a good reason, the commercial court has the discretion to extend it on the applicant's request.

§12.06 THE APPLICATION OF THE PUBLIC POLICY EXCEPTION

Questions related to the application of public policy as a ground for refusing the enforcement of a foreign arbitral award are traditionally difficult for the legal doctrine as well as the legal practice.

Applying this ground for refusal to enforce a foreign arbitral award, Russian courts take into account the requirements of public policy in the country of enforcement, that is, the notion of public policy developed within the Russian legal system.

The competent court must consider the category of public policy ex officio, regardless of whether or not the interested party referred to it. However, this does not preclude the parties from advancing their objections concerning the potential violations of public policy. In this case, the national court is not bound by the arguments of the interested parties.

The Russian doctrinal commentators are unanimous in recognising that the legislation does not fill the concept of public policy with specific rules.[4] For example, according to Article 1193 of the Civil Code, an otherwise applicable rule of foreign law shall not apply in exceptional cases where the effects of its application would be manifestly contrary to the principles of public order (public policy) of the Russian Federation, taking into account the nature of the relationship involving a foreign element. In such cases, the appropriate rule of Russian law shall apply instead, if necessary. Refusal to apply foreign law cannot be justified by a mere difference between the legal, political or economic system of a foreign country and the Russian Federation.

The Russian legal doctrine stresses that, in this respect, the national practice follows the international jurisprudence in its application of the New York Convention. In particular, foreign awards shall be deemed contradictory to the public policy and unenforceable in Russia in the following circumstances:

- where there are serious grounds to doubt the integrity and independence of the arbitrators who rendered the award;
- where the fundamental rights of the respondent have been violated, which prevented him from defending his rights;

4. *See*, e.g., Luntz L.A., *The Course of Private International Law: General Part*, 271 (Moscow, 1970) [Luntz L.A., Kurs myejdunarodnogo chastnogo prava. Obshaya chast. M., 1970. S. 271]; Karabelnikov B.R., *Enforcing and Challenging the Awards of International Commercial Arbitration. Commentary on the New York Convention 1958 and Chapters 30 and 31 of the Commercial Procedure Code 2002*, 329 (Moscow, 2008) [Karabelnikov B.R. Ispolnyeniye i osparivaniye ryeshyenii myejdunarodnyh kommyerchyeskih arbitrajyei. Kommyentarii k Nyu-Iorkskoi konvyencii 1958 goda i glavam 30 i 31 APK RF 2002 goda. 3-ye izd., M., 2008. S. 329]

- where the enforcement of an award may come into conflict with mandatory national legislation of the country where enforcement is sought or the provisions of such country's international treaties.[5]

Being contrary to public policy implies a contradiction to mandatory rules of public law. For the purposes of ascertaining the content of public policy, the rules of public law are the mandatory prohibitions compliance with which protects the common interests of society and the state. The doctrine recognises that such rules may include direct prohibitions as well as those rules from which prohibitions follow indirectly.[6] Examples may include the rules contained in the criminal, currency, and tax legislation.

In this regard, national courts play a major role in the interpretation of the notion of public policy, because 'it is impracticable and inexpedient for the legislation to attempt a comprehensive description of all cases where the application of foreign law would be inconsistent with the public policy, since it is impossible to foresee all the potential conflicts between domestic and foreign law that may arise in practice and lead to the necessity of applying the public policy exception'.[7]

However, one must note that the courts rarely apply the category of public policy. The Supreme Commercial Court endorsed this approach. According to paragraph 4 of the Information Letter No. 156 of the Presidium of the Supreme Commercial Court of the Russian Federation of 26 February 2013 'Review of Commercial Courts Practice Concerning the Use of Public Policy as a Ground to Refuse Recognition and Enforcement of Foreign Judgments and Foreign Arbitral Awards', commercial courts shall apply the public policy clause only in exceptional cases. Public policy must not substitute the specific grounds for refusing recognition and enforcement provided for by international treaties of the Russian Federation and the rules of the Commercial Procedure Code.

The commercial courts and the Supreme Court have reiterated on many occasions that a violation of public policy must be understood as a violation of fundamental rules of Russian law. For instance, the Judicial Board on Civil Cases of the Supreme Court pointed out that 'the public policy of the Russian Federation shall be taken to mean the basics notions of the Russian state's social system. The application of the public policy exception is possible only in those particular cases where the application of foreign law would produce a result unacceptable from the point of view of the sense

5. Karabelnikov B.R., *Enforcing and Challenging the Awards of International Commercial Arbitration. Commentary on the New York Convention 1958 and Chapters 30 and 31 of the Commercial Procedure Code 2002*, 331 (Moscow, 2008) [Karabelnikov B.R. Ispolnyeniye i osparivaniye ryeshyenii myejdunarodnyh kommyerchyeskih arbitrajyei. Kommyentarii k Nyu-Iorkskoi konvyencii 1958 goda i glavam 30 i 31 APK RF 2002 goda. 3-ye izd., M., 2008. S. 331].
6. D.V. Afanasiev, *Violation of Public Policy as a Ground for Invalidity of a Transaction in Russian and Foreign Law: Problems, Trends, Practice*, 137 (Moscow, 2006) [D.V. Afanasiev, Narushyeniye publichnogo poryadka kak osnovaniye priznaniya sdyelki nyedyeistvityelnoi v rossiiskom i zarubyejnom pravye: problyemy, tyendyencii, praktika. M., 2006. S. 137].
7. Krokhalev S.V., *The Category of Public Policy in the International Civil Process*, 34 (St Petersburg, 2006) [Krokhalev S.V. Katyegoriya publichnogo poryadka v myejdunarodnom grajdanskom procyessye. Sankt-Pyetyerburg, 2006. C. 34].

of justice that prevails in Russia'.[8] The Federal Commercial Court for the Moscow Circuit in its Decree of 29 August 2004 in case No. KG-A40-7948/04 explained that the violation of public policy of the Russian Federation or the fundamental principles of Russian law refers to an encroachment on the foundations of law and order or morality of a particular society, and not an inconsistency with the legal principles of an individual area of law. An example of a public policy violation could be the invalidity of a transaction on the grounds stipulated in Article 169 of the Civil Code, or the application of a rule of foreign law incompatible with the Russian legal system (e.g., polygamy). The Decree of the Federal Commercial Court for the Moscow Circuit of 3 April 2001 in case No. KG-A40/1672 elaborated further on the matter. The court indicated that an arbitral award would violate the fundamental principles of Russian law (be contrary to the public policy of the Russian Federation) if the actions necessary for its enforcement are prohibited by the law or are detrimental to the sovereignty or security of the state, affect the interests of large social groups, are incompatible with the principles of the economic, political and legal system of the state, affect the constitutional rights and freedoms of citizens, or are contrary to the basic principles of civil law, such as the equality of the participants in the civil transactions, inviolability of the property, or the freedom of contract. The Decree of the Federal Commercial Court for the North-Western Circuit of 20 March 2003 in case No. A56-34456/02 pointed out that the public policy refers to the basic principles that are universal, highly imperative, and have specific universal significance.

All those examples show that the category of public policy operates at a high level of abstraction. For this reason, the application of public policy by state courts is extremely rare and involves such violations that affect the fundamental principles of Russian law.

8. Ruling of the Judicial Board on Civil Cases of the SC RF of 25 September 1998.